THE ORDINARY ROUTE

Harold Drasdo

THE ERNEST PRESS

Published by The Ernest Press 1997
© Harold Drasdo 1997
Illustrations © Gordon Mansell 1997

A CIP catalogue record for this book is available from the British Library

ISBN 0 948153 46 6

Cover illus: Harold and Neville Drasdo on Rannoch Wall, Glen Coe, in 1951
Photo: Tom Ransley

Typeset from the author's disk by Stanningley Serif
Printed and bound by St Edmundsbury Press

For my mother, Ella Drasdo,
who is frightened of heights,
and remembering Mary Leonard

CONTENTS

FOREWORD

> History is written by those who survive, philosophy by the well-to-do;
> those who go under have the experience.
>
> W.R. Lethaby

I've been a serious climber, within the sense of this book, for fifty years now and an occasional writer on climbing and on mountains for forty. I'm in a small club. The casual nature of those writings, mauling a fixed idea, reviewing another writer's efforts, guidebook wars, hasn't given real satisfaction. A hope arose that the putting together of a book of reminiscence and reflection might relieve this discontent.

I had a simple plan for delivery, neat and easy to execute, but the book would have nothing to do with it. Insistent voices troubled me, dictating with such assurance that I had no choice but to copy out what they said. What they said, in fact, was intriguing but unreasonable, disconnected paragraphs and fragments without any hints on order or relationships. That's what took me so long.

The shape of the book surprises me, not its content but its silences, and I feel obliged to pass comment. It begins as autobiography, not in the plan, though that's allowed me to pay tribute to some of my teachers who've rarely or never appeared in climbing literature. Unfortunately, in abandoning that form, later companions of greater importance, some still close to me, fail to make an appearance.

In particular, I want to put squarely on record that Keith Carr, Andrew Maxfield and Gordon Mansell don't win proportional representation. Moving or sitting still, around the lives of these three there was a spinoff of improbable chains of events and they were the best story-tellers I've ever met. They also shared a priceless ability to turn discomfort, anxiety, even crushing defeat, into high comedy. (And unforgettable party people. I still hear recollection of occasions I missed: Keith, well away, strapping on an ancient leather motor-cycle helmet for a lengthy impromptu mime, "Blériot Crossing the Channel"; Max, shouldering through the crush to make his courtesies to a hostess, snapping the neck of her six-week-old kitten en route, and making his gallant attempt at recovery; Gordon formed groups of three into parties and groups of four into public disturbances. Their airy assumptions of expertise left swathes of destruction: Keith and companion, posing as consultant electricians and needing only a quarter hour to turn the enormous switchboard of a remote outpost of "the mighty Bowater Corporation" into a wall of flame; Max, assisting a friend with a six-week attack of sculptor's block — finishing the neck is the tricky bit — and detaching the head of the almost-completed figure with his first blow; Gordon as an insecurely seated trooper in the Horse Guards. It would be unfair, by the way, to deduce their abilities as climbers from those legends).

Keith, I think, never wrote anything and Max a couple of throwoff pieces and then they died, an illness and a fall. Gordon is alive and well and is recently returned from thirty years in Colorado and New Mexico; but he suffers from a delusion that most experience is oblong and is best put across on art paper or canvas. I ask myself: Have I missed an opportunity here, or neglected a responsibility? Perhaps it's just that I'm not a biographer. Or perhaps I saw that these three constituted a threat and might have crowded me out of my own book.

Again, the excursions described here are oddly selective. There's barely a mention of the two greatest cliffs in England and Wales, Scafell and Clogwyn Du'r Arddu, on which I've spent many incomparable days. Deeply satisfying alpine ascents have failed to win an entry and beautiful mountain areas, home and abroad, have been passed over in silence. My highest mountain, my nearest miss, my most agonising decision, resisted inclusion. On the other hand, although I don't see myself as a hill walker some simple scrambles are described at surprising length. I hope the principle of selection will make its own case.

I intended to include no published writing but the shape the book assumed made it impossible to avoid odd topics on which I'd already expressed myself; and three longer pieces fitted in so neatly that it seemed perverse not to use them. However, I'm the kind of writer who'd like to disown most earlier work so I've taken this opportunity to reconsider and to revise. I'd hope to be found accessible to anyone who likes mountains. Traditionally the problem of the technical vocabulary of climbing is solved by ending with a glossary. Instead, I've supplied a grammar and readers who've never tied onto a rope might refer to this. It's assumed that the climber will ignore it unless he's spoiling for a fight.

A few of the earliest routes described were close to the limits of the British climber at the times of their ascents, but not for long. Now they're open to tens of thousands and that gives me my focus. This book says that experience can't be measured by the absolutes of height and difficulty. It hangs on a long time-span of engagement, on an acquaintance with a variety of terrains and conditions, on a regular inspection of one's own limits and on the success of one's accommodations with or reprisals against the onset of ageing. And finally, of course, on imagination and on reading. Experience is more than expertise.

Lethaby's proposition looks hard to resist but his categories enclose a central area (which was, in fact, one of his concerns), the unacknowledged value in what we take as commonplace. I write in the hope that it's possible to see the world in Blake's grain of sand; I know we can find fear in Eliot's handful of dust. An alternative historian, a village philosopher, a man who's kept his head above water more by luck than judgement, I'd like to show the ordinary as rich and strange.

THIS OUR LIFE

We commonly do not remember that it is, after all, always the first person that is speaking. I should not talk so much about myself if there were anybody else whom I knew as well. Unfortunately I am confined to this theme by the narrowness of my experience.

Thoreau, Walden

Ogden Clough

BEGIN HERE: YORKSHIRE

Did you ever see the film *A Private Function*, a provincial comedy of manners released in the mid-eighties? If you missed it, well, it took a nostalgic and affectionate view of the Age of Austerity following the Second World War. The plot turned on the concealment and raising of an off-register pig, destined for the black market. The setting was the small town of Ilkley in the West Riding of Yorkshire in 1947.

The sense of authenticity was strong. Particular images conjured up the era. The pitiful weekly food ration is laid out; the war is over but some allowances are being cut rather than increased. A hand pens a careful line down the back of a woman's leg; it imitates the seam of an unobtainable silk stocking. The spotlit organist rises before the cinema audience; the Pathé-Gazette newsreels and the two features will be in black and white.

The background grasp of time and place was good too. Everywhere the utility clothing, the drab and standardised demobilisation suits of the men. In contrast, the hoarded prewar bits of finery of some of the older women. Everywhere the invisible organisation of the black market, a ghostly mirror of the war effort in its complexity and pervasiveness. The faces seemed right: old-fashioned, homely, innocent, sometimes beautiful, sometimes bucolic or even vulgar — 'downright common'. The sense of small ambitions and of dreams was right. One day it would

5

be possible to go away for a holiday, to Bridlington, Scarborough or Morecambe. Younger men fantasised about owning a motor bike, older men a car. Worry about the petrol coupons later. No-one considered saving up for a telephone; since nobody else had one, what use would it be? No-one had heard of television.

On country-town life in the North of England, to most viewers who remembered those years, this film must have seemed to say it all. And yet, as a picture of Ilkley in 1947, it was hopelessly, crazily beside the point. It missed what was happening over its head. I know. I was there.

Only a mile above the street scenes shown, the gritstone escarpment of the Cow and Calf looks out across the town and over Wharfedale. The Cow is a sixty-foot monolithic block, its front slightly impending; the Calf, a smaller cube, grazes the slope beneath, not straying far from its parent. Walk up a little to the left and you'll find yourself entering a hidden arena, properly known as Hangingstones Quarry. And there, on any weekend of that year, you'd have encountered a group of young people who seem, in retrospect, to stand outside that time. In all the busy action in the town beneath, circumstance was planning the destinies of the people. But in Ilkley Quarry the climbers seem to have been free of constraint, graced with certainty. A curve like an arrow-flight joins them to the way we live now.

It's a workable convention that British rock-climbing was invented at Easter 1886 by a Victorian gentleman, Walter Parry Haskett-Smith, with his ascent of the Napes Needle in Lakeland. Independently it was invented by the present writer, just sixty years too late, at the remote little outcrop of Ogden Clough on the moors of the Brontë Country. From time to time my wanderings led me to this neat little arrangement of rocks, rimming its tight ravine. In winter, in green and black, the corner-cracks seeping slime, it seems to hunch against the frigid wind. On a summer evening, westward-facing, it stores the sun in warm browns and golds. I scramble up the tiny chimneys. After a while I experiment with low traverses. And finally I succeed on one or two of the easier cracks, running back a few feet from the edge to stand in safety, trembling, bewildered and ecstatic on the empty moor. Now, briefly, I'll go back a bit.

If climbers write of childhood they often describe a series of exploits or excursions suggesting a fated propensity for the activity. Allowing only one concession to that format, I'll introduce myself instead by giving proper answers to three straight questions I've sometimes been asked: Where are you from? What is your sign? What kind of a name is Drasdo anyway?

Where am I from? I was born, in the February of 1930, in the city of Bradford. (City motto: *Labor Omnia Vincit*, Labour Conquers All. A slogan dreamed up, I believe, by the first mill-owners and recommended to a sceptical, ungrateful, and sometimes truculent workforce. Their own lives refuted it. City crest: skipping the trimmings, centrally, a boar's head with tongue removed. This illustrates a local legend, not important, and offers a feeble pun any story-teller will prefer to over-look.)

A curious incident was recorded by a Bradford newspaper in the summer of that year. A narrow moorland lane from Wainstalls to Oxenhope, unsurfaced at that time, crosses the plateau to the west of Ogden Clough. It actually achieves a greater altitude, about fourteen hundred feet, than the crag itself. At about the highest point there's a gaunt and isolated old inn, The Withins, in fact the highest public house in West Yorkshire. The landlord reported his astonishment at seeing a young couple ap-proaching by the rough track across the open moor from Causeway Foot, manhandling a pram towards his establishment. It proved to contain an infant of a few months and his customers were making a round trip of fifteen miles from Lidget Green. I claim no credit for this ascent having relied entirely on my porters but, yes, that was me.

What is my sign? I was born over the sign of gritstone with clay, shale and peat in conjunction. Alluvium and coarse gravels were in opposition with limestone in right ascension. That means that I'm ob-durate, resistant to change or pressure, corners rounding off very slowly. I'm rough-grained and incapable of acquiring a polish. I'm pretty reli-able. (It's strange that men have often believed the stars we're born under rule our natures and fortunes. If a man's character is his fate it's the bedrock, drift and subsoil from which he springs that shapes him and fixes his destiny. That, and the local weather.) However, I've been around a bit and learned to put on disguises.

"What kind of a name is Drasdo anyway?" It's an outlandish name, arriving on these shores about a hundred and fifty years ago. At the last count there were about twenty-five in Britain in two independent clans based on Bradford and Hull. Once, a member of the Hull group ar-ranged to meet me for a parley but we couldn't see any tribal resem-blance, though earlier forenames suggested common origins. The Hull group seemed smarter than our own. For many years Hannchen Margherita Drasdo ran the Drasdo Repertory Company. In living memory my own branch were poor whites with an unshakable belief in past dis-tinction. My paternal grandfather worked in Lister's Mill from the age of twelve until retirement.

An unsolicited investigation into the name produced curious results. Another twenty-five or so, widely dispersed, will answer to it in North America and only half that number in Australia, yet it assembles three hundred West Germans. In fact it probably comes from further east. (Drasdovitz, Drasdowitz, Drasdov, Drasdow, Drasdo, something like that: names simplify their way west.) We've never been sure which side we're on. In a Russian novel of the fifties, Dudintsev's *Not by Bread Alone*, a Drasdov is doing his bit for communism. In the thirties Hanni Stricker-Drasdo, a Swiss, received unwelcome letters from Otto Drasdo, a German, raving on about racial purity. He always ended with the salutation "Heil Hitler". Earlier again, Paul Julius Drasdo, in Hull, was the immigration agent receiving Jewish refugees from the pogroms and fixing passages from Southampton to New York. For myself, I'm a millenarian anarchist and sometimes a practical anarchist.

I've learned of only two historic personages, each with the name Johannes Gottlieb Drasdo. The first was Magister and Librarian at the University of Wittenberg in 1531. Perhaps he stood beside Luther as the Ninety-five Theses were nailed to the door of the church. The second was Librarian in the Philosophy Faculty of the same institution in 1786. His doctoral thesis, in Latin, dealt with the Bible in profane literature, early works to the time of writing, and is dated 16 October 1784. (Was the office hereditary? Did an earlier Drasdo hasten to look through the loan cards when somebody happened to mention that that fellow Hamlet hadn't come back from the summer vacation?) I stir uneasily. Each of these two produced a book of sermons. I nearly called this whole volume "Sermons in Stones".

The sooner we get rid of linear surnames the better. Mine hides the fact that I'm a full half Yorkshire, with threads of Irish, Scottish and Welsh as strong as the European element.

That explains everything and I can return to the world ignored in *A Private Function*. Of the few means by which young people could break out of the parochialism of the northern towns at that time, two were pre-eminent. One was through the door of the Public Library, outside my scope here. The other was through the Youth Hostels Association which opened up huge possibilities to the poorer adolescent. Of this class, at a weekly wage in 1946 of exactly one pound, rising to twenty-five shillings the following year, I was representative.

I used youth hostels for only a few years but they were a formative part of my education. To the north, sited in beautiful limestone villages — Malham, Kettlewell, Linton — they laid the Dales open. To the west, sometimes in more isolated situations, they gave access to the moors and each name meant a whole landscape — Wainstalls, Jerusalem Farm, Mankinholes. In them, one met people of all ages and conditions. I note in passing the strong radical tendency of most countrygoers at that time. Visitors made their own entertainment and sing-songs were likely to include Scottish melodies, socialist, communist and Wobbly anthems (sometimes in comic parody), dust-bowl, hill-billy and blues lyrics, the poetry of the poor. The atmosphere was always friendly and courteous. And there were the girls, a little older than myself and presumably inaccessible; but making style out of rags and looking clear-skinned and healthy enough, despite the meagre rations, to dislocate one's train of thought.

Public transport was comprehensive and efficient. Every weekend loosely organised walking clubs took the buses to Ilkley, Skipton, Haworth, Holmfirth and beyond. From the top decks they were able to admire the countryside and to look down on tightly packed cycling clubs heading out in the same directions. Living near the border between city and country (and torn to this day between both styles of life) I was advantageously placed.

Since the private game at Ogden Clough didn't yet have a name I still called myself a walker and cyclist in the summer of 1947. In Burley Woodhead youth hostel on the edge of Ilkley Moor I now noticed a card inviting anyone interested to join a climbing club. I stored the idea for the moment, having other projects planned. My brother Neville, aged fifteen, had begun to accompany me on hostel weekends and one week, starting from our own back door, we set off to walk to Scotland. Our roundabout route took us through the Dales and across to the Lake District. And there, on the road into Langdale, emerging perhaps from the woodlands beyond Skelwith Bridge, we became sharply aware that we were passing through some sort of psychic frontier.

From Elterwater next morning, our fifth day, we walked first into Chapel Stile, where Neville bought some Kendal mint cake at the little post office and store. He was so impressed with the list of expeditions on the wrapper that he later arranged to post his sweet coupons on and from then until the end of rationing Old Sanderson was to mail the dense hard slabs to Bradford once a month. We continued over to Grasmere and up to Grisedale Tarn for the descent into Patterdale. There, halting a moment by the tarn, we made a fateful change of plan. The top of Dollywaggon Pike was thick in cloud but, distinctly, a thin clear pathway zigzagged up the screes. Helvellyn was somewhere beyond. I can still summon up a residue of the mix of feelings and the gestalt of sense impressions — the stillness and soft damp of the air, the dizzying spaciousness of the place, the sombre colours, the muted sounds of sheep and human voices, the clatter of scree from above the cloudline. The impulse came to us simultaneously and without real discussion. I've no memory of effort, only of the charged air and of the freedom of the cloudy summit. We raced down Striding Edge transported by excitement.

That day destroyed the remainder of the walk. We trudged discontentedly back to the Pennines to finish at Twice Brewed youth hostel and to set foot on the further side of the Roman Wall before returning to Bradford by train. My demarcation line for the Scottish border, taken from Hadrian, was, I now realised, fifteen hundred years out of date.

I earned two weeks' holiday a year. A fortnight later, with another companion, I made a cycling trip to Mid and North Wales. Our route brought us back through Snowdonia and late one hot afternoon we pushed our heavy bikes, my three-speed defective, up the long ascent of the Nant Gwynant to Pen-y-Pass. Gorphwysfa, it's properly called, the resting place. It was cooler at the summit and a fabulous scene was arranging itself. Beneath us the Llanberis Pass was shafted through with evening light and drenched in astonishing colours, golds, greens, purples, black. After a while we remounted for the descent to Llanberis but, almost immediately, something happened.

It was a conversion as final as that of Saul on the road to Damascus. Simply, we passed three men striding abreast, sturdy booted figures in worn clothes, two carrying coiled ropes over their shoulders. Everything about them was just right. I could feel the justice of their claim to the place. Who were they, I ask myself now, who can they have been? Nearly fifty years later it's still quite possible that I might identify them if I tried. Almost certainly a Visitors' Book still exists, recording their names and ascents from some cottage in the Pass. And those names would be known to me — Longland, Edwards, Noyce, Barford, Morsley, Dwyer, some of whom I would one day meet. Almost certainly, too, they'd have been climbing on Lliwedd. In twenty years' time I'd be engaged in the arduous task of revising the guide-book to that yet-unheard-of cliff.

In a few seconds we'd left them and I knew the deep despair of being seventeen years old and having wasted my life. What was I doing, shackled to the road with this chain and rack, while on all sides the hills reclined in sensuous invitation? As we raced down to Nant Peris the majestic slopes unfolded and displayed themselves but I was no longer simply pedalling home. I was heading for Burley Woodhead and I was going to sign on.

Here's my card. I haven't looked for it for many years but it's significant that I've never thrown it away. A faded pink, folded to a three by
four-and-a-half inch face, it encloses within an embellished surround
the title: The Yorkshire Climbers (Mountaineering Club). Inside, the
facing page sets out the Constitution. The club badge may only be worn
by members who've led a rock climb of Very Difficult standard and
completed an eighteen-mile fell walk within the day. Lady members
may qualify by completing (a) or (b). The entrance subscription is five
shillings, the annual subscription eight shillings, payable quarterly. The
latter is waived for members called to His Majesty's Forces. No member shall be under sixteen years of age. And so on. No objects for the
club are stated.

Verso, the officers are named: President, G. Hocken, Esq; Hon. Secretary, G. Rhodes, Esq. (the G is for Charles); Treasurer, D. Hopkins,
Esq. (the s is redundant). And above, against name and address, in a
microscopic, oddly ornamented script, I've signed away many other
possible futures. It's taken weeks to get hold of this card. It's the nineteenth of October, 1947.

Burley Woodhead hostel was warm, welcoming and vital after the
darkness of the moorland road when I arrived to pledge myself. The
warden was the Gordon Hocken whose name appears as Club President.
Tall, spare, with long grey hair and a rare but engaging smile, he always
wore a threadbare, shapeless, once-white guernsey with flannels and
moccasins of comparable age. Courteous, well-spoken, preoccupied,
he gave an impression of intellectual resources not called on in his present
occupation. In fact, the youth hostels of Britain were staffed by the first
wave of postwar dropouts in those years. But Hocken, I guess now, was
also handling a personal misfortune in this way and he was later to return to the world outside. His duties prevented weekend climbing but I
was told that in Wales he'd climbed the Gashed Crag Route on Tryfan
with J.E.Q. Barford, whose one-shilling Penguin manual, *Climbing in
Britain,* became our bible.

Forgive me. I want to do a little name-dropping, though some of the
names I'll drop will be those of people not previously seen in climbing
writing. They can stand, I hope, for the great body of climbers who
made no first ascents, who never lived through or died in great epics,
who perhaps only joined the scene for two or three years but without
whom the sport would have been a much less rich experience.

So who was at Burley Woodhead that night, and who was to join us at
the rocks the following day? I rely partly on memory and partly on
probability. But I want you to see these people as clearly as possible.

So, before making these introductions, I have to say something about the unwritten Sumptuary Laws of the time.

The only suitable clothing cheaply available to climbers was surplus War Department stock. A hooded fawn-coloured cotton smock of a standard four-pocketed design cost eleven shillings. Loose, light, but with no rain resistance, these were the overgarment most commonly seen. Thin camouflaged overtrousers were also used though most of us wore cast-offs. White sea-boot stockings were often favoured and as headgear, according to season, a balaclava helmet, a Fair Isle type bobble hat, or an army beret. The only cheap rucksack was the limp and frameless parachute pack. A miscellaneous selection of working or walking boots was nailed for rock-climbing. Cheap black plimsolls were available but their use by the beginner was strongly discouraged as fostering a sloppy technique and as reducing the teacher's advantage.

This dress divided its wearers satisfactorily from civilians and from peace-time military too. But it didn't distinguish us sufficiently from the hiking community, a vexing problem. However, the rope might be displayed on the rucksack whilst travelling and a sling could be knotted or spliced to such a length that, secured by a war surplus snaplink, it formed a belt for the waistless smock. Critically, whilst the older hiker stuffed his trousers shapelessly into his socks and drew these up to the knee, the young rock climber folded his sea-boot stockings carefully to cover both the ankles of his boots and the turn-ups of his trousers. This imposed on him a stiff and careful walk or frequent stops for readjustment. (This gait strikingly anticipated that invented by Yul Brynner for *The Magnificent Seven*, dictated in that case by the need to produce, even after violent action, long thin unbroken cheroots from skin-tight hip or shirt pockets.) Finally, as an extreme and uncomfortable measure, the hairy jersey was sometimes worn inside the check shirt.

It's a commonplace that fashion in clothing eventually imitates styles developed for sport or warfare. Some years later anoraks and boots were to become acceptable street wear, as in subsequent decades duvets and thermal clothing were to pass from climbing to the world of casual dress, even of high style. Unhappily, in 1947 the only persons seen with hoods were old ladies in plastic rain protectors or an occasional pair of nuns. And the more oafish element in the northern cities could conjecture only a single purpose in carrying a rope: suicide. Therefore, on boarding a bus the climber was often the butt of laughter and loud jokes. Derision, however, is the burden the avant-garde learns to bear and we kept our composure, a correct instinct assuring us that history was on our side.

So who was there on that first weekend? Clearly I recall, late in the evening, a noticeable stir as a tall, hefty, bespectacled figure entered and removed a curious overgarment, apparently a hooded black serge cape. This was Don Hopkin, the most experienced climber and the central figure of the group at that time. Given to large, dogmatic generalisations he was prone to preface all important statements with the declaration, "I maintain....". He suffered a tendency to produce delightful malapropisms but his nature was so likable and his authority so unquestionable that notice of these was usually stifled. He relished the discussions and arguments he made strenuous efforts to provoke.

His close companion, Ernie Leach, already in his thirties, was a stocky little man upon whose face a sour expression alternated rapidly with a delighted grin. He was an equally formidable talker and his gravelly voice could be picked up at a good distance. His laconic comments still entertain those who can put them in context. They merit collection. Of all these Yorkshiremen he was the most Yorkshire, strong on dialect as well as accent. He loved climbing yet he had a poor opinion of most of those around him; "Climbers are the lowest of the low," he'd mutter to himself. Don and Ernie passed on to younger members what they knew of the larger world. They were acquainted with well-known figures further afield: Scottie Dwyer and Dick Morsley in Wales, Sid Cross and Jim Cameron in the Lakes. And they told stories of the great contemporary experts, Peter Harding and Tony Moulam in Derbyshire, Arthur Dolphin and Des Birch here in Yorkshire. With hardly a guidebook in print and no magazines, climbing was an oral culture. Anyone with news could take the stage but these two were our gurus.

Peter Bryce Thomson was certainly present that night. Medium height, solidly built, pale in complexion and with something interesting in his face, he had, or seemed almost to affect, a slight speech impediment. He wore the camouflaged twill-like garment known as a jumping jacket. These hoodless, pocketed, brass-studded tops, complete with epaulettes and crutch-strap, were very heavy and obstructed every movement but they made a man of the wearer. On Pete's head, at a jaunty angle, sat a peaked canvas Afrika Korps cap. He'd spliced an unusually long sling which he wore in the style of belt and bandolier, adding to the generally Teutonic image. A bunch of pitons often jangled at his waist. Pete was, in fact, an ardent admirer of the Munich climbers of the thirties, relating their exploits and quoting their reported battle-cries with relish. He wasn't a very forceful climber and the embarrassing moment when my teacher had to invite me to take over the lead wasn't all that far ahead. Some years later, high up a long rock climb in Skye, a gust of wind snatched the much-loved hat away and a desperate hours-long search of the enormous scree-slope beneath failed to locate it. At that Pete gave up climbing. Still, he stands as one of my heroes and I remember him with affection. A photograph admits that I copied the wrap-over sling.

Dave and Doris Gibbons may have been there. I never came to know them closely since they were in the older married sub-set of the club. Dave's age then would have been late twenties, maybe early thirties. Short, slightly pudgy, curly jet-black hair; complexion oddly pale, almost waxy. That fitted when I learned, forty years later, that he'd been a coal miner.

He was an inventor! Most of his ideas, it has to be said, didn't work out. His prototype rope-climbing apparatus consisted essentially of a locking spool with bicycle pedals and compensatory accessories. It was doomed from the start but no-one who watched the test trials is going to forget them. He addressed the problem of the unprotectable lead on outcrops and came up with "the shadow rope". An assistant at the top of the climb suspended a snaplink clipped around the lead rope above the second's hand. If the leader's nerve failed he shouted "shadow rope" and a running belay rose jerkily to his waist. There was slack in this system. On the other hand, Dave anticipated the Vibram soles we'd yet to see by nailing cut-outs from car tyres to his boots, an innovation immediately copied throughout the Third World. He looked at the holdless faces of the Cow and Bald Pate and with a miner's pragmatism chiselled a line of holds up each, actions which, surprisingly, drew only muted protest at the time. Unhappily he failed to lead his very steep project on the Cow and was obliged to seek a champion.

Keith Reid had an impaired arm and leg, polio maybe. Short, dark, bearded, with an intense downward and inward gaze, his rock-climbing was handicapped but he was a strong walker and often seemed to get into the lead as parties followed the very narrow paths through the heather. Irresistibly, the iambic metre of his stride communicated itself to everyone behind, to their exasperation. On a few occasions, at a considerable distance, the leader of a file of skylined walkers was correctly named simply by observing the activity of the whole party.

Now I see that this method of introduction is tedious and I'd do better to use incident. However, in case anyone fails to put in an appearance, as a courtesy I'll list the names of those who were or who may have been present. Gerry Hartley was there. And, very likely, Charles and Marjorie Rhodes, Des and Mary Morrell, maybe Jon and Valerie Stevens. Jack Bloor, Ronnie Hirst, Fred Williams. Jack Bradley, who was not all bad, was there. Also his angelically innocent-looking follower, Douggie

Bell, who proves on inspection to have been the agent inspiring or encouraging many of Bradley's delinquencies.

Anyway, here's Ilkley Quarry on that sunny autumn morning, as fresh and miraculous as the seventh day of creation. It's a roughly circular excavation over a hundred feet across and about forty feet deep. It lies just inside the lip of the moor and the natural edge and boulder slopes of the escarpment leave only a forty-foot entry, a dramatic gateway. It must have been worked at a fairly early period since no ancillary buildings or roadways remain. Once through the jaws the right wall, taking the sun, is seen as vertical but fissured with cracks. The others walls progressively fall back so that the further slope allows a simple scrambling exit or descent. Casual passers-by assemble on the top of the southern side to watch the action for a few minutes. The rock is an attractive medium-textured grit, pleasantly abrasive to the touch.

Pete Thomson and Gerry Hartley had offered to initiate me. The grading system was recited. The climbs were identified, following a theme here: Wellington Chimney, Waterloo Crack, Josephine, Napoleon, Blucher, Walewska. I see now that the teaching and advice was helpful, attentive and precise. They tied on with bowlines at each end of the hemp rope. I was in the middle with a butterfly knot. First we climbed Wellington Chimney and Fat Man's Agony, deep clefts in the left wall near the mouth of the quarry, strenuous but not difficult. Then, more serious, Josephine, a steep crack and traverse line up the right wall. How to pay out the rope around the body as the leader advances. How he had anchored himself to bring me up. Copy the leader's movements. This is chimneying, back and foot. This is hand-jamming. This is a balance move. This is strenuous, this asks for poise and delicacy.

There was a lengthy lunch-time adjournment at the Highfield Hotel, a quarter-mile away, where everybody reassembled so that the outside room was filled. The older ones drank beer, the younger ones had pots of tea. Patrons were expected to bring their own food; the management found the making of sandwiches a nuisance. People talked and talked, exchanging information, making plans. I listened carefully, not missing a word.

The afternoon began with a session on boulder problems and then we walked over to Rocky Valley, a series of natural buttresses forming a higher escarpment on this part of the moor. Beeline was shown to me and my two companions laid hands on the rock and made ineffective attempts to get both boots off the ground at the same time. ("Climbed by Dolphin." "Who's Dolphin?" "Arthur Dolphin. Best climber in Britain. Nobody else can start it.") Now I was taken up the two lines on

Cooper's Slab, the smooth and undercut front of the same buttress. I saw immediately the truth of what Gerry and Pete were telling me. The moves weren't so hard, the climb not so steep as Josephine. But there was no possible means of protecting the leader and there were no positive holds, reliance was entirely on friction and balance. A slip, a fall onto the steep bouldery slope beneath, and serious injury would be inevitable.

So that was that and I could read the future. I knew what I was going to do with the rest of my life. First, though, I had to attend to immediate problems. I needed nailed boots. I needed a rope and slings and snaplinks. And I needed an inexperienced companion, so that I could lead.

These difficulties were soon sorted out. My savings went with the purchase of a hundred feet of Italian hemp, two or three short lengths for slings, two or three ex-army snaplinks and a couple of handfuls of the soft iron nails known as clinkers and muggers.

Following Boas, historians notice the strong persistence of patterns in simple artefacts. Look at the man-made soles on a selection of boots today and for no reason of technology or logic some are found to imitate the nailing of the traditional climbing boot. For years my grandfather had first taught and then supervised the resoling and reheeling of my shoes. Now he advised as the massive clinkers were clinched through the welts of my walking boots and the star-shaped muggers were infilled. Equipped at last, my eyes fell on a supporter. And the day soon came when Ernie Leach's face lit up with amusement as he walked into the quarry, saw me negotiating a route of a month's acquaintance, and the identity of my second was disclosed: my brother, who was to become the more accomplished of the two of us on gritstone.

That's enough detail. A period of intense activity followed. I came to know Almscliff, Widdop and Laddow, each with its local devotees and particular legends, and a number of less-frequented crags. Mid-week, Neville and I applied a growing expertise to Ogden Clough. The club held alternate walking and climbing meets but, infatuated with climbing, I rarely attended the fell walks. At the same time the mystery of those distant Pennine venues seeped into me. The names: Simon Seat, Pen-y-ghent, Wild Boar Fell, Nine Standards Rigg, Boulsworth Hill, Kinder Scout. They might offer pleasure when I became too old for rock-climbing.

I'd been climbing for only six months or so when I got the letter I'd been expecting. My country needed me. This request, involving the suspension of a life-style, came as an inconvenience. In another two or three years' time there'd be a bitter competition between some Langdale climbers to win the fastest release from National Service. Amongst those about to appear in this book, the most rugged was out first as a persistent bed-wetter; I doubt whether he drank so much water again for the rest of his life. The fittest elected for a minor operation on his toes but the surgery made his style of marching even more grotesque; he was out in three months to make an unexpected recovery, soon becoming capable of running back from Scafell after a hard day's climbing. The most resourceful, who'd been priming himself on the classic texts of mental illness, indulged in some of the oddest behaviour the British Army can ever have seen; six difficult months passed before an Army psychiatrist (who found the appointments exciting) and a sergeant-major (who was racked by disbelief) were forced to agree that the Service would operate more effectively without him. The most argumentative produced a trump card, his Secretaryship of an Anglo-Soviet Friendship Society: he was refused the honour of bearing arms but was allowed to chop wood in Scotland. However, I didn't yet have the benefit of these examples and I'd not yet formed any views on the nation state. Further, the fantasy of a posting to some more mountainous country kept presenting itself.

The preliminary medical was brief but surprising. Heart okay, lungs okay, eyes okay; hearing okay, teeth okay, reflexes okay. Then the assaults on privacy which took each innocent conscript unprepared. The weary middle-aged doctor enclosed my private parts in a grubby hand and told me to cough. Okay. Before I'd recovered composure he ordered me to bend over. I complied warily, half-looking over my shoulder as he peered joylessly at his morning's hundredth backside. Okay. In fact I was fit in every respect except for a glaringly obvious problem.

He couldn't get over my hands. He sat at his desk for three or four minutes in total silence, lightly grasping between thumb and forefinger the tips of my middle fingers and reading not the palms for my future but the backs for my past. The recent fortunes of the gritstone climber are always written there. Large brown scabs, small red beads, formed striations in all directions on a sore groundrash. Finally he asked for an explanation but seemed unable to accept it. With enthusiasm I went through the technique of hand-jamming but he was a poor visualiser. He shook his head in impatient disbelief. He thought there must be some eczema there, exacerbated perhaps by this strange activity.

I was shocked. The young gritstoner is proud of his stigmata and he wears them like a badge. (But, displaying them to Don Hopkin after some gritstone horror, the master had complacently remarked, "You still haven't learned how to jam properly, Harold. Your hands have been *slipping*. I maintain that an expert climber never marks himself." And he spread before me his meaty and undamaged paws.) To lend support to my story I showed the doctor the detail of the fingerprints. All displayed that telltale circle, about a centimetre in diameter, within which the outer skin is worn away. (When I was to resume gritstone climbing, for a spell of three years I needed only to cut my thumb nails. The rock kept the nails of the fingers trimmed to just the right length.) In the end, anyway, he gave up. Physically I was more or less alright. As for my head, I didn't seem a dangerous case.

Shortly, the notice to present myself arrived. I was due a week's holiday with pay but my brother and a friend, both still at school, were free at the crucial time. There was no question about where to go. In our dreams we wrestled the Lakeland crags. We'd read every book we'd laid hands on, we'd questioned all who'd climbed there, we had handwritten descriptions of a number of routes. We travelled up by train with mounting excitement. And the moment finally came when we were walking up the road to the head of Langdale, seeing for the first time the shapes of hills, the patchworks of fields, the settings of buildings, a perfect integration about to form the primary landscape of my heart and head. Crags, boulders, trees, every straight and bend of the road would become as familiar as any scene of my life. And at last, here was the Old Dungeon Ghyll Hotel. I don't think we went in, there wasn't an outside bar then and we hadn't started drinking anyway. We continued up the last half-mile to our intended refuge, Wall End Barn.

For those few days in the spring of 1948 we were the only residents. The barn hadn't yet attracted the large and cheerful company it was to gather in the fifties and which was to lead, eventually, to its closure by the local authority as a threat to public health and perhaps to morality. It stands by the gate where the only road out of the head of the valley starts to climb to Blea Tarn before offering a return down Little Langdale or access to the spectacular westward passes of Wrynose and Hard Knott. Situated a hundred yards from the farm, it's a low strong building, perhaps thirty feet by sixty, with a single window aperture. The walls are of neatly coursed stream-dressed rubble, levelled on crude slate stringing. Any earth packing washed out centuries ago. The roof is slated in the diminishing courses characterising older Lakeland buildings and wears a thick carpet of moss. Recently it's been meticulously restored but for those who spent an important part of their lives there it seems a melancholy shell. I look at it now and a spear of grief runs through me. It's a hollow drum, still reverberating with a sense of absences, of irrecoverable youth and unquenchable optimism. The physical silence is dense and dismaying. It's all over now.

It's okay. You can look inside. During the day we leave the doors open to let in a bit of light. At night we close them and we use candles or, better, brothel cans, the smallest size of empty bean tin, half filled with paraffin and with a wad of bracken inserted to serve as wick. If space allows, we sleep on the left here on this deep bench of bracken intended for animal bedding. It's luxuriously comfortable and we use our ropes for pillows. (In the middle fifties, through some change in farm economy, the bracken won't be replaced each year. It will become beaten down, without resilience, and with the sleeper's every movement a thin dry choking, possibly carcinogenic dust will rise. Why's there been no follow-up of long-term users?) Look at the roof, massive oak crucks and purlins. In some (have I imagined this?) you see the mortisings of a yet older building. Notice that the rafters aren't sawn, they're riven. You can see that the slates are pegged, not nailed, since most of the torching has fallen away. The stream from Pike o'Blisco runs right behind the back so you can get water or wash there if you're so inclined. You can buy milk and eggs down at the farm, and sometimes bread. There's an earth privy down there too.

There wasn't a moment to waste, it would be dark in two hours. We dumped our gear, bolted some food, and rushed out for our very first Lakeland climb, Middlefell Buttress, right behind the hotel. Changing leads, we worked our way upwards, marvelling at the rock. Its solidity: hard, dense, nail-polished. Its colours: grey-brown to yellows and reds, frescoed with rondels of bright green lichen. On our walk up Langdale we'd seen no-one. Now, surprisingly, from the empty valley, a figure began to ascend the hillside and then to solo rapidly up towards us. He caught us on the wide terrace beneath the steep little final wall and introduced himself. It was Len Barlow, an experienced Lancashire climber and holder of a Guide's Certificate. Brian, more cautious than Neville and myself, was halted on this last pitch and Barlow promptly offered to lead. To my stunned dismay I heard Brian accept and thank him politely. Ungraciously, but with the recklessness of desperation, I insisted that Neville or I should try it first. After a moment's awkward silence, followed by a brief argument from which Barlow stood back, this was agreed or at any rate was what transpired. In fact the thing was easy but the narrowness of our escape from this appalling threat to our self-esteem left me gasping.

Amongst older climbers I sometimes notice a tendency to shunt early climbs, other than recorded first ascents, further into the past than they belong: even by some years. Apart from the last day of this holiday I've little memory of what we did but we stayed on the easiest routes. We climbed on Scout Crag and my brother reminds me that we were washed out of Great Gully on Pavey Ark. We had few route descriptions, there was a good deal of rain, and we may have spent a day or two on mountain walks. Towards the end of the week we made the adventurous journey over to Borrowdale. I've only a generalised sense of the impressions aroused by the ascent over Esk Hause and the processional tarns, Angle, Sprinkling and Sty Head, this indirect route presumably a scenic choice in hope of a view of Gable through the cloud. But, from the end of the day, two images with correspondences of strong emotion still remain. The cascades of Sour Milk Gill were thundering powerfully and creamily down the slabs opposite Seathwaite Farm. And in the little farm parlour there, where we rewarded ourselves with tea and scones, we found in the Visitors' Book the name of Howard Somervell, doctor, artist and early Everest climber. No doubt we added our own names, announcing our entry into the mountain world.

By the following evening, with two young fell-walkers we'd met, we were the unauthorised tenants of a small barn near Seatoller and only one full day remained. Brian decided to have a rest day whilst Neville and I would visit Pillar Rock. We set out early and marched up the Honister Pass. Then up over the flanks of Brandreth, down into Ennerdale, up towards Black Sail Pass and along the High Level Route. At last we found ourselves in the Jordan Gap beneath High Man.

The club elders, observing our rapid advances on gritstone, had cautioned us against excessive ambition in the Lakes and we had descriptions of only four short easy routes from the Gap to the summit. We disposed of these rapidly and sat on the top for a while, incompletely satisfied. It didn't feel all that late and we needed something more exciting. We knew what that had to be. An hour later we'd passed Looking Stead, contoured the slopes of Kirk Fell, followed the Gable Traverse to the Dress Circle, and were examining the Napes Needle. "It's that polished it shines int' dark," Ernie had told us. But it couldn't resist our momentum and standing on the top we felt that despite the weather the holiday had been richly rewarding. Darkness fell as we reached Sty Head Tarn but we were now on familiar ground and the stumbling descent and the trudge to Seatoller seemed only distantly physical.

My euphoria was shattered by our reception. Somehow it had got to ten or eleven o'clock. The two strangers reprimanded us heatedly and Brian supported them. Sick with anxiety, he'd been on the point of calling out the Keswick Rescue Team. Incredulous, baffled, we argued on, each unable to comprehend the other's view. His sense of the reasonable was confused, I thought. Yet he said he was going to be a doctor.

I tried to explain to him. He'd have to go to a university, it would take years, you couldn't do it unless your parents were rich. Thirty years later I met him by chance, a well-dressed prosperous-looking family doctor with a country practice nicely sited close to the Lake District.

In three days' time I was on an enormous barrack square at Aldershot, fixing my thoughts on the Needle while a distant but tremendous voice, full of sound and fury, seething with contempt, shifted me and my companions this way and that.

North-west face of Gimmer

22O35283

Once I'd been KBBW/44/3: that is, the third person, the eldest child, of
the forty-fourth household in the district of Britain known for identity
card purposes as KBBW. Later, I'd become LR91O7OOC: that is, a
subject to whom the state had made promises, attractive to the extent
that the promises of states are easily rescinded, in return for cash deduc-
tions and compliant behaviour. For the present I was 22O35283 and no
escape. What did it mean? That since some unknown date a queue of
men over twenty million long had been impressed before me into the
Armed Services? Many, perhaps, dragging their feet like me?

There were noticeable differences between dossing at Wall End Barn
and dossing at Oudenarde and Malplaquet Barracks at Aldershot. Later
I was to see that a good deal of the mindless unpleasantness of army life
was a charade or a response to desperate boredom and could have been
deflected by clowning along with it. From the beginning, though, I felt
at risk. Some instinct had taught me that invisibility is the best camou-
flage but though I kept my face blank I often seemed to attract a second
suspicious glance.

At the medical I'd been asked for my preferred choice of service and
I'd said that I'd like to go into the RAF and be posted to a base with a
Mountain Rescue Team. I was told that that wasn't possible at that

moment so I opted for the army. With its talent for putting square pegs into round holes the recruiting panel had then recommended that I should serve in the Military Police but, surprisingly, I was allowed to resist the offer. After a good deal of fencing the baffled interviewer, who kept going back to my school examination results in French and German, gave in. He couldn't put me into what I now asked for, the Pioneer Corps. My medical classification was A1 and this least prestigious of all units, armed only with picks and shovels, was restricted to men clinically handicapped for digging. Finally, with some reluctance, he allowed me to try my disappearing act in the Royal Army Service Corps, the next lowest echelon.

Perhaps two months passed before, following a guardroom interrogation as to why I had my army gym shoes in my pack, I was able to escape for a single day to the sandstone outcrops at Tunbridge Wells. I'd no information but found my way to High Rocks where, struggling up a strenuous crack in my cumbersome khaki uniform, I became aware that I had a small audience. The central figure in this party stepped forward and introduced herself, Nea Morin, a name not known to me at the time. She was accompanied by three older gentlemen, distinctly upper class, and by a sulking schoolgirl who looked as if she could think of better ways of spending the day. Years later I realised that this child, her daughter Denise, must have been close to my own age. Soon she was to become as skilful a climber as her mother and, eventually, an experienced ocean yachtswoman in her own right. After an exchange of conversation Nea gave orders and, relishing the first experience I can remember of travelling in a private motor car, I was whisked over to Harrison's Rocks, an enchanting glimpse of a pastoral south I'd never seen. Gritstone techniques require little adaptation to sandstone. I enjoyed myself on Birchden Wall and Slimfinger and was able to maintain the status of the Yorkshire outcrops as a training ground. No opportunity to repeat this excursion arose.

Then I was at Catterick Camp, getting occasional weekends free and two or three longer leaves. I extended my acquaintance with the harder routes at Ilkley and Almscliff and I revisited Langdale. I went back to Wales for the first time as a climber and spent a few days at Idwal Cottage. It was winter and I had no companion but I talked myself into a party from the Teaching College at Bangor and I made a few cautious solos. I also met a young American studying in England, Lorentz Hansen, and despite poor weather we climbed some harder routes on Tryfan. While the wind howled outside the hostel he talked about a paradisal Californian valley called Yosemite. Later, he sent me richly interesting copies of the *American Alpine Journal.* And I was settling in to make the best of my National Service, living for each break, when I was told that I was to be posted overseas. I was given embarkation leave and this was spent in the Lakes with my brother and George Elliott.

Elliott was not a member of the YCMC and was temperamentally disinclined to join anything. It was to be twenty years before beatniks and hippies became a visible presence in Britain but his more than shoulder-length hair made a preliminary announcement. Subsequently he made experiments with the shape of his life and died fairly young. He was spending a good deal of time in Langdale and in a scorching heat-wave would ring his surprised employers, an engineering firm, to say that the valley was cut off by freak floods and he'd get back as soon as possible. George was a beautifully easy mover, fast, assured and strong. More than anyone I ever saw, he climbed with joy. He could read, he had ideas, he was excellent company. He took us up Hiatus on Gimmer Crag, our first long Lakeland very severe. Technically it came as an anti-climax but I agonised over Neville's safety, coming last across the long unprotected traverse on a thin and lifeless hemp line. A letter of a few months later establishes that we reconnoitred the impressive East Buttress of Scafell on this trip but found it cascading with water.

At some time in the nineteen-fifties the Empire Windrush, a cruise ship, caught fire off Gibraltar and sank. It was a fine calm day and of the many hundreds on board not one life was lost. This news caught my eye. In 1949 it had been in use as a troopship, serving Malta, Egypt, Cyprus and Greece, and on our outward voyage, and also off Gibraltar, had suffered an engine-room fire. We were held up there for repairs for a week and I was able to make the delightful walk up the Rock, a gratifying and unexpected gift.

After a month-long roundabout voyage we arrived in Athens not a moment too late. It was the first year without deaths from malaria. And it was the final year of the Civil War, the fighting having only recently receded to the slopes of Mount Grammos and border areas in the north. However, I was quickly to discover that the personnel of the British Military Mission were confined to the city and I soon learned that it was best not to talk about one's hopes.

Rouf Barracks was situated in a western suburb of Athens. It was said to have been condemned by the Greek army and assigned to us. Its only memorable feature was its sixteen-seater toilet, a long partitionless wooden box with two rows of eight apertures back to back and set at just about splash limit over a stagnant sewer. It stood in a whitewashed corrugated iron shed and had lots of character. Rats waddled along the facing urinal gutters and vivid rapid lizards ran up and down the wall posts. Sunlight filtered in through the colourful blossoms of a flowering tree, screening the ventilation slots. Side by side, pants around their ankles, the young soldiers hid there for an hour at a time, re-reading with furrowed brows the comics of which the place had a small permanent library. In the quarterly rainstorms the sewer rose and most of the walled compound flooded a foot or two deep. Barefoot, in our summer shorts or rolled-up trousers, we paddled through the slurry.

The great marble whaleback of Hymettos looks down upon the city from the east. At sunset it visibly enlarges for several critical minutes and emits extraordinary pulses of light, shifting through apricot, gold, rose and violet, a phenomenon which drew written notice three thousand years ago. And this light actually does tint, as if on a stage set, the shadowed side of the white-walled buildings of Athens. The barracks being on the wrong side of the city, this spacious hill wasn't easy to reach in the time available and was outside our permitted bounds. A reconnaissance took me to the monastery of Kaisariani at the foot of the mountain. This attractive place, offering the cool shade of its trees and Byzantine church, was itself worth the walk. The naivety of the frescoes seemed to lend them an impressive strength. There were neither visitors, curators nor local people to be seen but some desultory excavations were in progress and the skulls of monks of long ago were carelessly laid aside in pits and tunnels.

A week or two later, obliged to travel fast, I walked up the hill itself. Spring flowers and aromatic shrubs I couldn't name extended my sense of release. My appearance on the ascent, conspicuous in uniform, surprised and seemed to please an amiable party of a dozen Greek hillwalkers. Unhappily their English was as rudimentary as my Greek and after a pause in which we could do little but exchange smiles and establish that I was heading for the top whilst they were traversing somewhere around the mountain we were obliged to part.

I allowed myself a tight hour on the warm clean scabby marble rocks of the summit. The smogs which were to swallow Athens in later years hadn't yet been imagined. It was a perfect afternoon and I knew exactly where I was. The geography was obvious and complete and I could tie the mythology and the history in. I was overlooking what is, absolutely, the most resonant landscape of the whole of the earth. Before anywhere else, this was where the action had been, and the thinking too. I told myself the stories and the facts and it didn't seem incongruous that, scratched on a rock at my side, were the names of two Germans with a date from the Occupation. Kindred spirits, presumably, and in a situation far worse than mine. I ran back down the hill, sweating in my khaki and watching carefully where I placed my feet amongst the sharp rocks. A single scratch on my boots would cause serious problems. Forty-odd years on, I understand, a road winds up Hymettos, Homer's Ymitos, to military installations on the summit. So here's a big conservation project: run these people out, efface road and buildings, remove every visible trace.

On one occasion transport was provided for a recreational visit to Corinth and from the old city I walked up the imposing craggy hill of the Acracorinth. Passing through archway after archway in the two miles of fortifications linking cliff and cliff I was impressed by the security of this stronghold, reinforced and extended to medieval times. The life-styles and manners of the inhabitants had deeply shocked St. Paul and he'd written them two strong letters. Once a round thousand temple prostitutes had served at the sanctuary of Aphrodite on the very summit here. Now the tide of human life had ebbed away and their daughters had moved to the streets of Athens with a sad little contingent on day and night picket at the gate of our camp. From this eminence I was able to look south into the Peloponnesus towards Mycenae and the plain of Argos. To the south-west, against the sun, were the empty barren mysterious foothills barring the way towards Arcadia and, further south, into the Deep Mani. I wasn't going to get there while the Army was timing me.

The authorities assumed that on the rare occasions when a lorry was made available for an excursion it would be used to visit a beach. In fact that suited almost everyone. Possibly there was a prudent intention to ensure that no-one was shot by snipers but more probably, since that risk seemed to be over by a year, it was simply a lack of imagination. I've nothing against Greek beaches and in recent years I've spent a good deal of time on more than a dozen Greek islands. But I recall a moment of deep frustration when, on the shore at Marathon, I looked up at the monument-crowned tumulus beneath which the Athenian dead are said to lie. I wanted to lay hands on some rock. Could I sprint up the very steep grassy mound and try to climb the monolith? Better not. The custodian was watching me suspiciously as I prowled around the base of the man-made hill.

For a couple of weeks the entire company was shifted out to camp at Varkiza, now apparently a popular resort and nudist beach. In this spell of training we put the then small local population, the flora and fauna, and above all ourselves, at serious risk; it seemed improbable that the organisation around me could defend itself, much less its country, but the exercise had its lighter moments. Long before dawn each morning, in our underpants, we were marched three abreast directly into the chilly sea, an indescribable confusion in the pitch blackness as those behind cried forward and those in front were trampled under. A similar confusion obtained in an air support operation. We laid out a well-marked dropping zone and grouped at a safe distance to enjoy the performance. A Dakota trundled over and dropped a few heavy bales into the middle of the company turning us from contented spectators to a panic-stricken rabble.

I was forced into small revaluations. One evening six of us escaped the camp unobserved and in a small taverna held a long and serious debate on the risk involved in shooting the feared and hated sergeant-major. Back at Rouf the opportunity would be lost so it was now or never. I argued against the plan on technical rather than on ethical grounds but I learned that it was possible to replace missing ammunition, knowledge which helped me avoid a spell in the glasshouse a few months later.

On the following morning I found myself following the man himself at the head of a file of a hundred soldiers. I'd given away that I could read maps, do tricks with ropes, and had other unusual skills; and I'd recently been promoted, an honour dangerous to refuse. At the rear of the file were the schoolboy officers, carrying tiny batons. In front of them came the whole company, cursing savagely under its breath and carrying Lee-Enfield 3O3s. I was next in line and, as some sort of mark of distinction, was carrying a Bren gun and tripod, twice the weight of anyone else's burden. At the head of the column was the sergeant-major, a tiny man with a very loud voice, bearing a sort of ornamental shillelah, his parade-ground staff. Despite the heat, despite the smart pace, and despite my load, I was thoroughly enjoying myself. We were crossing the low rocky hills of the Cape Sounium promontory, a scented air, an enchanting place. Without warning, on the crest of a rise, he suddenly stopped and like a freight train, colliding and gasping, deliberately dropping its rifles, the company shunted to a halt. Stooping, he picked the flower of a small herb and held it to his nose. He turned and offered it to me. "Know what that is, Corporal?" I'd no idea. "Wild thyme," he said impatiently, "wild thyme." And then, surprising me: "I know a bank where the wild thyme grows." That was near enough right and I realised that he was partly human.

Of course, I knew from the beginning that it was an enormous privilege to be in Greece. Industrial tourism hadn't yet been invented. If you visit the Acropolis today you'll be surrounded by thousands of others and you may have to look at the principal monuments from behind rope barriers. From our barracks I could walk there any evening in a brisk thirty minutes. Sometimes I was the only person on the hill. And sitting alone on the western steps of the Parthenon I'd look over the Saronic Gulf, at Salamis and Aegina, and watch perfect sunsets burn out beyond Megara and Eleusis, a panorama straining with associations and meaning.

The night city had other electrifying enticements. After a while I had the necessary disguise of white shirt, black trousers and shoes, and a convincing suntan. The hair was too short but was darkened by brilliantine and I was able to pass. The satisfaction of strolling casually beneath the military police signs defining the boundaries of the prohibited quarter was considerable. Soon I felt at ease in the tight little maze of streets packed with tavernas, ouzeris, and bordellos, alive with bouzouki music. It was possible to glance with hostile curiosity at the occasional nervous pair of redcaps scouting for British uniforms.

For all this, I was making a precise countdown of days to demobilisation. I'll keep my statement brief. The British Army made a man of me. It stiffened my character, strengthened my determination and taught the need for caution in potentially hazardous situations. When I went in I was innocent, open, candid and optimistic. Before I came out I was wary, resistant, and beginning to speculate that governments, in proportion to their strength, may be bad for our health. I knew, from our political lectures, that we'd intervened with tanks and machine guns to prevent the overthrow of the Greek government in the original communist uprising. I also knew that in the present crisis we were handing over to the Americans as guarantors of Greek democracy. Now I was hearing allegations that these same rebels were the former anti-Nazi Resistance and that we'd been protecting collaborators, who remained in office. (It would be years before I'd learn that while I was in Athens many thousands of those partisans were already in "re-education institutes" on the islands, camps in which slow learners died.)

I was also intrigued by a document, British Ways and Purposes, which I couldn't read since it was on the Classified List but from which various principles were sometimes announced to us. I realised that I couldn't subscribe to some of those principles. However, I judged it better not to draw attention to these misgivings while I was still within arm's reach.

Terrifyingly, the army being ignorant of my problem, I now found myself under strong pressure to sign on as a regular with instant promotion as an inducement. Each time I was called in for an interview I explained the importance of my mission in the Lake District but I was haunted by a very real fear that in a moment of complete mental collapse I'd comply. I hung on to myself tightly and on Christmas Day, 1949, was off Gibraltar again (where we again had an engine-room emergency) on my way home. A few days later, at Dover, I was halfway through handing in my equipment when the operation was abruptly stopped. Technically, a few of us still had time to serve. Almost weeping with frustration I was completely re-equipped, signing for everything a second time. Then, for six long weeks, I sat in Shorncliffe Barracks, without employment, without a book to read, and confined to the camp. All things pass and finally the day came when, having declined to buy my Army greatcoat for two pounds, much too lightly clad in Athenian street market clothing but with spirits soaring, I took the train north through a miraculous snow-covered countryside. I was free and I'd be home in time for my twentieth birthday.

The Flatirons, Boulder, Colorado

TRAVELLING LIGHT

I came back to Yorkshire feverish to climb but quickly a little adjustment had to be made. In Athens I'd spent a fair amount of time in a draught-free black-painted Nissen hut with outside shade temperatures sometimes passing a hundred. I'd been dreaming of walking and climbing in shirt-sleeves, clothes plastered to the body in a cool refreshing rain. In that February and March that wish was granted and that thirst was quenched.

There's a moving passage in *Tess of the D'Urbervilles* in which Hardy evokes a common experience of the English farm labourer of his time:

> To stand working slowly in a field, and feel the creep of rainwater,
> first in legs and shoulders, then on hips and head, then at back,
> front and sides, and yet to work on till the leaden light diminishes
> and marks that the sun is down, demands a modicum of stoicism,
> even of valour.

His agricultural workers had no choice. We were free agents but regular and total saturation came with our deal. It was to be ten or fifteen years yet before even temporarily waterproof clothing became cheaply available and we couldn't just drive away to a crag outside the rain belt. Quickly, there was an ancient familiarity about it, even a grim sense of ceremony as the process declared itself in sequences rather different from that of the field labourer.

In walking, in a matter of minutes, the sudden damp intimation in the socks became, with every step, a tidal squelch between the toes. The first wet rubbings pasted knees, thighs and elbows. The trickle from the neck and the rucksack straps began to explore the torso. With each stride the loose flannels remained glued tolerably to the front of the leg but slapped coldly and stingingly against the back. In driving rain one side learned the weather first. The earliest shower-proofed anoraks needed only a few seconds to concentrate the effect upon the front of the thighs. Amazingly, we sometimes stripped off afterwards to find a small dry patch, shielded by the sack. Often we dried our clothes on our bodies in the pub or the barn. At night we laid them on the bracken under our sleeping bags. Putting them on in the morning was hilariously distressing. It was the equivalent, I suppose, of the English Public School cold shower, if such a practice commonly existed.

In climbing, the rain dance was different again. In the folklore the water poured in at the cuffs of the raised arms and issued out at the ankles, though I've only seen this made obvious in caving when a rope ladder couldn't be kept clear of a waterfall. Certainly, raised hands on wet rock quickly lead water down the underside of the forearm and soon to the armpit; any high steps, once the knee is wet, spread the effect more rapidly than in walking. In continuous downpours we usually settled for crags close to the road so that we started off more or less dry. In fact, to climb technically difficult routes in wet conditions was regarded as convincing proof of a climber's skill and drive. After a few days' rehabituation in that winter I began to put on enough clothing to keep at least the wind out.

In my absence the scene had begun to change. New faces had appeared and older ones were missing. My gritstone and Yorkshire-based club was showing signs of fission. Other smaller clubs — the Phoenix Club, the English Electric Climbing Club, the Vibram Club — were now visible presences but they too were in a state of transition with parties recombining. Exempt from these tendencies by virtue of its insular and self-perpetuating nature, the Leeds University club was also in evidence; however, with the exception of Ginger Cain, and of Dolphin who'd remained an associate, its members didn't mix with other climbers. Within a few months there was to be a comprehensive re-grouping and the appearance of the loose alliance soon to be known as the Bradford Boys.

This shake-up of the smaller clubs was intensified and made irreversible by a single external cause. At Whitsuntide 1950 petrol rationing ended. Immediately there was an increase in the number of vehicles making longer journeys and the Lake District now became a feasible weekend venue.

Seven ways of getting to the English Lake District: to buy a vehicle and drive there; to steal a vehicle and drive there; to travel there by public transport with a proper ticket; to travel there by public transport without a proper ticket; to share the petrol cost with a vehicle owner; to gather enough support to allow the hiring of a coach; to hitch-hike there. There were other ways as well but there were obstacles to each of them and during the next three years these were the methods tested.

The ideal means, obviously, was to get a motor bike. Two or three of the older climbers owned bikes already and from that Whitsuntide relegated gritstone to an evening activity. Others had ancient machines within a year or so and most of us were saving up towards one. But that would be a long-term project and something had to be done now.

If you can't buy one, borrow one. This was an age of nicknames. It was explained of the Pale Man, spelling discretionary, that he had a head like a bucket, though whether the reference was to form or content wasn't made clear. It was usually understood as descriptive of his complexion. He seized a nearly brand-new bike and carelessly equipped it with number plates duplicating those of an unsold bike in a Bradford showroom. We were racked with envy when the glittering Triumph Twin was first exhibited at the Dungeon Ghyll. No-one asked about its provenance. In fairness, it has to be said that it was generally made free to anyone who wanted to road-test it and the curator seemed to become less and less possessive of his shiny toy as the weeks went by and he began to reconsider his position. His ordinarily evasive glance took on a trapped expression. Soon the bike was out on long loan and he didn't seem anxious to get it back. When the law finally reclaimed it from the hands of George Elliott it had clocked eleven thousand miles in a few months and, obviously, had travelled additional distances lying down.

I'd like to defend the Pale Man and to say: he wasn't really bad; he had to do it — *for love of climbing.* But that's not true. By chance, ten years later, I re-encountered Venus. A sometime Wall Ender, profiting perhaps from early observations in the field, she'd now become Miss Laws, a probation officer. It took a moment to accept her in this unlikely role as she updated me on his careers. Embarrassingly, and at unnervingly unpredictable intervals, now a car salesman wearing expensive suits, he'd been calling on her for references and once, I think, for an alibi. From wrecking bikes he'd gone on to wrecking cars. He needed a wheel in his hands. Later, at great expense to new employers, he damaged a vessel in the Thames on a dark night. No doubt his eyes were on the stars and he was dreaming of aeroplanes. His removal from the scene was a loss but he'd seconded me on the first ascent of Holly Tree Direct in Langdale so his name lives on in climbing history as well as in Court Records.

Although, on a local basis, bus services were excellent, they didn't permit the longer journey to Westmorland for a weekend. It was feasible by train but too expensive and too inconveniently timed for most of us. Of course, if it were possible to make the excursion on a platform ticket one objection to the shortened visit would be removed. Jack Bradley, with one of his followers, tested this possibility. Later he was to become a millionaire from time to time, as his empires rose and fell, and he was even briefly a Master of Foxhounds. But at that time he was an apprentice plumber, given to singing the Internationale, the Red Flag and Wobbly songs with apparent passion. His attempt to create a free public transport system within the shell of the old showed courage. The penny ticket would take him safely from York to Windermere but exit through the station there was impossible. An idea presented itself. Beyond Staveley, not far short of the terminus, the train reduced speed on a long uphill curve. I see him now, bravado leaking, face paling, as he hangs from the door. Really, it's much too fast. But with a companion watching and his reputation at stake it has to be done and he takes the punishing tumble down the embankment. Damage to clothing, severe bruising, and the intimidating jump itself discouraged continued experiment.

Most of us, anyway, travelled by hitch-hiking. On Friday nights we caught buses to the outposts of the West Riding conurbation, Keighley, Otley or Ilkley, and tried our luck. Occasionally, at Skipton where our routes converged, we'd find a spaced queue soliciting under the last street lights of the Gargrave road. Sometimes on Sundays there'd be a similar queue beyond Kendal on the return trip, a source of anxiety. The weekend's successes were diminished if we didn't make it back to Otley in time for reports and debriefing at Tommy's Café, a cyclists' hangout, or at the Black Bull later.

With modern road design, with greater traffic speeds and densities, with the distrust of male hitch-hikers by drivers and the distrust of male drivers by female hitch-hikers, with the car as one of the last outposts of privacy and autonomy, hitch-hiking has declined since its heyday in the fifties. That's a great pity. It had a lot to recommend it. It got us off the streets and onto the roads, it developed our conversational skills, it allowed us to meet an extraordinarily varied selection of people. We learned a more accurate physical geography and we put styles of agriculture and industry into proper contexts. We had a chance to see the countryside unblinkered by the tunnel vision driving would later impose on us. We got healthy exercise when we were obliged to walk for long distances. Our minds were stretched by game theory, strategy and tactics in computing problems of likely traffic flows, road feed patterns, signalling point advantages and hitch-hiker competition. We learnt to live patiently or we learned that patience must be a valuable gift. We spent time in places we'd never otherwise have made real.

Now I'll propose ease of hitch-hiking as proportional to degree of civilisation. It's a crucial index, like courtesy and openness towards strangers or foreigners, of the essential health or morbidity of a society. It forces a regrouping of West, East and Third World countries into entirely new blocks with much of the West relegated as a barbaric culture. It still picks out regions not yet sunk into decadence within each nation.

The signals are interesting. To this day there's no universal sign language for the driver, whose full-load, stopping-shortly, or turning-off-soon gestures may be meant to be informative or apologetic but remain ambiguous and capable of misconstruction. In the fifties the cardboard destination sign hadn't yet appeared and the hitch-hiker's signal said as much about the man as about his purpose. To stand for inspection at the roadside was as disturbing to some as to speak in public or to sell charity flags. With downcast looks these petitioners would raise a limp wrist a few inches but usually preferred to hitch whilst walking in order to avoid eye contact and the modest appeal risked missing notice altogether. The standard practice was to sweep a relaxed near arm with thumb upraised. Extraverts advanced into the road making policeman-like commands and mouthing pleas unintelligible to the driver. Responses to failure showed a similar range. Sometimes a philosophical shrug, sometimes a silent curse, sometimes a forgiving blessing. Even then, though, there were a few crazies who would break into a run after a departing car, first waving the arms desperately, then shaking a fist, shouting abuse, giving the Crécy vee-sign or, later, the American finger.

My own career as hitch-hiker began in Longdendale, Derbyshire in 1947 and ended, I hope, in Boulder Canyon, Colorado in 1975. Each of these adventures stays in my mind. The first occasion followed my first club meet. I was perfectly satisfied with Ilkley but since everyone was going to Laddow I had to follow. We arrived at this venue, not easy to reach, in ones and twos by different routes. After an enjoyable day the sensible members left to catch the last bus over the Pennines. An hour or two later the rest of the party began to speculate on ways of getting home. Quite suddenly, almost without farewells, the group fragmented in haste, heading off north and north-west across the moors and committed to a wide variety of plans. On a courageous impulse I went south, away from home. The logic was that I'd reach a road much more quickly by the descent to Crowden. That would give me more time to attempt to hitch a lift. If there was nothing on the road I'd walk the seven miles over Holme Moss hoping that there'd be late-night traffic in Yorkshire.

It worked. I'd seen no traffic as I descended into the valley and I set off in pitch darkness on the road over the hill. Within minutes a motorcyclist stopped, floated me over the watershed, and in a quarter-hour I was in Holmfirth catching a bus for Huddersfield. This incident gave cause for thought. I was home by ten or eleven. None of my companions reached home much before dawn and two had made an uncomfortable bivouac on Stalybridge railway station.

By 1975 the experience was unfamiliar. With my wife, Maureen, I was staying for a fortnight with old friends, Gordon and Maureen Mansell. Their home was on the western edge of the city of Boulder, within a few minutes' walk of that impressive frontier where the Great Plains meet the first declaration of the Rockies. Boulder Canyon slices through this escarpment. For our first climb the Mansells had recommended an easy route of about three hundred feet, Jackson's Wall on Castle Rock at the head of the canyon. Only a few yards from the roadside it proved a very pleasant opener, maybe severe by English standards. It was early October and to our surprise, before we were halfway up, it began to snow heavily. But the day was windless, the holds good and the rock steep enough for the snow hardly to lodge so that we weren't impeded. The Mansells arrived back from a walk with their young son just as we were descending, the snow stopping as unexpectedly as it had begun.

Two days later, towards evening, Maureen realised that she'd left her boots at the foot of the crag. The Mansells were out until late and, without transport yet, it appeared that we'd have to leave it another day before attempting to recover them. The chance seemed slim anyway but I decided to try to hitch up the canyon. It was only five minutes' walk to the mouth and within another five minutes I'd been picked up by two young men in a large and ancient car. On the shelf behind the back seat lay a fishing rod and two immaculate top hats. We'd only been travelling for a few minutes when the driver reported that the sheriff's car was tailing us. I learned then that hitch-hiking was illegal in Colorado, though I'd seen young people trying it in Boulder. There, apparently, a blind eye was turned, in view of the large student population. A story was quickly fabricated. The police car followed us for several miles but pulled in to examine another car hanging precariously over the edge of the ravine. Shortly I was dropped off at Castle Rock in darkness. I groped my way to the foot of the climb and to my amazement and gratification felt my hands touch on the boots, bone dry after two days of sunshine.

Now my problems began. There was almost no traffic going down the canyon but there was steady traffic coming up. Presumably one of these cars would be the sheriff's and if I stood on the roadside I'd be seen. Did it matter? I'm a British citizen, you're going to regret this. See what it says in my passport: "Her Britannic Majesty's Principal Secretary of State for Foreign Affairs Requests and requires in the Name of Her Majesty all those whom it may concern to allow the bearer to pass freely without let or hindrance and to afford the bearer such assistance and protection as may be necessary." Notice that: "requires". Any funny stuff and there'll be a gunboat on the way. The trouble was that I didn't have my passport, only my accent, a down-market version of R.N.P. In fact I had no I.D. at all, highly suspicious to American policemen, and as it happened I hadn't a cent in my pockets. By definition I was probably a vagrant. I could imagine the story Gordon Mansell would start to elaborate if I were taken in.

Boots in hand, for the next hour I stumbled backwards and forwards. When a car came down I ran to the roadside. When a car came up I ran back and hid behind a convenient boulder. Of course, the sheriff might be in one of the cars coming back down by now, from Nederland or wherever, on a return trip. Finally a big van, moving extremely rapidly by starlight only, suddenly flicked its lights on, exposed me, and ground to a halt. The window was lowered and a savagely bearded face was dimly visible. "What the fuck you doin' with those boots, man?" I explained, the back doors were opened and I was hauled inside, finding myself on a carpeted floor tightly wedged between an unknown number of large and hairy hippies. The atmosphere was thick with smoke and a joint, as they used to say, was pressed into my hand. As I drew on this I was aware that it permitted a silent inspection of my illuminated face. For some reason the vehicle's lights were snapped on only a second or two before reaching each bend in the road. Otherwise we went barrelling down in total darkness but the driver knew the shape of the canyon. Nobody spoke. Dropped off at College Avenue, I was home in minutes and, slightly disorientated, was surprised to discover I hadn't spent much more than two hours on this refresher course.

It's not easy to summarise the experience gained by the years on the road. I can't even say that prediction was impossible since, starting each weekend journey at the same time and place, I soon found that two or three drivers watched out for me and were happy to pick me up. Who was the portly old man, a whiskered Dickensian figure in pork-pie hat and chocolate three-piece suit complete with gold watch-fob? He drove a pre-war Wolseley, would take me from Keighley to Skipton, and seemed to regard the arrangement as a part of his social calendar. I was often questioned carefully about my strange obsession and I was often wished well. On a number of occasions I was even told that my philosophy was interesting and I sensed that the driver was reviewing his own life as well.

This was in contrast with another view. At work I was sometimes rebuked, mostly, surprisingly, by younger people: hitch-hiking was a form of begging, it was wanting something for nothing. My reply that I didn't cost the driver anything, and that I looked forward to the day when I'd own a car and could settle my debts, was dismissed with contempt; it strained imagination to see me as a car-owner. Once, sack on back, starting the four-mile midnight trudge home from the centre of Bradford on a Sunday night, I thumbed a motor-cyclist. He pulled in two hundred yards beyond me. "Are you a hiker?" he called back. I wasn't a hiker, I was a climber, but I agreed for the moment and jogged up the road while he throttled his bike impatiently. He let me get almost there. "Well, hike then!" he shouted and pulled smartly away, delighted with himself. He didn't know that it didn't matter. I'd been hoping to save some time but, instead, I'd enjoy the walk for itself.

Generally drivers seemed to be interested in the hitch-hiker, who has no licence anyway to interrogate the driver in any depth. Sometimes, though, they'd explain themselves to the therapist in the passenger seat. Occasionally they'd preach to the young man and once I sat through a stiffening fifty-mile discourse on Moral Rearmament. (Twenty-five years later, by contrast, I couldn't get a young man out of my car at his drop-off until he'd completed his testimony on how to be saved.) With not many cars on the road and hardly a lady driver ever to be seen the fantasy of being picked up by a rich, amoral and glamorous older woman was never fulfilled. Just once, a girl did pick me up, immediately introducing herself as the fiancée of an older climber I'd already met.

Hitch-hiking can be uncomfortable and even dangerous. I recall an uneasy couple of hours on the back of a flat-bed lorry bombing down the Great North Road in a snowstorm. The driver was keen to get home before the roads closed. My companion and I sat with our backs square against the headboard, nothing to hold onto, our bare hands spread on the icy metal bed. On every curve the lorry slid a little on the road and we slid a few inches ourselves towards one or other of the unguarded sides.

Leaving Ambleside one rainy afternoon I was picked up by a twenty-year-old driving an expensive new car. He was going to Kendal but decided he'd run me as far as Levens Bridge. I demurred, embarrassed, but he said there'd be a little more traffic coming in there, true, and the rain would probably be lighter, also true. I could see that he wanted to drive and needed a just cause. On the A6 he started to open it up until, not far from our destination, he lost it on a mild curve. We made two revolutions, first horizontal, then vertical, passed between two large trees, and finally the gleaming car was at rest on a wide grassy verge, the engine still purring sweetly, the windscreen missing. The weight of the rucksack on my knees had pinned me comfortably to the seat. A neat five-foot length of turf was tucked across both of us. We'd had a miraculous escape.

The driver was apparently in deep shock. He was clearly uninjured but sat there in silence, gripping the wheel fiercely. I couldn't get a word out of him. I got out and inspected the car. Not a mark anywhere on wheels and sides but the whole roof slightly depressed. All the other windows intact. After ten minutes of questions and uninvited suggestions it began to come out. His elder brother's car. Permission to drive it to Ambleside only. And worse to come: his brother's firm's car.

I felt an unreasonable and unatonable guilt. He couldn't even bring himself to drive home. I got him to a phone box where he made his difficult call. I offered my name and address but he didn't want to know me. It was hard to find parting words. In the end I simply had to walk away, leaving him with a problem only reducible through the perspective of months or years.

It was clearly more effective to hitch alone but sometimes, for company, we worked in pairs. Standing on the roadside outside Kendal, homeward-bound, my brother set me right on probability. We'd been there more than two hours. That was exceptional, I said, it could only be minutes now before someone stopped. No, he said, it doesn't work like that. Other things being equal, the chance in every minute is the same. This car might be the one, or we might be here all night. I heard his explanations with a shock of disbelief. And I realised for the first time the direction Neville's interests were taking.

The longest times I ever stood were in France. Outside Sens, two young Danes had first call. "Ça va long, ici," one of them shouted as the hot afternoon wore out. But after five or six hours a big camion finally stopped, they persuaded the driver to invite me aboard as well, and I was shifted a couple of hundred kilometres closer to the Alps. The next day the difficulties continued. I'd got onto a minor road and I saw that a crisis was approaching. I was in a bad area. It was where Estragon and Vladimir, heading for the Pyrenees, had been stranded for so long that they'd had to seek temporary work as grape-pickers.

I can't suppress the feeling that Estragon and Vladimir are my brother and myself and I'd better explain. When *Waiting for Godot* was first staged the critics saw that it was something special but they couldn't think of a context with a reasonable fit. Beckett knew well enough that theatre directors don't hitch-hike yet he took the precaution of casting his heroes as clowns so that attention would be concentrated upon predicament and language rather than on social significance. When the first director, in France, had the inspiration of presenting them as tramps, a convention followed ever since, Beckett must have smiled. It was so close to the truth that it didn't give the game away. It's been said that Goethe knew the art of hiding things on the surface and I think that's true of Beckett.

The stage directions are minimalist ("A road. A tree. Evening.") but it's actually set just east of the point where the road from Killary Harbour and the Twelve Bens meets the Clifden to Galway road. (Connemara is deliberately named a couple of times.) We're waiting for an Arranged Lift. It was a fish lorry (Beckett says a horse and cart!) but when you're desperate anything will do. We've pinned our faith on this Irish promise. Every hitch-hiker will be familiar with our shifts between suicidal despair and resurgent faith and will be at home with the humour of the absurd which was invented, in fact, by hitch-hikers. At the beginning of each act Neville struggles to get his boots off to inspect his blisters. (We've walked down from Glen Inagh.) In the middle of each act we discuss splitting up to improve our chances. At the end of each act, in the same memorable closing lines, we resolve to walk a little further to change the variables: but, somehow, we can't quite stir ourselves.

> Vladimir: Well? Shall we go?
> Estragon: Yes, let's go.
> (They do not move.)

All that's wrong with this reading is that the play appeared a couple of years before either of us reached Connemara. Also, we never went together, we went with other companions. Anyway, he pretends the inaction was near Mâcon. I was twenty miles away, near Bourg. I did the sums. I'd less than three weeks free and I'd only enough money to buy food to support so many days' climbing. I was spending it here. Better to sacrifice some of it and a couple of mountains than to eat my way through money and holiday by a roadside in the Departement of Ain. I gave in and caught a train to Chamonix.

The shortest time I ever waited was at Hellifield in Yorkshire. It was a paralysingly cold winter night, I was inadequately clothed, and I got stiffly off the back of a motor bike at the bus stop in the village centre. I felt I was on the edge of hypothermia. There was a queue of a half dozen people at the stop, hunched, unspeaking, standing patiently. I asked how long for the next bus into Skipton. A quarter hour. As I was being answered I heard a car approaching. I walked back a few feet, the driver stopped, and I was on my way to Skipton. I'd been on my feet for twenty seconds. I couldn't help wondering whether this incident cracked the Yorkshire reserve of the silent figures.

The most satisfying journey made by hitching was a climbers' Grand Tour taken by Neville and myself through England, Scotland, Ireland and Wales in a fortnight. The symmetry of this trip was only spoiled by the fact that we didn't seize a climb in Scotland, not being aware that rock climbs had already been made not far from our route through Galloway. During this expedition we succeeded in crossing Ireland as an unpromising party of four, my brother having recruited two startlingly beautiful girls as companions for the Irish leg of the enterprise.

Longer journeys always held an additional element of uncertainty: where would the night be spent? This expedition offered a pleasant surprise. Passing through Galloway, all traffic having apparently finished for that day, we found ourselves at Newton Stewart and still twenty miles short of Stranraer where we were to catch the early morning ferry. The girls I'd yet to meet would be on the boat train and it was clear that, for certainty, we'd have to catch that six o'clock train ourselves. The stationmaster was locking up for the night but he sold us tickets and we asked if we might spend the night on the platform. Obligingly, he suggested we use the waiting room if we didn't mind being locked inside since it gave access to the ticket office. To our delight we found a substantial fire still burning and long capacious well-padded leather benches on which to throw down our sleeping bags. In the morning we were roused by gentle touches on the shoulder. Pint mugs of very sweet tea were thrust into our hands and we were told that our train would be along in twenty minutes. That was British Rail.

It didn't always work out so well. For the Christmas of 1951 we were staying in the barn at Gatesgarth in Buttermere, a dozen persons, a Bradford group and a London group. The hills were under deep snow. On Christmas Day, ordinary rock-climbing being out of the question, we decided to try to force a route by any means up a then unclimbed wall of High Crag Buttress. Mike Dixon, Neville and myself each led a short pitch, resorting to combined tactics, jammed ice axes and a lasso move, before Pat Vaughan was finally stopped on a steep unpromising wall.

I'd been enjoying myself and hadn't been able to tear myself away though I was supposed to be at work in Bradford on Boxing Day. I waded over Honister Pass in darkness, the road not negotiable by vehicles, and found as I trudged down Borrowdale that nobody was travelling in that valley anyway. One memory stands out clearly. Passing the brightly lit Swiss Lodore Hotel, sounds of music and festivity emerging, the main doors opened and two quite young women came out. They were in immaculately chic white evening dresses and each held a glass in her hand. They walked across the terrace to the balustrade and looked down on the road where I happened to be passing under the only roadside light for a number of miles. Sack on back, in my sodden clothes, I was noticed and in the still winter air I heard the clear English voice that carries so much further than the speaker realises: "Oh, the poor thing!" The words were said with real compassion. Obviously I was a tramp, friendless and homeless. Snarling under my breath I put my head down and strode on, irrationally confident that my day would come.

So, if you were around then, where did you spend Christmas night, 1951? I spent it on a park bench in Keswick. It wasn't too bad. The bench was on the riverside but beneath a broad road or railway bridge so that I was sheltered, the snow having turned to intermittent rain. On Boxing Day, however, the roads remained almost empty so that it wasn't until seven at night that I started my day's work.

Just after the appearance of *A Hitch-Hiker's Guide to the Galaxy* a more useful and rather better-written survey, based on first-hand research, appeared in one of the minor climbing club journals: "A Hitch-Hiker's Guide to the A6." It listed and graded the various emergency dosses offered by that long avenue. It wasn't a road we often used but we had a similar familiarity with the Kendal end of the A65 and for the Lakes generally we collected and exchanged information on all identified shelters. Some of these could be almost crowded on Friday nights though none compared with the so-called "Station Hotel" at Ingleton, a train in a siding sometimes accommodating a hundred pot-holers and walkers on a weekend.

Nights to remember. In Stonethwaite, with Dennis Gray, I scouted desperately for cover. Then I noticed that the top-lights of the windows of the tiny primary school were open, no problem for a climber. I slid in and found water available so that quickly we had our Primus stoves running. And there in the corner of the hall was a four-foot-high pile of gymnasium mats from which we built ourselves beds of the preferred degrees of resilience. Church bells woke us pleasantly to a fine morning. We arranged everything as we'd found it, checked that no trace but our fingerprints remained, and slipped quietly away with a silent blessing on Cumberland Education Committee.

A night in Sligo Town, cold, on the hard floor of a box-wagon in the station. We'd been kept up late in a bar where, after a bad start, the local teams proved unable to beat us at darts. Well after midnight the door swung open and the Garda sergeant ducked in. We expected the session to end but he insisted on standing for the honour of the town. We beat him too and staggered out to seek shelter. In the morning we rose very early, stiff and fearful that we might suddenly find ourselves rumbling back to Dublin. Immediately, we got a lift to Donegal Town. Still, no-one was stirring as we crossed the wet cobbles of the empty market-place to picket the Killybegs road. Dead central in this wide expanse, the single scrap of litter, a discarded contraceptive spoke of the secret life of the town. Illegal, disgraceful, it had travelled through some unimaginable smuggler's route to reach this distant outpost.

(Rest in peace, Mike Downing, companion on this trip. Not a climber but a searcher. Scenes, experiences, situations, fun. Amused by my fanaticism he followed me up climbs with zest and an intrigued curiosity. A gregarious being, who cracked only once during our lonely spell in the Poisoned Glen, begging me almost in tears to hitch down to the coast for a full day's drinking. Whose name appears against a single climb. And who, in 1976, forgetting that I and perhaps a few others loved and needed him, shot himself in the little town of Midway, British Columbia.)

A night in a beautiful house in Ambleside. The householder, walking his dog at midnight, saw me casting my eye over possibilities on the edge of the town. Housebreaking hadn't been invented in the Lake District then. He questioned me and was shocked by my immediate purpose. He insisted on taking me in, made me a drink, and after I'd declined to soil the sheets of his immaculate guest bedroom he permitted me to roll out my grubby sleeping bag on his luxuriously thick lounge carpet. In the morning he cooked me a full English breakfast to set me on my way. The whole episode was embarrassing. I thanked him sincerely but tried to convey that I was the spearhead of an invasion the like of which Lakeland hadn't seen since the Vikings. Best to lock up daughters, barricade doors and windows and let my comrades look after themselves. They were competent at that.

A contribution from my brother: In the West of Scotland he'd walked all evening without a lift or a sign of shelter. It was pitch black. He had no torch, tent, primus stove, matches or tin opener, though he had a tin of beans in his sack. He was hungry, footsore and tired. Finally he made out on the verge what he first took to be a dump of road-mending material. Stepping closer, he discovered that it was covered by a tarpaulin. It might be possible to sleep beneath it. Lifting the edge he eased his hands under what felt like a huge turnip. Was the dump a clamp, a store for cattle perhaps, offering food as well as shelter? Then, as he hefted and weighed the object it gave out a blood-curdling scream. Understanding came instantly: he was inspecting a tinkers' tent and handling a tinker's head. Appalled, fearful for his life or health, the someday Dean of Life and Health Sciences at a great Midland university sprang to his feet and gasped out an explanation. Immediately, a chorus of voices, terrified, confused or belligerent, broke out:

"There iss a fe-llo trrying to strrangle me!"

"Iss it the po-liss?"

"What iss happening. It must pe four in the pluidy morrning!"

"I think there's only wan fe-llo. Will we get oot and grab him?"

"He said he thought you wass a turrnip!"

That's the beginning of Nev's story.

Mostly, these are tales of forty years ago. This way of life made our climbing of the early fifties possible. I imagine that I clocked up almost fifty thousand miles and I've only paid a fraction of it back. Still, when I can pull up safely on today's congested roads it pleases me to offer a lift, to give local advice if asked, to wish a stranger safe journey.

Did you ever see the BBC's first climbing documentary? It was made about 1958 and it's archive material now. Mostly it profiled Joe Brown, moving easily up Suicide Wall, on the Cromlech boulders, on Cloggy. For completeness, though, it recorded two figures loitering outside what was then the Police Station in Altrincham, the start of a route to Wales. Watch this pair for technique. A car approaches, the driver pulls up and leans across to wind down the window. A practised team. The presentable one steps forward and is shown full-face as he politely states their destination and asks whether there's space for two. The other has withdrawn to the wall, arms folded, not crowding the driver, smiling amiably. The other was Geoff Roberts.

Deer Bield Crag

THE LAKES

Who were the Bradford Boys? Unlike the Creagh Dhu in Scotland and the Rock and Ice in Wales, groupings fairly comparable in lifestyle and number but of which one was either in or out, it's hard to draw a line around this loose association. The difficulty showed up first when Dennis Gray offered a tentative list of a named team with footnoted reserves in *Rope Boy*. It came to a head thirty-three years or so after the diaspora when Duncan Boston decided to organise annual reunions of survivors at the Old Dungeon Ghyll Hotel. These reunions were open to Wall Enders from the start and were soon invaded by others who'd climbed in Langdale in the late forties and early fifties. In effect they've been hijacked, but without diplomatic protest and with everyone's consent.

There seems to be agreement on only two points. First, that less than half the number came from Bradford; and second, that one boy was visibly a girl. In fact the name was accepted by a number of West Riding climbers as a means of self-definition, though it was probably first used by other parties to label a new presence in Lakeland climbing. If the Boys had a fixed address, that address was Wall End Barn. But from 1951 other climbers, especially from Lancashire, began to share that address in greater numbers and some miscegenate climbing liaisons were quickly formed.

So who were the Bradford Boys? Of all attempts to answer this question I prefer Einstein's: it depends on the observer, his speed and track as he travelled through. Following the reasoning you'll see that it's possible to fix names and disagree on dates or to fix dates and disagree on names. I choose to fix dates and from my stances they run from the de-rationing of petrol at Whitsuntide, 1950 to the events of the summer of 1953. Names can come out as needed.

If Wall End Barn was the barracks of the Boys, and shortly of a fair number of girls too, our postal address must have been the Old Dungeon Ghyll. (Some years later, only just in time, I was to pick up from the bar a six-week-old letter from Geoff Sutton which would shape the course of my life decisively.) A happy circumstance for Lakeland climbers, the hotel had recently passed into the hands of Sid Cross and his wife, the former Alice Nelson. They'd been one of the more powerful teams of an earlier generation and their marriage is wittily commemorated in their two steep contiguous routes on Eagle Crag in Buttermere: Half Nelson and Double Cross.

A native Cumbrian, easy in manner, Sid Cross had distanced himself from his working-class origins by unremitting hard work. He'd started out as a cobbler and had also worked in a tannery. You never saw such hands. His charm and sense of humour, his prestige, and his limitless fund of anecdote endeared him to the wealthier climbers and walkers who stayed at the hotel. However, perhaps he saw in the young Wall Enders an echo of his own beginnings and enthusiasm, and he took an interest in our progress. Cool enough to be able to handle the difficulties and embarrassment occasionally posed by some of our number, he turned the new outside bar into a haven of warmth and conviviality.

You've seen the barn already, you'd better take a look at this famous bar. It's formed in part from a converted stables with a couple of stalls nicely sized for benches and tables. The floor, walls, seating and serving arrangements are perfectly suited to contain a clientele often wet, always noisy, sometimes offensive and occasionally dishonest.

Today, when a newcomer steps inside this bar, his eye will rest for a moment on the five by three oil painting mounted on the wall. It was the work of a young London artist, Shirley Parfitt, a regular visitor at Wall End. Years of smoking fires, perspiring drinkers, and steaming clothes and boots, far from damaging the panel would seem to have enriched it. Now it has the dark glowing colours of a quattrocento master. Centrally, a bearded climber reposes, floating, caped, cast as Bacchus. In his left hand he bears a flagon which can only hold Younger's Ale, in his right he raises an ice axe. The Langdale Pikes are seen in the background and in the middle distance a voluptuous white-robed girl, reclining passively and availably beside a tent, gives a strong alternative focus. Cherubs hover around and one amongst them reads the third series Great Langdale climbing guide, permitting the critic to assign the work a date no earlier than 1950. A scroll unfolds a message or motto: Festerat Wallendia. (To fester, intransitive verb, dialect, obsolete: to live, not unhappily, in discomfort and squalor.) This slogan now allows the critic to date the canvas as not later than 1957 when the barn was closed. Finally, the inclusion in the scene of the hotel rather than the barn might allow him to guess correctly that the work was commissioned by the landlord himself. Altogether it's a jokey, well-executed pastiche.

A residual mystery about this painting is the use of Jack Thornton, also known as Black Jack, as model. Could it be simply that he was the Wall Ender most easily persuaded to exchange a climb on a fine day for an afternoon with glass in hand? Or might it be that Parfitt had taken some dislike to him? By plan or accident, she fixed him for good. She set him in amber. For years afterwards he was obliged to loiter near the painting in the same threadbare clothes. To this day he's been unable to shave off or reshape the beard. He can't lower his glass in case some new visitor fails to make the connection and nudge a friend. Hands up those who say art can't rule our lives.

To those who played parts, these three years are the Golden Age of British climbing. Are there any objective arguments for that conviction? It might be said that from 1950 onward climbing was to become a popular sport, not just in the sense of numbers but as an activity open to anyone. Certainly, working-class climbers had won recognition earlier but their exploits had almost always been confined to the areas in which they were living. From now on they'd operate throughout Britain and progressively further afield.

It might also be claimed that the step from the very severe grade to what was to become the foundation of the extreme grades was somehow the most significant in the history of the sport. At first glance that claim seems to rest mainly on an accident of language, the near-exhaustion of an adjectival classification system. But let's pretend for a moment that the present grades represent equal increments in difficulty, a supposition that ought sometime to be examined. Now let's borrow a statistician.

Set out a graph with a vertical axis from Mod to E10 and a horizontal axis for the last hundred years. Plot the years by which ten routes of each successive standard of difficulty had been accumulated and draw the curve. Surely what you'll see is a slow ascent up to the early fifties, possibly with plateaux spanning the periods of the world wars, and from the fifties onward a steep unabating rise to the present day.

And also, of course, that time was the very end of an ancient civilisation, one in which without deliberate choice individuals and subcultures could remain untouched by styles promoted by the mass media and tended therefore to evolve distinguishing identities spontaneously.

Now how can I represent what those years meant to me? If I were to write down all I remember of people, landscapes, incidents, the climbs, the moves I made, I'd fill many books. If I were to attempt an objective history I'd have to spend years in cross-checking and assigning values to the often discordant and sometimes feeble memories of my friends. What I'm going to do is, I'm going to cut just three cards out of my pack, turn them over, and say what they mean. Well, I admit it, I marked the cards. It's the only way I could hope to represent so much by so little. As a matter of fact they're not my highest cards but they make a trick.

The first card says Deer Bield Crack. It stands for consolidation, in this case our ambition to repeat all the great classics of the Lakes. Shortly the effort would begin to centre on the climbs of Birkett, Peascod and Dolphin, all three close to the ends of their productive careers. But initially we had the harder earlier routes to measure ourselves against and amongst the prestigious lines of the nineteen-thirties Deer Bield Crack had, if anything, increased in reputation through the years.

In the February of 1951 I found myself spending a night in Grasmere Youth Hostel with Peter Greenwood. Our awaited partners had failed to arrive, perhaps through road conditions. The hills were deep in snow.

Greenwood — short, compact, powerful, almost Latin in appearance and volatility — is in the history books as an outstanding climber but his restless energy diverted him into very varied adventures. He ran into problems with policemen, licensees, hostel wardens, girls, other climbers. A Berserker spirit ruled his nature. In the barn one crowded and noisy night, following some earlier difference, he insistently provoked a member of a group not known to me until his patience was rewarded. The visitor, a Bradford area gritstoner known as Pablo, was considerably bigger than the tormentor. From the dimly lit further end of the barn we heard a solid smack as he hit Pete, and then, an alarming crack as Pete's head struck the crudely cobbled floor. We pacified the visitor and his friends, carted our deeply unconscious hero back to his corner, and manipulated him very awkwardly into his sleeping bag. For a good quarter of an hour then, sitting in vigil over him, we held a drunken and uninformed debate on the nature and seriousness of concussion. Ought we to get medical advice? How would we do that without transport?

How and where might we get access to a telephone long after midnight?

The discussion ended when he woke up suddenly, snarling curses. He was going to kill Pablo. He started to struggle out of his bag. Just in time two of us caught hold of it, twisting it tight over his shoulders and against his neck. He couldn't get his arms out but at the same time we could hardly hold him. He bucked and heaved and it was as though we were pinning a dangerous beached fish by the gills. Three or four others laid themselves across the strait-jacketed body but with a maniacal strength he kept raising them a little, like a boat lifting to a swell. After several long minutes, as abruptly as he'd wakened, he collapsed and fell into a deep sleep. Warily, we sat around him for an hour or so. He seemed to be breathing alright. Always the same. A fight, a climb, he couldn't believe in defeat.

In Grasmere, then, we ran through possibilities and the idea that the steepness and aspect of Deer Bield Crack might have kept its major difficulties snow-free occurred to us. Pete was uneasy, having already agreed to do the climb with his capable new second, Fred Williams. An odd streak of consideration and strong loyalty in his make-up sometimes took me by surprise. But the others hadn't arrived and it seemed the only worthy objective.

Deer Bield is a strange one. It's possible to project character into most cliffs or mountains and it's not difficult to list the associations and components we've built that character from. Deer Bield, by contrast, is for me one of the very few crags in which I sense anima, a concentrated self like that of a wild creature, not intentionally hostile but not tameable. It seems to crouch in the hillside.

It was a wild morning with periods of calm interrupted by sudden furious squalls of snow. We had the remote little valley of Far Easedale entirely to ourselves. As we approached, heads down against the blast, the cloud cleared and we looked up to see a remarkable sight. The whole right flank of the buttress was a featureless sheet of almost vertical snow and it amazed us that the major fault of Deer Bield Chimney hadn't produced any surface ripple to mark its presence behind this scooped white shield. The line of the Crack was clear, though. As we stared up at it a savage flurry hit us, making us turn for a couple of minutes to hide our stinging faces. I wondered whether, if it persisted, we'd even find the cliff again, not a half-mile up the slope and boulder-field. It eased, we reached the foot of the fissure, and we saw that it appeared to be almost free. We could see some unfrozen streaks of melt-water seepage in the main pitch and the crag had the greenish cast it always develops in winter. Perched on a couple of protruding rocks we changed, audaciously, into socks over plimsolls.

The notorious crux chimney is approached by eighty feet of steep disjointed cracks. From a distance this chimney appears as a dark vulval slit and no clear sense of its difficulty can be formed. Closer, the left wall is seen to be set back. On reaching the foot of the thirty-foot cleft its unsuspected depth is revealed. In fact it pierces the cliff, the nether opening forming Deer Bield Chimney but the connection being too tight to pass. Looking up into the holdless slot it's seen first to widen and then to close. At half height the right wall shows an interior overhang forcing the climber out into a shallow hanging chimney. A few feet higher it looks as if it tries again, nearly boxing the exit with a block overhang. Clearly it's going to involve a protectionless gutwrenching struggle with inelegant wriggling, desperate palming, possibly the painful use of knees. Imagine a geometer forced to ascend between two frictionless planes set so close together that it can't properly flex its back.

Following the description I climbed up well inside to reach the stricture. Here, beyond reach, I happened to notice a deep and distant chockstone, a possible means of protecting the traverse out. Within a few minutes I'd so exhausted myself by trying to cast some linked slings over it that I could do nothing but slide back down for a rest. My indirectness had tried Pete's patience and he pointed out that a runner there might jam the rope at a later stage. Seizing his chance and ignoring guidebook advice he set off on the outside, heading directly but without security for the upper chimney. A commentary of curses, groans and laboured gasps accompanied each move. We were wearing far too much clothing but it had seemed too cold to leave anything behind. Finally he was up. When my turn came I persisted with the traditional line. On the traverse I found that by drawing my knees up to my shoulders I could wedge myself to rest without the use of hands and could even make progress in that way at some risk of cramp. I joined him in a small recess below a narrow crack and continued, brushing snow off now, to a big bay beneath the exit pitch.

This little corner isn't twenty feet high but it overhangs in both directions. However, an opposing facet on the left wall may allow a bridging technique. At the top the two walls separate to give access to an alcove in which the climb finishes and through this aperture cascades of snow were being projected intermittently. On reaching it, left leg still bridged out, I found the roofless sentry-box half-filled with snow. Right arm and shoulder locked securely inside the shears of rock I dug for holds. Just as I realised that my hands were now too numb to use I discovered that I'd manufactured some sort of little iceberg, founded presumably on a rock spike. Bare fist painfully clenched, knuckles red-raw, I stirred and pounded the snow down and then, using hand and wrist as an inanimate hook, I hitched the rope up over it, sawed it down with my body, collapsed, and was lowered off.

It was his day but in view of the cold he decided to keep his gloves on. Risky, I thought. He wasn't tall enough to bridge so he asked for tension to help reach the exit. There, he looked at the problem for a few seconds, then told me to get ready to catch him. I'd assumed that he'd fix a sling and by then it would be my turn again. Startling me, he managed somehow to clap a gloved hand high on the iced jaws on either side, called for slack, and then propelled himself up and through in a single powerful move, almost a vaulting action. The snow was still pouring out. Without belaying he wedged himself in the little niche and pulled the rope in quickly. "Make it fast," he shouted, half-dragging me up. It took me, I suppose, thirty seconds. In that interval the snow had built up over him, burying legs and back, pouring over his shoulders, dividing in two streams around the balaclava-masked head.

Blinded by spindrift we raced up the hillside and made a wide, stumbling detour to avoid the margins of the crag. At one point we found ourselves thigh deep in powder and the absurdity of wading this in stockinged feet halted us for a while, weak and helpless with laughter. We got back to our boots and with relief we worked our numb feet in. Then, as we picked our way back down the hillside, the cloud cleared to reveal an ascending figure, Fred Williams. Generously, he congratulated us. "Doesn't matter," he said. "I guessed you'd have come here and I knew you'd have done it." They didn't know it yet but a closer fight with Deer Bield lay just a few months ahead of them. My big effort there was still five years to come.

How trustworthy is memory? Our climb is twenty frozen images now, some stored in the muscles as well as in the mind's eye. Visually everything is black and white except that a hint of colour comes in as we pick out Fred, a sense of the sun attempting to break through. The rest of the day is blank. Are angles and dimensions subtly distorted, has inconsistent material been edited out? I've never been back on the route to try to kick-start recollection.

Ten years later, driving up to the Cairngorms, I got out to stretch my legs at Castle Rock of Triermain. A car pulled up behind and someone called me by name. I walked back to the driver, dark-suited with collar and tie, an attractive girl at his side, strangers both. He laughed. "You don't recognise me?" I shook my head. "Pete Greenwood." Briefly we said where we lived and how we made a living. Climbing? He'd given up, I never give up. He thought back for a while, gunning the car intermittently as if in impatience. "It burns out," he said (angrily? wistfully? philosophically? — I couldn't tell), and drove rapidly away. Another twenty years on we'd meet again and David Craig would even inspire him to climb again.

I turn the second card with reluctance. No surprises, it says North Crag Eliminate. It annoys me to have to play it but it makes a good illustration. It stands for onward purpose, the making of new routes. And since it's my best-known effort in the Lakes, perhaps it would have been perverse to have suppressed all mention. Other climbs cost me more, others scared me more, others took more natural lines, others were achieved in a more satisfying style. But this route certainly winds up to a committing final pitch with engaging positions, nice moves, perfect rock.

Rawdon Goodier has suggested that though climbing is often thought of as a romantic, anti-scientific pursuit the first ascent is really "the equivalent of the scientific discovery to which the author's name is attached, the guidebook description equating to the scientific paper." That's the truth. New climbing and scientific research are fixed equally on problem solving and the thirst for recognition. New routes are dated, just as the great scientific journals print dates of receipt and acceptance so that there can't be any argument about precedence. The question of whether sole title to a declared project ought to be recognised has come up in climbing too. The maker of new routes and the researcher feel a similar pride in their discoveries, forgetting that the discovery was simply out there waiting and in a few months or a few years would inevitably have fallen to someone else. In this they're unlike the artist whose achievement, whatever its value, is not accessible to others.

Friday, the first of June, 1951. The weather seemed set fair for the weekend. Don Hopkin and I had a rare petrol-sharing lift to the Lakes in the Stevens' huge open tourer, an ancient Sunbeam which attracted admiring glances even in those days. We spent the night at Keswick Youth Hostel. On the Saturday we caught the bus to Seatoller, walked to Scafell and climbed Central Buttress, the most famous route in Lakeland at the time. We were back early enough to move on to Thirlmere and to find an unoccupied building, an old smithy, in which to sleep. I'd persuaded Don of a new possibility on Castle Rock.

In climbing Overhanging Bastion a few weeks earlier I'd noticed that it would be possible to ascend directly to the top of the gangway from a balcony in the middle of the headwall. The problem lay in how to reach that point. Wanting an independent start I set off up the bramble-defended corner to the left of the Gossard. In this corner I took an anchor which the engineer studied for a very long time in silence, two jammed knots linked in opposition. Finally he announced that the idea was clever but that he was reserving doubts on the uncertain squeeze-factor of the knots. As I continued I noticed that he was allowing me sufficient slack to permit a groundfall if I were to tear through the safety-net of brambles. Shortly I found myself at a fine old yew tree pressing against the under-cut headwall.

From a perch in the top branches of the tree a steep and very narrow offset seemed to offer a way through the overhang. I tried this almost successfully two or three times until, stepping back, I missed the branch I'd launched from and crashed noisily down to Don's considerable alarm. Giving up on that I went round to the left and shortly we discovered that it was possible to make an airy traverse right round onto the front. This traverse took us straight above the tree and now I noticed good finishing holds to the left of the offset. As I brought Don across to join me I'd time to study a narrowing gangway disappearing leftward into the over-hanging wall. We completed the planned exit and he suggested a name, The Barbican. Waiting for our secure lift home we felt we'd had a perfect weekend.

That might have been all. But, standing at the foot of the crag the following summer, I saw a surprising sight. A jackdaw, sailing across the headwall, suddenly wheeled and disappeared straight into the face of the cliff directly above the gangway. Interesting. Not visible from beneath, some ledge or fissure or tiny grotto broke the apparently fea-tureless wall.

I returned with my brother. We modified the Gossard start, succeeded on the bulge, and I reached the end of the narrowing gangway. Here I found a frustrating obstacle. A hidden crack ran up from its end, good. But a heavy two-foot splinter of rock was projecting from this crack and it was clear at a glance that it was precariously balanced. It couldn't be bypassed and its weight was too great to allow me to cast it off whilst making a difficult move. Depressing. The only solution was to descend on a top rope to kick it down. So I backed off and finished up Barbican. Then Nev held me as I descended a fingery and very exposed arête and moved across to the crack which I now saw to form one side of a huge wedged flake. I lowered myself and touched the splinter cautiously with a toe. Instantly it was gone and an impressive explosion sounded from the ash wood beneath. Excellent. Apart from the moves from the gang-way the whole pitch was clearly climbable, though fairly sustained.

Unfortunately it was now too late in the day to start again.

A twinge of guilt returns. I'd persuaded Nev of this possibility and he'd supported me. Now he wouldn't be free for several weekends but I couldn't sit still for so long. Also I'd had to discard my badly worn rope and I hadn't much confidence in Neville's rather shabby rope either. But see who comes here. This is the sixteen or seventeen-year-old Dennis Gray, in appearance an underfed, streetwise fourteen-year-old; ready to go anywhere, do anything, bubbling over. And that looks like a brand-new coil of nylon over his shoulder, though maybe only half-weight in calibre.

We arrived at the Thirlmere smithy in the early evening, having to force an entry this time. It was too late to climb the thing but I couldn't resist another reconnaissance. The bulge above the yew tree gave too long a move for Dennis so I fixed the inactive rope in a useful place, he pulled and I pulled, and we were able to admire the big pitch before finishing up the Barbican again. We were on the route quite early in the morning and this time I tied a series of knots in the inactive rope to help Dennis help himself.

The big pitch. Do it like this. Take up a position at the end of the gangway: left hand and wrist palm up under the bottom left corner of the flake to give an elbow rest; right hand jammed as close as possible; right leg still out high with toes locked under the flake; left foot braced on anything you can find. Now cross over with your right hand, yes, for the hidden crack round on the left. Break the rules and bring your left knee high up briefly as a spacer. Release the left hand and palm against the wall now to counteract a swing. Then the right foot comes across high to get into a layback position, the left hand joins the right, a move or two up and it's over. You're in a comfortable resting place at the top of the flake with a full-weight sling on a big spike at your side. Well, that's what memory says after forty years. Happily, I invented these lovely moves by instinct in the time it takes to read of them. Alright, do it the way they do it nowadays.

That's probably the crux and I'd already been down to this resting place. A surprise was in store. I made the ascending hand-traverse round the corner to a niche, a second good resting place. Here my problems began. On the descent and subsequent re-ascent I'd used the shallow little vertical groove in the arête. It had neat spaced finger-holds, lichen-covered, but starting footholds were missing so it asked for a pull-up, then a one-handed cling and reach to begin. I had only the one good runner and I was a long way out from the stance. The position was very exposed. I tried it a couple of times and went back to the niche. It felt serious now.

I saw an alternative. From the niche itself I could make a long ascending stride into the groove, avoiding the bad move. Still not easy, and if I were to slip the rope might drag briefly but damagingly down the arête. I needed some protection in the niche and there was only one solution. I had no hammer but I happened to be carrying two or three pegs. Using a loose rock from the floor of the niche I tapped a peg awkwardly in. It was in a very weak position, a vertical crack facing exactly the wrong way. (One month later, on the entertaining second ascent, Joe Brown was to lose his third man on the previous pitch and his second man was to lose a plimsoll on this pitch; the master would shake this peg out by hand.) But it looked real and often that's all that's needed. A minute later I was on the top.

North Crag Eliminate stands amongst the best routes in the area but I've described its ascent in such careful detail in order to restate the dilemma inherent in the making of new routes on British crags. The crux pitch couldn't have been climbed without the prior removal of the block on aid or by top-rope or abseil; and, as it happened, I hadn't rehearsed the most difficult moves. The fact remained: I'd looked at the end before reading the book. And this had robbed me of the fuller satisfaction other new routes had given or were to give — say, Grendel on Scrubby Crag, a cliff I'd only seen on a single earlier visit, or Hubris on Deer Bield, a route made in vile conditions with some recourse to aid: ascents made gratifyingly, from the bottom up. However, it's the case that the pleasure or anguish a new route will subsequently offer to others is independent of the style of its first ascent.

With that, I turn my third and final card and this one is a surprise. It's blank, it says nothing.

It stands for failure, for frustrated purpose. It must mean that, for me, losing has often been more memorable and more useful than success. The situations I remember best of all, in the Alps and elsewhere as well as in Britain, are those final moves and positions in which I found myself blocked. I find victories unsustaining but I can live indefinitely on images of impassable barriers, unattainable holds.

From many failures I choose what was in one way the most conclusive. From the moment I first saw it I felt that Dove Crag offered the grandest possibilities in the Lake District. It had only a single route, Hangover, up the whole of its steep or impending frontage. Accompanied by Don Hopkin I made what I called the third ascent, Dolphin having reported his as the second, but many years later I was to learn that Scottie Dwyer had repeated it during the war years. With Tom Ransley, I went some way up the right-hand side of the North Buttress and some way up the central area of the South Buttress. In retrospect, these probes were unrealistic considering our equipment, and perhaps our skill as well, but they satisfied the need for arousal. Finally I launched out into the area left of Hangover. We'd climbed that route to half-height because the obvious chimney approach looked wet and dirty.

This time I was with my brother, who climbed at about the same standard as myself. He was, perhaps, not so obsessively driven and he was to make fewer new routes. But he was technically adroit and seemed to have wide tolerances for rock type and situation so that his own discoveries were to range between the gymnastic twenty-foot Bald Pate Direct at Ilkley, now graded at E2, and the impressive thousand-foot Nose of Sgurr an Fhidhleir in Coigach, the original line, also said by some parties to rank Extreme. In our earlier years we often climbed as a pair and it was probably only my seniority and his indulgence that gave me a bit more than my share of the pleasure of leading. As time went on he was to discover in the research paper in optical neurophysiology a more compelling satisfaction than the new climb, so that nowadays we too rarely find ourselves exploring as a team.

From the top of the little chimney above the initial slabs I swung left around a rib into a steep grassy groove (up which Brown and Whillans, independently, would make probes in a year or two) and then round a further rib into a second, cleaner groove. Nev joined me and I set off up this weakness, the boundary of the South Buttress. Every few feet I arrived at small ledges or remissions in the groove and at each of these I found long loose splinters of a curious shape. Crudely, they were like aeroplane propellers, waisted, triangular in section, the angular spine on the back conforming to the bed of the groove, the tips chamfered towards that spine so that each stood upright in perfect balance. When I threw them into space they gave out sensational battlefield noises in descent, gratifying to the leader but alarming to the second who was unable to judge what margin of safety he was being allowed.

All this was very enjoyable. But now I arrived at a similar obstacle scaled up. It might be possible to dislodge it without danger to myself but it was far too heavy to control the risk to Nev. For some time now he'd been making or transmitting small signals of unease or of positive dissent. I studied its balance carefully. It seemed to be securely seated. It was more irregular in shape and offered its own holds. I climbed delicately over it and finally found myself at an abatement in the groove with more extensive views. However I was still without any real protection and this attractive nook, which would otherwise have made a stance, offered nothing. On the right rib a pinch-hold almost made a perfect thread. If I'd had a hammer a gentle tap of the pick might have changed the whole situation.

At that point we were startled by a shout from the foot of the crag. I looked down to see two climbers. This was astonishing. Who were these people? I'd believed myself the cliff's only devotee in those years. Then one of them asked if we were on Tarsus, an enquiry which amused us. Tarsus is a modest slabby severe round on the flank of the crag. The scenery around us wasn't a territory of severes. We redirected them and they moved off.

An appealing groove continued directly from where I stood. It was less steep and was formed in perfect rock with not a loose hold in sight. On the other hand its compact nature would set delicate problems and everywhere there was a thin dry scurf of lichen. The groove cut through the skyline with no hint of protection or remitment and common sense prevailed. The wide left wall was blank so I looked round the rib on the right. Here, a huge scooped flake rested on some narrow invisible ledge against a short vertical wall. It seemed too big for my weight to affect it so I hand-traversed it, stood up on its further end in a little corner, and was able to feel flat holds on the lip of a steep slab beneath a big overhang. I rested there for some time as reason contended with desire. No, I was too far out. I reversed back to the groove and my thoughts now fixed on the pillar above Nev's head. It didn't give a technical problem but in descent one mightn't exert just the same forces as in ascent.

Confession time. There was nothing from which to abseil or lower off. But beneath us the visitors now reappeared, having decided not to climb, and they hailed us again. Without hesitation I asked if they'd be willing to try to fix me a top rope, explaining my anxiety about the block. With security I might somehow bypass it. Readily, they agreed. It was the only time in my life I've asked a stranger for help on the mountains.

I estimated that it might take an hour to arrange this assistance. I could only describe how to recognise the top of Hangover. I didn't know the ground above us or whether good anchorage would be available. I didn't know how competent these mystery men might be. Even with his friend relaying messages it would probably be difficult for the man with the rope to locate me, out of sight and probably out of hearing. Yet on a second attempt and within ten minutes the end of a rope fell down into my hands. Briefly I considered climbing upwards. It didn't make sense. They had a long rope and it was dawning on me now that our own rope might not have taken me out in a single runout. If no stance were to offer itself new problems would arise. I descended carefully over the pillar which now seemed safe enough, shouted my thanks and untied.

Mortified, cursing my weakness of character, I traversed back and we marched up the finish of Hangover.

I'd been in the area where, in the sixties, Mordor would join Extol. Great difficulties lay ahead and, in fact, our rope was probably too short to take us out in one. So it all worked out for the best. And the memory of that groove, the pose in the corner above the flake, the sense of possibility all around, have given me something to live on and to stir my imagination ever since.

The three years came to an end. In the first winter I remember Saturday nights when, with a young local shepherd, Pete, Dennis and I were the only customers in the Dungeon Ghyll bar. By 1953 it would be crowded through the year. A bus for which we'd petitioned would make occasional journeys all the way up the valley. Some climbers would arrive at Wall End on motor-bikes and others (Terry Parker, Pete Shotton, Jack Thornton, Vivian Stevenson) would have become the unofficial custodians of the barn. A lively company of girls — Marie, Kathleen, Mavis, Eileen, Valerie, Doreen, Connie, Sheila, Shirley; and others, for whom I have faces but whose names have gone — would have nonchalantly redesignated it a unisex dormitory. In the interval we'd climbed hundreds of routes in the Lakes, we'd stretched ourselves on some of the hardest climbs in Wales and Scotland and we'd had some stirring adventures in the Alps.

Some of the Bradford Boys might not be willing to close the era so conclusively in the year of the ascent of Everest. Alf Beanland, Jim Lyons, Duncan Boston, Dennis Gray, Ernie Leach, Colin Fearnley, John Ramsden, my brother: all were to continue their activities from Yorkshire for a year or two or for many years. But by that autumn the scene had certainly changed. Don had moved to Morecambe, Pete to Keswick, George Elliott had married and had immediately gone to sea. The Pale Man was in hiding, Tom Ransley had moved on, and so had I. And, in that August, something beyond our sense of the possible had happened.

South Ridge of the Aiguille Noire de Peuterey

AN END

"Where were you when you heard that Arthur Dolphin had been killed?"

I was entering the main street of Courmayeur, where he is buried. I'd just got down from the Noire. After climbing the South Face of the Géant, Arthur had slipped during the unroped descent of the easy but exposed plinth of the Aiguille. I was in time for the first funeral I'd have any cause to attend.

It was an afternoon graveside service under a scorching Italian sun. Present: André Collard, the Belgian with whom he'd been climbing; Jack Bloor and Mike Dwyer from Yorkshire; Geoff Holmes, from London; the British consul from Turin; and Keith King, and myself, and the priest. I think that's right. The cleric raced through the ceremony, perhaps in a shortened form for this unknown foreigner of some unknown faith. The words, having no meaning for me, ought to have been powerless. But the frantic haste of performance, the urgent shouted rhythms of the declarations, actually and strongly communicated a poetry of desperation through the barrier of language. Man's days are as grass.

I'm not sure in what sense I could say that I was moved. Perhaps, for most young men, grief is always contaminated by a sense of the drama of violence on occasions like this. I remember, in fact, feeling a kind of anger, an intense wish to get away quickly. I even felt a real anxiety that I might faint if I were to stand still much longer in an airless heat that seemed insufferable. Eventually the coffin was lowered and the first shovelful of earth was thrown down upon it. The soil was dry and full of stones and made a loud, startling, conclusive rattling on the wood. With that, tears I couldn't conceal suddenly ran down my face and within a couple of minutes all those who'd known him had joined me for solidarity.

He'd never been one of us. He was older and from a different social background. He'd been a hero before we'd started climbing. But he was transparently innocent. His schoolboy humour, his childish delight in weak puns and tongue-twisters, his interest in people and his enthusiasm for the sport overrode any barriers. Having spent several years establishing himself as the leading Lakeland expert he'd found that, from behind and immediately, new challengers were arriving. His instinctive response was to inform and to encourage us. We'd begun to join him for highly competitive Wednesday evening bouldering sessions on gritstone. After his ascent of Deer Bield Buttress he'd written out descriptions for Pete and for myself and invited our opinions. On hearing of North Crag Eliminate he'd glanced at the line and then suggested that we meet for a day on Castle Rock, an invitation so daunting to me that I never took it up. By the summer of 1952 he'd already accepted Pete in an equal partnership which immediately produced routes as impressive as anything seen in the Lakes up to that date. That partnership was over now. He'd made space for us and left us on our own with his monuments.

At Duncan Boston's first ingathering in 1986 we were all thinking back to the end of those years and to the courses of our lives. One thing struck me. Jack Bradley had arrived, still larger than life and once again a focus of attention during the weekend. Never a very good climber but always a moving force, his picaresque adventures built a legend. After forty years, and now his death, it's still tasteless to report some of these tales. He had a mischievous, often cruel sense of humour and I pass over this.

He also had an extraordinary ability to effect narrow escapes. Once, his party of four spent a weekend in Gaping Ghyll, bivouacking in the Sand Caverns. On the Sunday night, wet, muddy, hungry, and with combined resources of a shilling and eight pence, they were faced with the task of hitch-hiking back to York. Jack led them into a moorland transport cafe and ordered everything the group could possibly eat. His simple plan was to offer their services afterwards for washing up. The lengthy meal drew to a close and no-one else came in so that the only washing up would be their own. The proprietor chatted with them, a likeable man, and finally delivered his bill for twenty-eight shillings. Jack picked up their single shilling, put it in a slot machine, drew out thirty shillings and paid up. Is this story true? Ask Mike Hollingsworth? I tell it as told to me within a month of the event.

I'd last seen him in Ambleside bus station in 1954. He'd just got the sack from his job as plumber or bricklayer but he had four pounds in his pocket. He was about to hitch up to Skye where it would last him a fortnight and he could think up a scheme. Twenty years later Valerie Brown drew my attention to an article in a women's magazine. Four ladies had written on what it was like to be married to a millionaire. And there was a photo of Jack, confident as ever, standing on the steps of his manor, his lady on his arm, two or three well-groomed dogs at their feet.

Yes, that was the unsettling thing about this and subsequent reunions. There were too many millionaires for so small a gathering. The fact made a poor fit with the ragged-trousered, easy-going bunch I remembered from Wall End Barn. We almost all came from working-class families. We almost all left school at fifteen or sixteen. But the ways in which these fortunes had been accumulated didn't seem specially uplifting. Jack had run building firms, haulage firms, had even made the first commercial aluminium gliders. These enterprises had varied in longevity and reputation. Would I have stepped inside a house that Jack built? I'd have taken a pretty good look at the outside first.

The property developer who'd arrested one of my falls, now nursing a tray of drinks through the crush, seemed to have made smoother progress than Jack. Apparently he was into nursing homes. Were they the sort of ventures in which the life savings of Britain's aged are rapidly eroding? The figure wedged in the corner was apparently here by chance. I'd never seen him in the barn anyway, though he was one of Dolphin's associates and was certainly in Langdale in those years. He was said to be the inventor of the spirograph and his name appeared on those expensive children's toys. The senior partner of a juke box and pool table empire wasn't present though he'd used the barn from time to time. His consortium was shortly to be sold for more than ten million. The lady I'd taken on her first Lakeland climb wasn't here either though her sister (not badly off?) was with us. No doubt she was hard at work, ministering to the neuroses of the affluent by promoting a G-plan diet.

I looked around in curiosity. There were others I guessed might be members of the same club. I turned to Mike Dixon in perplexity. "Are you a millionaire as well, Mike?" I asked. He was amused but chuckled a little uncomfortably. He shifted his feet. "Well," he said, with some reluctance. "I suppose so. But it doesn't really *mean* anything nowadays, does it? Not like it used to." He brought himself back to the present and fixed a stiff price for the second-hand, obsolete, slightly faulty word-processor he was about to sell to me.

At the first reunion we checked through the dead and the missing. We'd never meet George Elliott, Alf Beanland, John Greenwood, Frank Weirdon, Alan Bullock, Dave Gibbons, or Charlie Salisbury again. Mountains, other accidents, and now, dismayingly, illness or old age. Some, like Pete Thomson and Ernie Leach had been located but refused to associate with climbers any more. ("Climbers are the lowest of the low.") Others were lost and now someone asked about the Morrells. Oh, they'd been in the art world, hadn't they, they'd moved to London. Then they'd separated. They were thought to have been on the fringe of the drug scene, they were probably dead by now. I'd never really known them to talk to, they were older than me, but I remembered Mary well.

A hot day on Gimmer a lifetime ago, the cliff under siege. My partner and I were sharing a narrow ledge for half an hour with Mary, her husband and the friend who was their frequent escort. We were blocked by a very slow party in front and we were pressed by a queue of teams behind. There was no breeze and the men were sitting shirtless, soaking up the sun. Mary, daringly, had also removed her shirt and was filling her bra with outstanding success. Beautiful girl. Suddenly she made some exclamation, an expression of impatience, of exasperation, of oh-what-the-hell clouded her pretty face, and with the panache of a magician Mrs. Morrell flicked off the bra. Shocking. No big deal nowadays but this was before perfect strangers on a rock-climb high above the Langdale valley in the reign of King George the Sixth. Also electrifying. Mr. Morrell stared moodily into space. The rest of us tried to concentrate our attentions upon the contours of Pike o'Blisco but found ourselves, every two minutes, casually scanning the skyline from end to end.

Scissors cut paper, paper wraps stone, stone blunts scissors. Amongst other things this is a book about the appeal of mountains. Now I have to report that in an instant, it seemed, the sun had perceptibly dimmed, the greens of the valley had become a little parched, even the rock was somehow just dead rock. Notice was being served that life would be filled with competing claims.

I relate this incident for another reason. Only a couple of days after the suggestion that Mary was probably dead I discovered that she was

alive, well, and still living in London. She was, unbelievably, the closest friend of my closest non-climbing friends in North Wales. But she
was a surname further on, and though they'd often spoken of her as an
artist they'd never thought to mention that she'd done a little climbing
when young, or that she came from Yorkshire. A year or two later I met
her. We wouldn't have recognised each other but an hour of reminiscence gave me serious cause for thought.

She'd only climbed for a few years, gritstone, the Lakes, Wales, Skye,
and the climbing world she remembered was grossly different from mine.
It had centred on days of unhurried fun on classic easier climbs. Nobody ever got hurt. And, for her, the mountains would remain forever
fresh and miraculous, untarnished by familiarity. "The best years of my
life," she said. By contrast I'd gone on and I'd come through carnage.
Say, twenty-five or thirty climbers I'd shared a rope with had died climbing, and a similar number I'd known on first-name terms. That sort of
count is common to most climbers of my age. So what Mary had to say
made me consider my investment in mountains. Might a law of diminishing returns operate even here?

And, yet, my own life has been full of compromise. I could never
have believed that possible in 1953. In that autumn, belatedly, I'd be
going to college. Abandoning the idea of a career in hospital administration I intended to qualify myself as a teacher of English. From that
summer forward I'd have long holidays and soon I'd be earning enough
to travel more easily and to buy some decent equipment. I felt certain
that I was capable of more difficult climbs than any I'd yet done and I
was confident that great achievements as climber and mountaineer lay
ahead of me. My plan was simple. I'd test every one of the enticing
unclimbed lines I'd noticed in Britain. I'd get to grips with the most
famous routes in the Alps. When I was too old for serious alpine climbing I'd visit the Himalaya. And when I was too old for Himalayan mountaineering I'd take up skiing.

In every detail this plan came to nothing. The summer of 1953 was to
be, precisely, the end of the most intensive phase of my climbing. Until
then all other activities had been subordinated. From then on, climbing
would have to mesh with other purposes. While some of my contempo-
raries soldiered on I amused myself. In the summer of 1956 I'd be in
Paris with a girl-friend, wandering around the Louvre and exploring the
Left Bank. Five years later, as old acquaintances began to go on Himalayan expeditions I'd join an expedition a hundred thousand strong for a
four-day Aldermaston March; my longest roadside vigils would be at
Holy Loch and at Greenham Common, before the women discovered

the place. Ten years on and I'd be driving to Tangier, enjoying sun and sea. Fifteen years and I'd be on the road to Istanbul admiring buildings and great cities.

At the same time, I never considered giving up. At the end of the spell in Paris, Frank Davies passed through, I negotiated a loan, and unforgivably let the girl find her own way home. In no time at all, it seemed, we were on the summit of the Aiguille de Roc. After one Aldermaston March, married now, my wife and I went straight on to climb in Cornwall; from an affray at Holy Loch we sailed magnificently away down the Clyde so that a couple of days later we were on the Rosa Pinnacle. On that first drive through Spain I stopped by the roadside to look at an impressive rock peak of which I couldn't discover the name; a few years later I returned to make a route on it. The Istanbul trip was broken up by mountain excursions.

Further, although I lost any need to prove myself against others I enjoyed periods of strenuous activity whilst writing rock-climbing guides. I went on from teaching English to work in Outdoor Education, moving to the mountain area in which I live to this day, spending a great deal of time on the hills and staying in touch with new developments. I kept my eyes open for every chance at home or whilst travelling. And I learned that I'm an incurably serious climber in this sense: that whatever anxieties or responsibilities I may have on my mind, these are erased the instant I lay hands on rock; and that however badly I may be performing from time to time, once engaged I've no choice but to check my limits. Finally, the images of climbing, the kinaesthetic memories, the resultant set of impulses, are a permanent and substantial part of the life of my mind.

My brother once reflected that for decades after the death of Dolphin we still considered him our unmatchable master; whilst in fact, despite his famous routes, his career was brief, his travels restricted, his experience limited compared with our own. It sounded like heresy but on consideration I had to accept it. The rest of this book, by transect, by device and by abstraction, is an attempt to make some sense of my own experience.

THE USES OF ADVERSITY

And there are some things which may not be advantageous,
yet still I call them good.

Plato, Protagoras

Nantillons glacier with Charmoz, Grépon and Blatière

ON FALLING OFF

The climber's attitude towards the fall is strikingly ambivalent. This confusion has even been acknowledged by his institutions, the climbing clubs.

The nineteen-fifties saw the appearance of many new clubs. For some the technical entry qualifications were set higher than ever before: the Alpine Climbing Group asked for an impressive list of successes and terminated membership when the list ceased to lengthen. By contrast, the Dublin-based Newton Club asked only a single accomplishment, an eighty-foot free fall. That seems a curious threshold and it's a reasonable guess that it must have been the minimum flight achieved amongst the founding fathers.

The Newton Club faced a vexing problem. It could appoint President, Treasurer and Secretary, and have no members, or it could have three members and no officers. The club was determined to be recognised and it showed extreme ingenuity in keeping up appearances. But no new candidates came forward and it was torn between its wish to maintain standards and its boredom with the same three stories.

Inevitably, the rule was relaxed. Totalling-up was allowed. The striking of rocks, or other climbers in passing, no longer disqualified. Splashdowns into sea, river, lake and Irish bog were recognised. Slides were still ruled out but skiers who'd tumbled over natural precipices were invited to apply. The club had a motto: "G". And it had its own tie, bearing, it hardly needs saying, the simple device of an apple.

Typically, climbers treat matters of gravity with levity. One informal group, the Spencer Couloir Club, restricted itself to those specialists, novice and expert alike, honest enough to admit that they'd ignored the warnings and saved themselves half an hour. For a number of years the Cromlech Club awarded its Iron Cross to the member achieving the longest fall in the year under review. This decoration held an ambiguous prestige, sharing the status of the yellow jersey of the Tour de France and that of the dunce's cap. It was an honour everyone wished to have held but for which no-one wanted to compete.

An obvious platform for any reflections on falling would be the use of one's own credentials. But if I were to copy out my C.L. — curriculum lapsus — in careful detail, and if I were to add to it those falls of second and third parties in which I was involved, I could hardly spare a glance at people, times, scene and consequences. Instead, then, I'll select just a few falls with strong sentimental associations.

I fell off inaugurally on Yorkshire gritstone in the winter of 1950. Not important, but it was a beginning. In old army boots I was attempting the first ascent of Short Circuit in Ilkley Quarry. As I was completing the last move, with a peg runner at half height, something happened. My quick-witted second sat down to take in slack, my toes just brushed the quarry floor, and I didn't feel the least bit subdued.

A fall in Langdale off what is now the Pinch Finish of Jericho Wall was a bit more stimulating. Pete Greenwood had taken a bold stance at the top of the flakes. He had good foothold but the rock was impending and he couldn't stand in balance. A hanging stance was uncomfortable before the era of the sit-harness and the belay plate so he had one arm wrapped around the pinnacle. He was paying out single-handed over his belay loop and across his waist, dangerous. I went round the bulge and found myself precariously placed. The very steep slab was crusted everywhere with a dry grey lichen. I moved leftwards towards an easier position but felt the lichen crushing, rolling like grit beneath my toes. I was still very uncomfortable. I realised I hadn't much time and I looked at the choices. To reverse these difficult moves on the powdery footholds: dicey. To continue with speed and resolution to less steep ground only ten feet above: brave. But before I'd quite made up my mind between the two possibilities a third occurred to me, a back somersault, and I was hanging in mid-air and not even turning. I was looking across the valley at the juniper-covered slopes of Lingmoor, still catching the evening sunlight. Either the mountain or the observer was upside down.

Pete seemed upset. He was shouting swear-words at me. He went on and on. I was getting myself right way up and trying to work out what had happened. It was hard to believe but it was true. He'd had a moment of blind panic. Here was a revelation. He could take these terrific dives and usually his determination would only be strengthened. Now he'd seen it from the other end, and from a bad stance, and it had shaken him. Gradually, though, the abuse began to falter and I sensed that he was being visited by an idea. I'd got my weight off him by now. He grew two or three inches, five-eight, five-nine. Obviously, he licked the palm of his hand and sucked the web of his thumb. He rubbed his ribs. He eased his shoulders and squared them. He'd held me one-handed and he'd done the right thing. If he'd let me go and killed me he might have burned through his belay loop and followed me down.

He was recovering fast. "You climb down," he says, "I'll give you a tight rope if you want." He was about back to normal. "Don't bother with runners for me," he says, "I'll untie and solo down." We got back onto the ground. It was too late to do anything else. But, suddenly, each of us was perfectly satisfied with his role and his performance.

Remember Nietzsche: "Whatever does not kill us makes us strong." Remember Zweig: that tales of close calls constitute "the original definition of what is worth talking about." I wish you could have seen us. We strode down to the D.G. bar like giants.

Over the next couple of years, as leader, I fell off from time to time, always in one of two situations. The first of these suggests a good question but, addressed to Hollywood's reply to Nietzsche, it hadn't been formulated at that date: "If you're so smart, Mr. Drasdo, how come you got your socks on outside your shoes?" Well, it was what I was taught: that the only way to get up the harder routes in the rain or in wet conditions was in stockings over plimsolls. I could list some impressive successes in that footgear. Gradually, however, it became clear that the adhesion frontier of the stockinged foot isn't well defined and occasionally I was washed away.

In the second circumstance I simply pulled off loose holds. We were often on new routes or on the earliest repetitions. It was in this situation, cartwheeling off Alph on Pavey Ark, that I first hurt myself. The following day I had to admit that my hand wouldn't work and to seek advice. I was advised I had a scaphoid fracture. For the first time, now, I read the small print and for a tedious ten weeks I carried a plaster cast around. The only happy discovery was that a wrist cast is extremely effective in wide cracks on gritstone, making a fist jam completely painless and marvellously secure. Embarrassingly, the cast eroded rapidly and needed reinforcement twice.

From that time onward, partly perhaps through changes in my circumstances, partly through those slight and unconscious shifts in the set of the mind, I seemed to stop falling and for years I thought that phase had ended. A slide at Chamonix added a small new perception. Is a slide a fall? The intellect derides the application but the body keeps muttering that it felt like a fall. I'd come down about four hundred feet before stopping myself in an ice-axe arrest. I was astonished by the effort this demanded and by the physical beating this variably frozen but almost uniform snow-slope had been able to administer.

Many years passed. If I were to describe my last and shortest fall it would be at greatest length since it proved the most consequential. It left me with two souvenirs, a slightly twisted finger and a rather beautiful three-and-three-quarter inch Smith-Peterson pin, retrieved eventually from my right neck of femur. I have it by me now. It's been recycled as a necklace.

In a supporting role I attended the falls of friends and I paid back a few debts. Out of this rain of bodies I have to declare that Peter Greenwood easily came foremost for sheer bravura.

He impressed me on Great Central on Dow. It was a clear sunny morning but the rock was wet and very chilly to the fingers. Dennis Gray had led the first bit, I'd led the South America Crack and Pete was engaging the crux, Bandstand Wall. We were climbing in socks. It was only a short fall but he fell very slowly so, as he fell, he turned around, looked about him, made a graceful body swerve, spread and raised his arms to just above shoulder level, put his toes neatly together and finally settled on the very tip of a pointed, slippery, boulder-like projection on the edge of the ledge. We stared open-mouthed for a couple of seconds, then grabbed him. He stepped down, did a little jogging on the spot, dried his hands, blew on his fingers, set off again, did the move and fell off the next move. Having rehearsed the part he took it more quickly this time and, having rehearsed our parts, we seized him immediately. But I had the eerie feeling we weren't even needed. On the third attempt he went straight up.

I'll go through that again. I don't want it to be said that I exaggerate, but, is it possible to fall very slowly, or even slowly? Yes, it would appear so. There are three stipulations. First, that the fall is seen end on, so that there's less apparent movement in the timelapse than for the same fall viewed from the side. Second, that the faller is profiled against a neutral field, ordinarily the sky, so that there's no blur of background transits to emphasise velocity. Third, that the faller describes a slight arc. Then there's a moment like that in a clay pigeon shoot when the skeet, still having forward motion, seems for an instant actually to halt at the apparent limit of its trajectory. So, in a fall, the eye abstracts a single position. The faller is stilled in a dramatic gesture, giving an image of tremendous potency. It has halted ten thousand motion pictures. It has inspired the covers of a wallful of paperbacks.

Alright. But wasn't he just about to tumble over the second time? Well, maybe. Or he was just correcting his balance. Memory suppresses conflicting detail. I want to say how it was but sometimes that means how it seemed. The impression was of an Olympic gymnast seen on television. The impact was strong since we'd never seen an Olympic gymnast because we'd never seen a television set.

We set off for the third or fourth ascent of Ivy Sepulchre. The description allowed two aid pegs though only one was in place. I was clipping in when Pete started barracking me. He'd recently ignored the peg on Kipling Groove and he was going to make this trick his trademark. Here, the peg was clearly obstructing the vital hold so, inviting him to demonstrate, I came down. He went up and saw the problem but couldn't admit defeat. Surprising me, he turned round and faced the grossly overhanging corner-crack. Have you ever seen Cumberland wrestling? The contender's legs are spread wide, his hands on his adversary. They wrestle for a throw. Pete put his left hand, right arm and foot into the crack, braced his left leg high out under the overhang and wrestled it Cumberland style. It seemed an unlikely solution but in two or three powerful moves he had head and shoulders above the bulge.

It looked as if he'd done it. But then he dislodged some chockstones deep inside the crack and these began to stack up against his body. From time to time he'd dart his left hand down and scoop one out. Then he'd part his knees like a bomb bay and discharge a whole salvo but the crack kept supplying reserves. Fifty feet below, in the centre of the target zone, tethered by long slings to a tall sapling, Neville and I kept colliding in amateurish attempts at maypole dancing. Finally it all got too much, he resigned his position and came whanging out in a hail of rocks.

Once I was quite relieved to see him fall. He was after the unrepeated Gimmer Girdle and he had a second but the second wouldn't go without a third. I was called in unwillingly, since I'd be descending last on the Grooves Traverse which none of us had seen and which was said to be hard. There he was, then, on the eleventh pitch and, watching from Gimmer Crack, I saw that he was struggling. Then he fell, was checked, and unbelievably started again, forty feet, eighty, a hundred and twenty and still going on, half jumping, then bouncing, tumbling from ledge to ledge at the foot of the crag. Too late, at the end of its tether, the rope made a final effort and hauled him up fifteen feet to a ledge he'd just vacated. Two passing walkers hurried up to comfort him.

The middleman's hands were badly burned. Managing an awkward rope-length of slack I got up the rest of the Crack and helped him across and up. Then we descended Junipall Gully to rejoin Pete, who had hurt his ankle. He was in a foul mood. As I remember, he said nothing to the middleman, who stood a little off, head bowed, cuddling his hands. Instead, he turned on me. He'd borrowed some of my line slings and now he said that they were dangerously long. As he'd been making a delicate move one of them had snagged and jammed under a tiny downward-pointing spike and he'd slipped in trying to free it. We helped him slowly down towards the valley and gradually a more philosophic temper overcame him. He began to speak thoughtfully about his future, which was not to include rock-climbing. It was to centre instead upon the Gaiety in Bradford where, apparently, he was already hugely admired for his virtuosity as a ballroom dancer.

I could see the point. He'd still be leading, there'd still be the savage competition and the trophies. Briefly, I imagined him in the Tango Finals. That would be something worth watching. And at the Gaiety, I supposed, the only recreational injury to be feared would be the broken heart.

Sometimes, in the fall, the element of epic or heroic is subsumed in the tragic, a category I defer. More often, in my experience, that element is undercut in comic deflation. I've even known seconds — maestros of the banana skin — who could turn small incident into large spectacle. I've already discussed iconography, allusion and the influence of patronage in Shirley Parfitt's painting in the bar of the Dungeon Ghyll Hotel. Now — watch carefully — I'm going to stretch out a hand and I'm going to release the bearded central figure from the picture. Like that. He stands before us, blinking. Still a young man! Gently but firmly, I'll detach the pint glass from his fingers (he resists a little: there!) and I'll put it to one side. We'll let him keep his pipe, he won't go on the hill without it. Now I'm going to stand him at the foot of Godiva Groove on the north-west face of Gimmer. We're only a few yards, in fact, from the ledges where, five years earlier, Pete ended up.

He was in high spirits that day. A beautiful morning, the rock bone dry. There's not much traversing on the climb and he had a new local expert, Terry Parker, in front of him and a former local expert, myself, behind him. Compulsively, he kept checking everything again and again: pipe, tobacco, matches, and the bowline and numerous hitches still securely tied.

We were about halfway up before he slipped. He'd been reporting any redundant slack in the rope ever since we'd started but he went down a few feet and then, just clear of the rock, he floated across to the left for fifteen or twenty feet. As he was swinging he made a clockwise quarter-turn — I saw his worried face — and then he just touched the rock with a saucy bumps-a-daisy. Instantly, amazing us, delighting us, he made a strange popping noise, gave out a small puff of smoke, and burst into flames. And for twenty or thirty seconds he danced in the sky, bawling his head off and trying to stamp himself out.

There was an occasion on which I didn't show to advantage myself. Winter fifty-two or Spring fifty-three I was set on making an ascent of the then unclimbed Kilnsey Crag. It was an almost universal opinion at that time that limestone was dangerously unreliable. I already knew this to be unfounded but we were anxious not to discredit the belief. It reserved an arena for aid climbing, an essential technique for some of the routes in the Western Alps and Dolomites on which our ambitions were fixed.

Kilnsey rises from the green floor of Wharfedale in a long grey bulging wall. It was finally climbed some years later after a determined siege by Ron Moseley. The film of *Moby-Dick* had just been released and a friend in the team said to me that the cliff, festooned in siege ropes, tiny figures clinging to it or hammering away, brought the closing scenes to mind. When I repeated the remark to Dave Nicol he cast Moseley as Ahab. That was right. There was no more obsessively driven climber operating in Britain in the fifties. The whole image was appropriate. Everything about Kilnsey — the random drainage vents, the bitumen stains, the succulent, almost littoral character of the little plant life it holds, the swell of field surging against the cliff — everything suggests its marine origins as if the leviathan had freshly surfaced from the ocean and the waters had, only a moment ago, cascaded from its flanks. (For a quite different sense of Kilnsey, I ought to add, see Chiang Yee's painting, "Cocks and Hens in front of Kilnsey Crag", about 1940, in one of the Silent Traveller books.)

The second visit provided the entertainment. I want you to see this clearly. I've picked the one line leading towards some sort of exit weakness because I'm worried about security on the smooth grass slope above the crag. Here, a vertical rebate in the wall gives a left-facing reveal a few feet wide. A peg crack runs up the middle of this reveal. We could climb it free but clearly there's loose material and we're here to practise pegging. I suggest that my companion, Keith King, should take this pitch, since I've already led it on the earlier visit.

What happened was my fault really, though he shouldn't have done what he did. First, I'm not belayed. What can he do with me? Drag me across the field to the road, and get me run over by the only traffic we've seen, a farm horse and cart? Second, in view of the loose rock I've moved off to the left. Third, since it's always fun to see someone struggling, I've moved further left again so that I can watch him without cricking my neck. So he works upward, remarking, as I had last time, that the pillar forming the right side of the crack gives a noticeable vibration. I'm close to the foot of the wall but looking straight at the facet. The ropes run diagonally from my hand, then rise vertically through the snaplinks.

In aid climbing, when the leader falls, the pegs strip from the top down. Except on this one known occasion, when they stripped from the bottom up. It was a contingency for which neither of us was remotely prepared.

In retrospect, the mechanics were simple. The idiot had pounded an absurdly thick peg into the top of the thin crack. The crack had expanded slightly and the lower pegs were marginally eased. The other idiot was sitting dreaming in the position best calculated to exploit that weakness. Finally a moment came when he asked for tension. I set my heels against something, leaned back, and gave him tension.

For the next few seconds we were really busy. He was into particle physics, I was into wave physics. He was dropping like a bomb but in a distinctly stop-go sort of fashion. Yes, in quanta. Much against my will, I was gliding across on an interception course in systematic undulations. First I was snatched into midair and then I was mysteriously released. I just managed to get my feet in front of me. But as subsequent pegs pulled and as he disposed of each new increment of slack the angle of the ropes increased, tending to lift me more directly. At the same time a pendulum action was being initiated, working to lower me. And so it went on until, still only just above the ground, I hit him like a homing missile.

Keith King lives in Penrith. You can get his address from the local phone book. If you ever have an hour to kill in that town, look him up, hang around his corner, and see if you can spot him. I'll give you a clue. He is the old man with the head hacked out of oak burr. The torso and limbs are to match but it was only our heads that met, in a ringing concussive detonation. A flash of light lit the skies over Wharfedale. I think I let go the ropes then. Apparently we woke at about the same time, possibly only seconds later, in a heap and groaning with shock and pain. Then, little by little, we found ourselves laughing. Until finally we were possessed by that debilitating laughter in which the one who's just about to control it restarts the one who had it under control.

While I'm at Kilnsey I'll finish this story. A bit at a time we climbed carefully onto our feet. We had sore heads. We had lumps. And his pride was hurt. He stood there, fists bunched, still swaying a little, and scowling up at the top peg from which a rope still depended. We bounced on it. Solid. With a top rope who needs pegs? He went up and I followed. Then I continued up the groove, some moves free, then pegging. There was a moment of surprise when I broke in my hand one of the small keyhole-shaped gadgets we'd bought cheaply to supplement our war surplus karabiners. They'd been sold as parachute hooks, a chilling thought. The groove arrived at a loosely imbricated bulge but here a horizontal crack ran left across the wall. I crossed it and arrived at an exposed and narrow ledge. He joined me and I started to peg an insecure wall to the foot of the exit weakness.

Call me Starbuck. He was the one sane man on the *Pequod*, the first mate and the first of the three harpoon boat chiefs. He said: "I will have no man in my boat who is not afraid of a whale." It didn't work, nobody even listened. The crazies just piled aboard and he had to die with them.

Keith was no threat. Now don't misread me. He seemed to have no personal ambition, he was content to follow me around on my tick list. I'd take the harder pitches and he'd take the easier. But once or twice, when a description wasn't specific, he found himself faced with the crux. He'd complain but it wouldn't stop him. As a second he was brilliant. It was all a huge joke and he'd urge me on even when I was in extremity. Except that on a few significant occasions, when he thought I was getting the pair of us in over our heads, he fell silent.

He was saying nothing now. After the traverse he'd pointed out that he'd shaken the pegs out by hand and he'd said this in an unusually serious tone of voice and as he said it he fixed me with his eye. I'd explained that it didn't matter, the corner peg was solid and the rest had been locked in by our weight on the etriers. I was having second thoughts myself, though. I could see into the weakness now. It was vegetated but still so steep that it would have to be pegged to clean off the loose material safely. The time and effort required wasn't easy to judge. And I was deep in this calculation when a third factor intruded in the shape of Miss Elizabeth Duckworth, who was waving and calling to us from the road. It was her fault, really, that we didn't make the first ascent of Kilnsey Crag.

Betty Duckworth was a fairly recent arrival at Wall End. The occasional visitor might have gained the impression that, like the fair Briseis, she was being passed from hand to hand through the tents of the allied camps. In fact it was the other way round. She was on a tour of inspection which found most of us wanting. I'd have considered her at some length here but I learn that she's now retired from her position as County Librarian for Cumbria, a post in which she might have wished to buy up all copies of this book. Even then, she was going places. We were hitch-hiking, she had a little car. It was there on the road beneath us. In a half-hour we could be walking up to a sunny gritstone edge. Suddenly it seemed ill-mannered to leave her sitting waiting for the rest of this cold afternoon. I depegged back to the stance.

We still had to get off. I looked again at our anchors. All our pegs were crude lunch-hour apprentice jobs, copied not from specimens but from our explanations of the idea of the peg. They were ring pegs, flat blades and offsets of mild steel, a stupendous weight. I had in one short blade, not much to look at. But the other was the pride of my collection, a huge bowie-knife shaped ring peg, a piece of metal sculpture. With this, the inventor or artist had followed his impulses. It was made, he told me proudly, of stainless steel. I'd driven it hard into a little pocket. Keith was the heavier so he abseiled first from this dagger while I held him belayed from the blade. He didn't like setting off and he didn't like the move into space, ten or fifteen feet down. And he'd no sooner left the rock and relaxed when there was a crack like a pistol shot and a little plate of rock had blown away from one side of the abseil peg. Our eyes met. Nothing to be done. Standing uncomfortably upright I took as much of his weight as I could on the safety rope. Down he went, slowly and smoothly. I didn't like setting off either. But now Keith had swung on the peg so I took out the other and followed, making a countdown of height and injuries as I descended. For one reason after another I never returned. Many years later I saw that the first Yorkshire Limestone guide had recorded our attempt: "their monster abseil peg is still in place." I note, incidentally, that the free climbs which nowadays reach our ledge directly don't attempt to go higher. Perhaps we did make the first ascent of Kilnsey Crag?

Looking back at this short selection I imagine two extreme responses. The modern expert will say: we log up mileages like that in a month. Hold on, I was remembering the hard fall. In all but one of these recollections we were tied on with a bowline round the waist. The first fall mentioned was on Italian hemp and all but one of the others were on the original, rather slippery laid nylon, sometimes only half-weight in calibre. The falls were held by gloveless seconds with a waist or even a shoulder belay.

The non-climber, on the other hand, will say: all this sounds like lunacy, you're alive through luck, not judgement. That's true to a degree, as it is of all survivors and story-tellers. Still, it appears that we saw most of the risks and that our primitive safety systems worked remarkably well.

Beyond the particular, my knowledge of the fall is in three tenses. I look back at past falls and I say, that taught me a lesson, that amused me, that simply energised me. On the actual present experience of the fall I reserve the most acute observation I've come across to serve as a conclusion. For myself, I can find little to say. It was only the cliff that flashed before me, never my life. The mind, it seems, makes a mute but startled exclamation and the event is over. I might be wrong. Maybe I gave myself no chance. Some principle of prudence grouped nearly all my falls within twenty to forty feet while the fearless Greenwood explored the full rope's length and its stretch as well.

There remains the future fall, the possible fall, and it's this that all climbing is importantly about. The body is programmed before every other emergency to attend to its balance, that is, to avert a fall. In fact, climbers hardly ever fall through loss of balance. They fall through loss of strength, loss of adhesion or loss of libido, aside from objective causes. But any preliminary signals of those threats will activate the whole system. And it's when a fall is anticipated, and when this anticipation is long-drawn-out that the idea of the fall most strongly defines and declares itself. Far more alarming than any fall I ever had, I relive just one of these disturbing memories.

Decided to do Gallows Route on Buachaille Etive Mor. We were told it had been repeated only once, by the originator himself, John Cunningham. Was Cunningham any good? He'd arrived in Langdale and he and his partner couldn't follow Neville and myself up Perhaps Not in White Ghyll. True, there were extenuating circumstances but in climbing one doesn't make excuses for other people. We knew nothing about the Gallows but one of the Creagh Dhu had showed us where it stood.

At the stance before the big pitch I couldn't find a really good anchor. Never mind, get some runners on quickly. I crossed the initial traverse without hesitation but with some surprise. It had looked simple but I'd found myself making readjustments in mid-move. I knew I'd done it expensively and I ascribed that simply to my footgear. The standard black plimsoll had lately vanished from the market and the only alternative was the Bata baseball boot. At a glance these seemed attractive, disposing of the worry that a plimsoll might slip off the heel. In fact they had a welt and the glazed yellow sole seemed to give no real adhesion. At the resting place I couldn't find any protection for the first overhang. Feeling distinctly committed I went over it, not difficult. That got me to the second overhang. It was only a bulge really. There was still no protection. Wide awake now, and feeling oddly tired, I pulled over it and looked up the long groove above. The angle had relented but I couldn't see any obvious spike for a sling, any thin crack for a jammed knot, any big resting place. What do we do now?

Clausius said it: entropy is always increasing, call that the Second Law of Thermodynamics. Energy bleeds away, everything grinds to a halt and falls to bits. I knew exactly what to do. I got down from the bulge and rested briefly. Then I got down over the first overhang and rested a moment again. Beneath the sleeves of my anorak I could feel the hard swelling of the forearm tensor muscles that's delicious at the end of an afternoon's bouldering but is bad news on a big mountain pitch. I set out to reverse the traverse, couldn't see how I'd done it, and knew suddenly and with certainty that the next move was the terminus. Fast, ragged, I just got back to the resting place, third visit. I'd failed to get up and I'd failed to get down.

I looked back across at my brother. I said: "I'm going to come off on this." He said: "Better not. You've seen this belay. This stance doesn't help. We could both go." I said: "When I come off I'll be as close as I can get." He looked unhappy. I turned away and for a long time I watched the Rannoch Moor, where nothing was happening. Until, surprising me, a strong impulse of determination, no, of glee welled up, actually wanting to fight it out.

Boltzmann said it: $S = K \log W$. Entropy is the product of the constant Boltzmann found and the logarithm of a particular statistical probability. All systems incorporate entropy. But, even in the clockwork world of physics, probability, not certainty, is the last word. So what about the world of human purpose? Nothing is certain. In the end, disorder rules. In the meantime, islands of stability or continuity, seeming like miracles, survive the storm. Maybe this was just part of a pattern. I was going to be scared stiff lots of times, I was going to nearly fall off lots of rock climbs lots of times. That turned out to be true.

Alright, I can hear you, I know. I'm just gutting the equations for the poems and junking the hard bits with the commercial value. But I wrote the note down years ago. Now, to my amusement, I meet the same thoughts again in James Gleick's book on Chaos. The use of the Second Law by writers is misguided, he says. Then, using the strategies and weapons of the writer, he tries to put the sums into words and to describe systems in which order survives, patterns persist, at least on a temporary basis. Well, temporary is okay. Temporary will do for now. As a matter of fact, I never expected more. I set off on the traverse again and when I got to the far side I was still there. Cunningham! Maniac! I lunged for the belay loop, something to hang on. Deliberately, Nev blocked me. Gasping, I had to hold onto his shoulders, looking the very picture of the man who's been there and back. I convalesced for a few minutes. Of course — there was always the possibility that Cunningham had made an abseil inspection. Some people did that. There were even people around who top-roped hard lines first. Still, not a bad climber, Cunningham. When I was able to talk properly I said that for now we'd go and do something else, and we'd get some first-hand information, and we'd come back another day to do this thing.

There is a Doctrine of the Fall. It says that we're spineless, we know what the grades are and we know what we're capable of and we just give in. It's attached to the Biblical account of the temptation of Eve and Adam by the serpent and it uses the fall as metaphor. This Christian teaching takes a really hard line. It tells us that our weakness is congenital, coming to us straight from Adam, and it abuses us when we show evidence of this inherited characteristic.

Question: What are the longest survivor falls so far claimed?
Answer: Those of Tomlinson and Lucifer. References: Kipling's Selected Poems, 'Tomlinscn'; The Holy Bible, Isaiah 14:12, Luke 10:18.
Objection: Not proper falls. Tomlinson was pulled, Lucifer was pushed.

That's an oblique approach to a fascinating point. What is the crucial, most obvious difference between life on earth and life in heaven? It is this: that in heaven there is *no more falling.* The people have wings. Sceptical, facetious, I suppress the temptation to make jokes. The problem remains, whether you believe the Cosmos was dreamed up in the mind of God or whether you assert that heaven was designed on the drawing boards of earth: this bizarre discrepancy still cries out for explanation.

It has to be said, too, that religious metaphors of the fall are strong and natural. Notice that they belong to a group of three, the elevation metaphor, the ladder metaphor, the fall metaphor. The elevation metaphor, whether used for spiritual or worldly purposes, deals with condition and works by opposition. We feel high or low, elated or depressed. We have scores of names for these states and stations.

The ladder adds dimensions of effort and aspiration, risk and failure, progress made and ground lost. Where there are mountains the mountain may substitute and where there are forests the world-tree may stand in but possibly the ladder has precedence. Perhaps it first comes strongly into Christian theology, and almost certainly it arrives in Christian art, when John Climacus borrowed Jacob's Ladder for use as a teaching aid. But, like my friend told you, the image isn't exclusively Christian. It's found in the Egyptian Book of the Dead. Amongst the Greeks it's found in Plato. Amongst the Latins it's found in Porphyry and Plotinus. (Here's a research project: Establish the region and period of origin of the game of Snakes and Ladders. Check whether its pattern of colonisation relates to the spread of the Christian faith.)

The fall metaphor dramatises an instant. Whether religious or secular it has a strong psychosomatic aptness. When we regret a moral choice it's in our heads that the judgement is made. But it's in our bodies that we get that sinking feeling.

There is a Freudian slip. It draws attention to the world of dreams. Expeditions of highly-qualified field scientists have made long treks through the landscapes of the night, trying to record and classify the action. Weird goings-on. Yet, while they can't agree what it's all about they agree very closely on what they've seen. All these grownups nearly crying because they can't seem to get their vests on or tie their shoes or pack their bags or catch their buses: social-conditioning dreams. All these couples, gliding into each other's arms, sometimes suggesting possibilities, destinies even, that hadn't yet occurred to the daylight zombie. These are families of dreams. Now, when we get down to particular events, all the ethnologists are in agreement: the most popular occupation in dreamland is falling.

This seems very odd. In this context I can't help noticing two other strange dreams. First, the levitation, floating or gliding dream. Second, the downhill-movement, sliding, skiing, surfing dream. The temptation to put the three together is strong. In an old terminology, that would give the falling dream as an anxiety dream, the levitation dream as a wish-fulfilment response to the same anxiety, and the downhill-movement dream as an intermediate type with the fall held somehow under control. Notice that the three dreams have some curious correspondences with the three metaphors but don't make too much of it.

The question of why people should dream so much of falling is something else. I have an intuition, not supported by enquiries, that climbers dream intensively about falling, perhaps with some referential detail, in the first phase of their intoxication; and that as time goes by they probably stop having falling dreams altogether. If this were so, it would be mildly interesting. What is really interesting is why civilians should dream of falling.

The computer-function theory of dreaming proposed by Christopher Evans is ingenious and persuasive. Yet it disappoints us by having nothing new to say about the falling dream. It has to rely on earlier suggestions, as that the dream is triggered by small bodily sensations, a delayed heartbeat, a pause in respiration, the slight gastric movements of digestion, and so on.

The bolder explanations of the falling dream are two, perhaps only one. The first is that it is pre-human, going back to our remote ancestry in the tree-tops and to the subsequent struggle to stand upright without the use of the hands. It's been shown that in infant baboons the principal innate fear is of falling and it's been asked whether the 'startle reflex' of human infants might not spring from the same origin. The second would be that falling dreams refer only to the dreamer's infant struggles to walk and that therefore they might be regarded as the first example of social-conditioning dreams.

It would be interesting to know more. Surveys of dreams have usually used college student populations or have solicited respondents from magazines and newspapers. Dreams have been recorded since the dawn of writing but it's unlikely that there have been any systematic studies outside Westernised societies. Do aboriginal peoples without riding animals, brought up in low huts or tents on treeless plains, dream about falling? Can a man born quadriplegic have these dreams?

Humpty Dumpty fell. And Jack and Jill. And Alice. Even in nursery rhymes, even in children's stories, there's some mystery about the fall. Icarus fell. It wasn't because "the wax of his wings melted", don't believe it. It was just politics: the Chief Priest loaded a parable and shot him down. Rome fell. And Troy, and Mexico, and Singapore and Saigon. Cities, cultures, empires that took centuries to build are laid to rest by the little word. The ambitious modern novelist can't resist checking for a charge in the old idea: Albert Camus, *The Fall*; William Golding, *Free Fall*; Colin Thubron, *Falling*; Jim Harrison, *Legends of the Fall*. In *The Monkey Wrench Gang* the new bridge spans the gorge of the Colorado: "Seven hundred feet down. It is difficult to fully grasp the meaning of such a fall." The fall has been merchandised: the ultimate soft fall is now on offer to everyone in the bungee jump. A fallen woman, falling in love again, morale will fall. The verb has conjugated itself and its freight right through the language, which is to say, right through the way we think.

In some aspects of contemporary rock-climbing the fear of falling seems to have been disciplined but that control is provisional and precarious. Just inside the back of the skull, just outside the oval of vision, the real fall is standing by. And before all the dreams and beneath all the symbolism and behind all the jokes the fall suggests some simple, deep, central, premonitory meaning. In this, the climber is expert, but it doesn't take a climber to see it. Iris Murdoch goes close to the heart of it in a few lines from *The Sea, The Sea*:

> Falling, what the child fears, what the man dreads, is itself the image of death, of the defencelessness of the body, of its frailty and mortality, its absolute subjection to alien causes. Even in a harmless fall in the road there is a little moment of horror when the faller realizes that he *cannot help himself*; he has been taken over by a relentless mechanism and must continue with it to the end and be subject to the consequences. "There is nothing more I can do." How long, how infinitely expansible, a second is when it contains this thought, which is an effigy of death.

ON GETTING LOST

In Daniel Boone's autobiography, ghosted in his old age, the American frontiersman makes an entertaining boast: I was never lost in the woods in my whole life, he says, though once I was confused for three days. Another version exists in which he describes himself not as confused but as bewildered. A good word: bewildered, trapped by the wilderness. Compare: benighted, caught by the night.

The distinctions between being lost, being confused and being bewildered can't be stated with precision. Roughly, when we're lost we don't have the faintest idea which way to turn; salvation will be by luck or by rescue. When we're confused the seen landforms allow two or three correlations with the mental landscape or with the area of the map we believe we're occupying but we can test these options. When we're bewildered we're detained by the wilderness though we may still have an ongoing strategy in mind. In Britain these shades of meaning are usually academic. Unless bad weather, illness, injury or schedule play a part, it's unlikely that we'll suffer anything worse than brief disorientation in our road-dissected hills.

Even here, though, it's certainly possible to get things wrong. And although I've mislaid myself once or twice in larger landscapes it seems to me that similar sensations are to be found in the smallest domestic misadventures. In confining myself to these I find a core of value in the experience itself, freed of more serious considerations.

In fact, our small yet sometimes complex and often cloudy hills, our short winter days, are rich with opportunity for the carefree or careless. Getting lost is especially a possibility for the rockclimber, who rarely carries map and compass and who's often incompetent in their use. Generally it can be said that, like primitive man, he's base-orientated rather than north-orientated. That is, he becomes familiar with the skylines around his area of operation; gradually he triangulates outward from known landmarks, assisted by folklore, by hill paths and by the brief instructions or simplified sketchmaps in climbers' guidebooks; he visits higher and more remote crags beyond the boundaries of his valley: until the day when, clad in cloud and overconfidence, he finds the known world has displaced itself. So, for example, Keith King and I once made the long approach from Langdale to climb on the East Buttress of Scafell. We didn't have map or compass but we didn't need them because these were our hills. In thick cloud, neither admitted to the other his enormous relief when we found ourselves at the recognised cairn of Scafell Pike, just a few minutes from the cliff. Disconcertingly, Mickledore Gap failed to appear and a long time later we felt an equal relief on recognising the shore of Angle Tarn. It was too late to start again but at least we were nearly halfway home.

Once our party gave itself a day's break from rock-climbing in the Poisoned Glen in Donegal. Secure in the care of two friends and local experts I followed Frank Winder and Betty Healey over the granite pavements of the Derryveaghs to finish on Slieve Snaght. There we told each other how much we'd enjoyed the walk. Night was drawing in as we emerged from the cloud to find ourselves at the remote and uninhabited head of Glen Barra.

At about this time a French climbing expedition sailed a chartered boat from Iceland for Cape Farewell, the mountainous southern extremity of Greenland. The party, aiming off insufficiently, failed to make landfall and finally its only certainty was that it was in the north-west Atlantic. "If we can miss Greenland on the way out, how will we find Iceland on the way back?" the members asked themselves. In the event they were located and redirected after an extensive NATO search.

In Glen Barra, in our more modest dilemma, we had similar misgivings. It was only a few miles back over the hill: but without torch, map or compass, in darkness and cloud, with no clear paths over the Bearnas or Ballaghageeha Gaps and with the massive cliffs of the Poisoned Glen obstructing our descents, we felt it unlikely that we'd get back before daybreak. On the other hand it was forty miles by road, most of it little travelled in those years. If we were to walk to Doochary it might be possible to get bed and breakfast, except that we hadn't enough money.

However, this was in the nineteen-fifties in the west of Ireland, where the wildly improbable was not unlikely. On the high ground towards Glen Veagh, a hallucination surely, the lights of a vehicle appeared and began to inch downward into Glen Barra. We ran down to the half-surfaced track and stationed ourselves alongside. Eventually a battered little van, probably the only traffic of the day, perhaps of the week, trundled slowly towards us. First in line, I solicited the driver politely in the style of the English hitch-hiker. It was still just light enough to be able to see his face and I watched in dismay as he deliberately averted his head and drove carefully around me, actually mounting the opposite bank to pass. Betty was also unsuccessful. But Frank, fifty yards down, had stationed himself at a rocky narrows and, feet astride, stood his ground. Reluctantly the driver lowered a window two inches and asked what was wrong. He'd typed the situation as a reprisal for Johnson's Motor Car or as a commandeering by deer-poachers. Our explanations were accepted and after a bone-shaking ride we got out at Doochary. There, in a bar, we found a cheerful party priming itself before driving to a ceilidh at Dungloe and the offer of a lift was spontaneous. And at Dungloe we found a traveller awaiting a taxi to Dunlewy and happy to accept a small subsidy.

Most British climbers will tell similar stories. I'm one of the community of mountain-goers settled on or close to the slopes of the Carneddau. We know its cwms and summits very well. There's no point more than two or three miles from a road-head though the road perimeter is fifty miles or so. Every few years the telephone rings and a hesitant voice starts to explain, to the growing delight of the listener, that the party has been on Carnedd Llewellyn and visibility was really bad on the tops. The speaker is at Dolgarrog, or Aber, or Bethesda. The car is at Ogwen, or Capel Curig, or Ro Wen.

Map and compass are a serious impediment to the enjoyment of movement. If there's no sense of physical risk the temptation to leave them in the sack, even on unknown ground, is often irresistible. The consequences can sometimes be entertaining. Before traversing Skiddaw for the first time I studied and memorised a route. After the summit I didn't pay close attention to distance travelled until windows appeared in the cloud and I realised I was nowhere near my intended descent. If I didn't get back to it I'd face a long walk on the road. Hastily I got the equipment out and just managed three quick bearings for a resection before the mist shut in again. The result, as is always the case if this operation is done quickly, produced the triangle sometimes known in navigation as a cocked hat. In this event I had an extended isosceles triangle lying on its side and neatly framing the name of a shoulder of the hill. I looked with appreciation at its wholly appropriate title: Cockup.

Happily, even when map and compass are continuously and carefully used, it's possible to make mistakes. Driving from Sheffield to North Wales one mid-winter afternoon, Maureen and I made a stop at the Snake Inn and decided we had time enough for a short walk. This old hostelry lies in the gap between two of Derbyshire's finest hills. I knew the plateau of Kinder Scout, to the south, and its intricate fingerprint of peat groughs as well as I knew my own hand. To the north stands Bleaklow, a more massive, less well-trodden mountain and a summit I'd never taken in though I'd made a few excursions across its flanks.

In the event we decided to walk as far as the end of Alport Dale, a tight little valley leading deep into the heart of the hill. This entry, which neither of us had ever seen, was full of interest. In this valley the early Methodists had held their annual Love Feasts or Feasts of Charity. Setting the tone at the start we saw the remote barn where, three hundred years ago, outside the reach of the law, George Fox had preached in safety to the first Quakers. Very quickly the depth of the snow increased and after passing beneath the huge collapsing stacks of Alport Castles we found that the shallow little river was now iced over. We were wearing wellingtons and these proved more useful than boots. As the ravine closed in, deep banks of soft snow forced us to cross frequently from one side to the other and from time to time we broke through into a foot of running water. I checked our progress by counting off the tiny tributaries, all shown though not all named on the old one-inch map I was using: Glethering Clough, Nether Reddale Clough, Upper Reddale Clough, Miry Clough. The lighting now had a grey or sepia cast with the only sombre relief given by the few small streamside outcrops and trees and by the occasional bogburst staining the snowslopes above us.

Then, at last, we were at Grains in the Water, the steeply enclosed terminal bend and the mysterious place-name that had tempted us up the valley. We shared a flask and some food in this magical sanctuary in an atmosphere of calm and seclusion so strong that I wanted to delay our return. And as we sat there a character defect that's often led me into difficulties began to assert itself with a tempting proposition. We had to be back in Wales in reasonable time, yes. But why not just climb up onto Alport Head to set foot on the ridge itself? There wouldn't be any problem in retracing the route in the dark.

Maureen acceded willingly. We climbed up the headwall and I checked the compass as we entered cloud. Soon we were standing on the whalebacked watershed in a strong wind. Nightfall was on us yet still the impulse argued. Now we'd be returning in darkness whatever we did. We were only a mile from an unvisited summit. A shorter return to the road would be available from there. Why not?

All right, then. But we'd have to be careful on the unknown descent. And striking the precise summit, a minimal elevation on the plateau with no confirmatory trig point, wouldn't be easy in these conditions. Surely there'd be a cairn, anyway? I took some compass bearings and distances by torchlight, shielding the flimsy map awkwardly from the wind as I estimated times of travel in minutes and glanced at my watch. Then I asked Maureen to count paces. The rough ground, heather with occasional peat steps, rose only gently and was made uniform by snow.

It's easy to let body and instinct outvote or overrule the compass and known tendencies have to be resisted. Facing squarely into a bearing we sidestep minimally but consistently away from the wind. In ascending or descending traverses we gain or lose a little less height than the compass advises. After a quite short time in a cueless environment the style of movement perseverates on changing aspects of a slope until the dogmatic compass, swinging crazily away, insists on a showdown. Without the compass, on featureless and level ground, a blindfold man is said to complete a circle in seven miles. A woman, it's reported, in two.

These tendencies are overcome only by rigorous discipline. Correctly, in these conditions, the one holding the compass stands still and directs the other to the limit of visibility and hearing, just a few yards perhaps, corrects the position, joins the other and repeats the process. I couldn't be bothered with all that. We just pushed on together as I fixed on an unburied tuft of heather, an odd rock, an exposed bank of peat, a ripple in the snow. The wind and the spindrift impeded us a little but I was sure we were making a reasonable pace. Curiously though, for each leg, the time ran out long before the pace target. I compromised and strained for some object in the darkness but the summit could have been anywhere. Now we were surely descending a little, now rising again. We continued, admitting finally that we'd crossed or bypassed the highest point. And suddenly we were out of the cloud and able to see the lights of vehicles on the Snake Pass and the glow of the Lancashire conurbations. We were well to the west of our intended descent. The map was stuffed away and we enjoyed a surprisingly easy and pleasant traverse back by Alport Low and the Old Woman to Doctor's Gate Culvert. Four miles of road remained but we were moving rapidly by now.

The following evening I studied the map again in disbelief. Bearings and distances had been correct. We must surely have walked right over the high point but the lack of any confirmation was galling. Maureen, who never uses maps, listened as I reasoned aloud. Then she passed a remark about Alport Head. I'd never mentioned the name so how did she know of it? Because it had said Alport Head on the plaque. What plaque? The plaque I'd been watching her read.

I'd seen her glancing at what, side on, seemed a rough flake of rock, crowning a little cairn. I'd passed round the other side of it. It was a memorial to three teenagers who'd died there in a blizzard a few years earlier.

I argued on. Was she certain she'd counted the paces correctly? It's easy to drop a hundred, perhaps more than once. She insisted her counts were right. Of course, she added, she'd adjusted the figure for her shorter stride. Well, I'd also made allowances for that. And she'd corrected for the head wind and difficult going. I'd made allowances for that too. Teamwork.

The use of map and compass, even in Britain, is sometimes essential to a particular purpose and is often prudent. But it's a precaution to be weighed carefully and to be taken with some reluctance since it always diminishes the experience. Far better, if possible, to see the landscape with fresh eyes, curiosity and innocence our guides; to have the scene reveal itself as we move without pre-knowledge of what the next bend in the valley will reveal or what prospect the col is about to disclose. Call it the conservation of aesthetic impact.

That's not to say that careful navigation can't offer great satisfaction. To take a long shot over open and featureless country, allowing no overviews, and to hit the destination perfectly brings a positive swell of pride. To this end it's better to use old small-scale maps since they encourage free and uninterrupted macronavigation. Unfortunately, at satisfactory scales, it's hard to find decent maps of the hills of Britain. The expanded metric maps most walkers carry impose a different style now, a tedious point-to-point accountancy, a halting inventory of trivial features.

Crucially, the pleasure of navigation itself is suddenly in question. As I write the size and weight of satellite positioning devices is rapidly reducing. The mobile phone has already been put to use by climbers. If these two aids are combined with map and compass, skills we've been refining since time immemorial become obsolete. Pressures from responsible authorities, from rescue organisations, from insurers, may be brought to bear on organised parties. Even the solo hill walker may find himself threatened.

I've made a single memorable ascent of The Cheviot. I'd never visited the area and I had no walking map but I happened to have a compass and we had a road atlas in the car. Looking at this I guessed that although no detail of the hill's topography was shown the summit itself was probably accurately placed. It's true that I'd have preferred to make the ascent by way of the College Burn to see the cliffs of the Henhole which I knew of through climbing legend. The blank map offered no help there so I simply drove to the nearest marked village to the summit. It turned out to be only a large farm at the roadhead.

A bearing on the top showed it to be shut out from this point and the direct approach to be a steep and stupid line. However, bypassing the mountain, the valley rose steadily to a high col from which the summit might be visible. If we were to reach that gap and to fix it with back bearings, and if we could estimate the distance to it accurately, we might be able to separate the hill itself from any confusing neighbours. Carrying the large leather-bound atlas we set off up the valley.

As it turned out, any approach would have worked. The summit had no rivals. We'd had a late start and we reached the peat-bog-moated top just as the sun was setting but in time to admire as spacious and breathtaking a panorama as I've seen on mountains anywhere. Looking into Scotland no trace of human presence could be seen. No roads, no buildings, no pinprick of light in the darkening valleys beneath us. Beyond these valleys range on range of hills receded giving an impression of a land abandoned or still uncolonised by man. This was at New Year but on a perfectly still and surprisingly warm day. To the south a sparse scatter of lights revealed a few isolated farms. And further, as we sat there, at colossal distances the towns and cities of the North of England began to declare themselves in pools of light.

I saw then that what I was lacking wasn't a walker's map. I needed, on a single sheet, the whole of Northern England and the Borders. I wanted to be able to name those distant cities and those shadowy ranges without tedious transference of bearings. I wanted to know just how far our horizons stood that evening.

Maps, I think, offer their greatest pleasures in the home and the most fascinating maps are those of countries we'll never visit. They induce a dreamlike pleasure as the mind considers place-names and the eye follows rivers and roams amongst mountains. They're a poem without beginning or end.

Getting lost, however briefly, is a luxury. It may mean inconvenience, unwelcome further exercise, hunger, thirst or expense. Surely, though, it's one of the most vitalising experiences wild country can offer and we ought to be properly grateful when it comes. It can't be arranged deliberately, simply by leaving map and compass behind. That's a good move but it usually only offers us exploration. Something has to go wrong, there has to be an interval of suspicion or a moment when things won't fit, when sets of assumptions have to be discarded and the slate of the mind is wiped clean. Then, the strangeness of the world crowds us. And shortly or finally, the revelation comes. We accept the baffling landforms for themselves, cross a metaphysical boundary and discard the bad template as comprehension floods us. It's a moment for rejoicing. We were lost and are found again.

The Dru

ON PLANNED BIVOUACS

To bivouac: "to pass the night in the open air." The word comes through French from the German *beiwacht*, extra watchman or lookout; later, *biwak*. The origin is military, implying outlying sentries in a state of weary vigilance. Immediately it carries suggestions of emergency, of a disturbed, uncomfortable or uneasy night. The definition quoted is interesting in itself. One wouldn't expect a lexicographer to have any field experience but I imagine I read a sly humour in the phrase "to pass the night."

In walking, the bivouac has often been thought an event worth celebration. The first English writer to describe a night out in this vein is probably John Taylor, the Water Poet. He should also be credited with the invention of the sponsored walk and in 1618 he described his planned journey on foot from London to Edinburgh, a journey he actually extended to Aberdeen, passing through the Cairngorms. A number of nights were spent without shelter:

> In heaven's star-chamber did I lodge that night,
> Ten thousand stars me to my bed did light.

In mountaineering, perhaps more surprisingly, the bivouac has often inspired a full-blown romanticism, extended to this day by Will McLewin.

"There are so many stars. They seem not to be distant points of light but a net hung across the sky....An unbroken night's sleep is a disappointment."

The most evocative description I've come across is that in Robin Fedden's book on the Encantados. This lyrical passage is convincing too. On a clear night the rotation of the earth no longer rests on reason: our bodies tell us that the earth is turning; and this is confirmed when we doze and awaken surprised to see that Cassiopeia has swung round by two or three hours. "Perched with a rope round my waist," Fedden says, "I saw the machinery of time. I saw it, the whole grave procession, from midnight to morning."

Even some of the strongest and most enterprising spirits on the most arduous climbs give voice to similar emotions and tend to pick out the same ideas. "One is in limbo," says Royal Robbins, "cut off from the crowd, suspended between mighty efforts of the day past and the day to come." He commiserates those who can't sleep because they've grown accustomed to too soft a bed. They should enjoy the night watching Orion or the Great Bear "tick the minutes off the celestial clock."

The disenchanted will want to point out that, though Robbins had certainly been around and was as hard and as cool as they come, a good proportion of his nights out were spent on big walls in California under starry skies. And that Fedden, whose main experience was of desert journey bivouacs, was writing about the sunny side of the Pyrenees. (In fact, Fedden's observation that "the earth moved" is a bit unfortunate, recalling a much-publicised night out twenty years earlier and a few miles further south. Hemingway's hero, of course, had the inestimable luxury, in one account, of lying on Ingrid Bergman.) It's clear, anyway, that in general good bivouacs are all good in similar ways. Bad bivouacs all differ in their styles and degrees of vileness.

For British climbers working a way into the harder Alpine routes in the early fifties the matter of the bivouac set a teasing problem and folk wisdom soon produced a Northern proverb: "if you carry bivvy gear you'll bivvy." That is, if a party carries precautionary equipment on a climb just possible in one day the weight of the gear will itself make a bivouac inevitable. And even the carrying of the gear won't guarantee a comfortable night as we were to discover on the South Ridge of the Aiguille Noire de Peuterey.

The first British ascent of this classic route, one of the longest pure rock climbs in the whole of the Alps, had been made the previous year. Keith King and I were hoping for the second but on arrival at the mountain we found that it had just gone to Hamish Nicol and Pat Vaughan.

Further, another pair, Dennis and Gwen Greenald, were still on the route. This couple was making what seemed very ambitious excursions for a husband-and-wife team at the time. In fact their total of bivouacs for the season was alleged to have exceeded the aggregate for all other British climbers in the Western Alps that year. Their determination impressed me. I wasn't aware at that time of their secret which related to the profession in which they were engaging or training to engage, that of child psychology. To one who's looked deeply into the minds of children, nothing that mountains can do is likely to ruffle the composure.

We considered the strategies of these two parties, as shortly disclosed, with interest. Starting at the same time, the first team had carried no gear and had completed the route in a very long day. Burdened, the Greenalds had enjoyed, if the word is appropriate, two bivouacs. Surely we could move as fast as Vaughan and Nicol? Yet the route had a serious write-up. The French guidebook stated that retreat was problematic after the abseil from the third tower, Pointe Welzenbach. To add spice, the crux doesn't present itself until the fifth tower. It seemed to us that the first party had been in a secure position. Travelling light, they might inspect the main difficulty before the Greenalds reached the abseil and if they were to change their minds they'd still have a means of escape. If, at a later stage, they met with any problem, backup might eventually arrive.

In the event we decided to carry the gear. Partly, this was because by the time we were on the climb there'd be no-one left in the valley who knew who we were or where we were; partly, because we'd been preparing ourselves for months for this sort of exercise and we'd just now carried our monstrous loads over the Col du Géant. My basic resource was an ex-services air-sea survival suit, a huge kapok-filled sleeping bag from which arms and a hood extruded. It was complemented by a similarly-shaped waterproof envelope in a bright yellow rubber-coated fabric. I'd divided both parts at hip level so that in extreme conditions I could wear either upper half whilst climbing, whilst for the bivouac I could button the pieces together. This merman-shaped cocoon resisted compression and was forced into a large sack only with great difficulty. Keith had a similar outfit except that his, I think, was provided with legs as well. My two-pint Canadian Solus paraffin stove would be left behind and we'd use Keith's benzene-fuelled appliance, the prototype, we were later to learn, of the first sophisticated petrol bomb.

The South Ridge of the Noire is a beautiful thing. The approach route is a scramble rather than a hut walk and at that time the best line, hardly marked, was easily lost. We lost it but made our way nevertheless into the deep and spacious bowl of the Fauteuil des Allemands, the Germans' armchair. The original tiny unwardened refuge stood against and in the shelter of a tall overhanging cliff on the eastern side of the cwm. It offered an excellent view of the ridge, one tower of perfect red or yellow granite succeeding another.

We were at the foot of the rocks as dawn came. The climbing was mostly easy but we were obliged to haul our awkward and heavy sacks on some of the steeper and more difficult pitches, a time-consuming process. After passing the Rubicon of the third tower I counted the difficulties out: the Ressaut en Demi-lune on the fourth tower, Pointe Brendel; the crucial groove and traverse on the fifth tower, Pointe Ottoz; then the last pitch of five; then the last pitch of four. It was clear now that nothing was going to stop us but it was also clear that we'd have to bivouac. We were prepared for that.

At the very last moment I got it wrong. Darkness was close and over the last hour heavy cloud had formed on Mont Blanc and was rolling down on us. We were a few easy minutes from the top of the lower summit, but we didn't want to spend the night there if a storm was about to break. Neither did we want to go back to an excellent bivouac site we'd recently passed, since speed in locating the descent might be vital in the morning. I was returning to the crest of the ridge by a snow gully when I noticed a chimney leading into what seemed to be a deep cave some distance up the right wall. I indicated it to Keith as he joined me and he led through up to it as the daylight faded. In dismay he called out that it had no real floor, simply a forty-five degree slab; however, it had a level ten-foot ceiling. All it offered was shelter but it seemed risky to continue to the exposed summit if there might be a threat of lightning which, notoriously, turns this ridge into a death-trap.

I joined him and saw the problem. He'd been able to place good belay pegs but there was almost nothing to stand on. He'd installed himself in a squatting position on some sketchy footing, restrained by these anchors. Three feet below him I settled myself, also squatting, a good foot-jam for my right foot, my left in a sling on the slab, secured by the tight ropes. Cautiously and awkwardly we put on our bivouac jackets and balancing the stove on his knees Keith prepared a hot drink and soup. The lower halves of our sleeping outfits had been carried for nothing.

Not a good night. But it was interesting, even amusing. He seemed to suffer more than me, wrestling with the ropes, half-sliding off, trying new positions, cursing. I slept surprisingly well, except that every hour or so I was awakened by an agonising cramp in my right thigh. This was an ailment I'd never experienced and each time I was obliged to rise to my feet and shake out until the pain subsided. However, snow had begun to fall now and I was able to look out at the heavy flakes with equanimity, even with pleasure, from the security of our shelter.

We discovered in the morning that a capacious ledge lay on the west face, just beyond the head of the gully. We'd have reached it more quickly than the cave itself. However, it faced into the wind and several inches of snow had fallen. Perhaps we'd have spent just as restless a night in brushing it off. Now the snow had stopped, the sun was trying to break through the cloud and we were perfectly dry.

On the most serious alpine climbs safe and comfortable bivouac sites may be few and far between and the guidebook will draw attention to their positions. Usually these will determine the planning of the ascent. Yet the simpler the excursion and the more choice on offer, the more difficult a decision may become. This was borne home to me by a curious experience on an easy two-day walk in the Isle of Arran. With Gordon Mansell I was taking a group of students from Brodick to Lochranza by way of Glen Iorsa. The weather was set fair and we decided to carry no tents and to settle down in the heather towards the top of the glen wherever fancy might suggest.

Of course we'd looked over the route, which didn't even present scrambling, on the map. But when we got into the glen we found, a thing without precedent, that the landscape was as simple as the map. As climbers we knew Glen Rosa, the parallelling valley to the east. It shows fine and massive cliffs. Standing by the little river of Glen Iorsa we were looking up a perfect textbook model of a glaciated valley, immaculately scooped, the floor and lower walls destitute of a single feature.

The sun declined and we still had to decide where to stop. The problem had presented itself immediately, no one spot was better than any other. We looked for some small tree to settle down by. Nothing. We looked for a bush. Nothing. A rock. Nothing. We moved along the meanders of the little stream searching for a shingle beach, a small bank, but we could find no object to which we could attach a few words to say where we'd lain down. Only the vast trough of the glen and the level heather all around us. In the end we simply gave up, throwing down our sleeping bags to spend the night homeless at the dead centre of nowhere. It seemed oddly unsettling to lie beneath the sky without a single describable object to which the mind might belay itself.

I find myself reluctant to describe some of the nights I've spent out in Britain as bivouacs. The word, qualified by mountaineering, seems to imply some degree of emergency or to suggest at least a little positive action in improvising shelter. It seems more correct to say that I slept out. Yet, inconsistently, though the presence of a roof seems to exclude them, I think of the nights I've spent in deep caves or abandoned mines as bivouacs.

A site, at first glance perfect, may turn out a nightmare. My most disappointing bivouac was again with Gordon beneath the North Face of the Dru, ominously close to the spot where, a hundred and fifty years earlier, Frankenstein had argued with his creature. We'd been told of excellent possibilities on the Rognon and there we found what seemed a perfect structure. A colossal cube of rock was supported two feet above a spacious rock floor by small but solid blocks. Ceiling and floor were dead level, the space available was many square yards in extent. We inspected this edifice carefully. It couldn't move, could it? Come on, be rational. And if the weather were to change, as it was beginning to appear that it might, we'd certainly stay dry.

After cooking we wriggled awkwardly in towards the centre of the slot. I now had an excellent duvet jacket. I worked my legs into my rucksack and drew the extension up to my waist. I rested my head on my rope and composed myself for the night. That worked for ten minutes. The block was set against a steep slope and ice-cold air, descending this slope, was flowing through the crevice like water. The duvet felt marvellous but it had no hood and my face began to freeze. It was impossible to sit up but on one elbow I eased the collar up around my ears. Another ten minutes and my hips were painfully chilled. That made twenty minutes. The rest of the night continued at its own pace.

Morning brought the relief of movement. We were away at the first hint of light into a ghostly cloudy dawning. Two of our friends had been sleeping somewhere in the same confusion of boulders and we could hear their voices but we couldn't place them. We hurried up to the North Face and went up the couloir and snowslope to the foot of the difficulties. Here we could confirm what we'd suspected, that the rock was holding ice. The cloud was thickening and a wind was beginning to blow. We descended rapidly and, hearing voices again, stared for a long time into the dangerous approach couloir of the West Face, their objective. We exchanged shouts, they were directly opposite us, yet we couldn't see them. Then we caught a movement and we identified two mites, a fraction of the size of the figures we'd been looking for. A big face. Paul Ross and Joe Smith were more determined and nowhere near as bright as Gordon and myself. They fought their way upward with great difficulty until the storm had sufficiently terrified them, and then they fought their way downward, for many hours, with greater difficulty still.

My most comfortable bivouac in the Alps was on the North-west Ridge of the Grands Charmoz, with Keith and four Irish climbers. It was to be our first hard route of the season and we weren't yet acclimatised. We came to a strange arrangement to climb in convoy in three parties of two, sharing out the more difficult pitches. This gave us a sociable day but advance was hopelessly slow. At five in the afternoon we reached the sensational pendulum before the final bastion, a point Keith and I were to reach three weeks later at nine in the morning, having set off at the same hour. From the start this first attempt had really had the character of a reconnaissance. Without attempting the pendulum, two or three pitches below the crux, we began to retrace our steps and finally settled down on a roomy though exposed ledge in a secure position. The night was fine but not too cold and I slept well.

Frank Winder, however, had fortified himself with Benzedrine or some such amphetamine at a quite late stage in the day on the assumption that we were in for a committing push through the final difficulties. After midnight he was still highly charged. I woke from time to time to see him pacing the ledge like something from Hamlet and muttering in passionate tones the poetry of Yeats. I knew these poems by heart myself ("Some day we shall get up before the dawn...") and Frank had an unforgettable voice; on this occasion, however, I was able to ignore the pair of them. Descending in the morning I felt happy in returning the broad grins of ascending French parties on the glacier with their politely mischievous enquiries: "Bon bivouac, messieurs?" "Vous avez dormi bien, messieurs?" Speaking for myself, I said that we had.

I see now that I'm crossing the line. On this attempt we had the equipment to reduce discomfort though we hadn't positively planned to spend the night out. The distinction leads towards the crisis of the forced bivouac.

ON UNPLANNED BIVOUACS

The unplanned bivouac isn't always worse than the planned bivouac though that's its marked tendency.

In Yosemite, more than twenty years after the night on the Charmoz, I was climbing with my wife. She'd always been a keen hill-walker, more so than I, but she'd no obsession with rock-climbing. It seems fair enough to persuade anybody to sample a day on an outcrop but I've never tried to entice people onto longer or more difficult climbs unless they show enthusiasm. As time went by, however, on odd occasions she'd accompanied friends in a party spirit on routes harder than anything we'd done together. She'd even had a day out with Joe Brown. What was that about? I'd never known him offer free tuition. All this seemed curious. Finally I'd asked if I could climb with her again from time to time and she'd agreed. I discovered or rediscovered that although she didn't like strenuous routes she was a stylish balance climber, able to follow climbs difficult enough to satisfy the pair of us.

Here we were, then, in the place returning English climbers nearly always described with the same word: Paradise. It's true that those amongst them who'd visited Tuolumne Meadows, up above the valley, restricted the expression to that sub-alpine world. However, I realised before we went there that these last were a special breed, indifferent or hostile to the society and amenities of the valley itself.

For four or five days we enjoyed ourselves on the smaller cliffs and on the short routes making sorties up the lower slabs and exfoliation flakes of Glacier Point Apron and El Capitan. To satisfy my curiosity we went up the steep starting pitches of the East Buttress of El Cap but I couldn't bring myself to persuade Maureen that this longer excursion, about which I'd heard conflicting reports on the condition of the rockfall area, was a reasonable proposition for a dilettante. However, I felt a very strong need to do one or two routes reaching the valley rim and I settled first on an ancient classic, Royal Arches.

As we walked up the slope behind the Ahwahnee Hotel I described the excursion to Maureen as a reconnaissance. It was already after mid-day and our topo gave a time of six hours for the climb. At that speed on this late October day an ascent would finish at dusk. In any case we'd no idea whether the normal descent set off east or west along the rim, nor whether it was complex or difficult. This was an inspection then, and tomorrow we'd get out earlier and go straight through the Arches.

(Inside a week we'd know all about the descent, which lies to the east of Washington Column. We'd climb the old South Face Direct on the Column. We'd hear cries for help from two climbers who'd started to abseil the gully between the Arches and the Column. We'd find we couldn't drop them a rope without knocking down rocks as well. We'd indicate the exit, easily accessible to them, of the route we'd just climbed. We'd wish them goodnight. And we'd make our descent in brilliant moonlight. Then, no more than five feet from the road, ducking under a holly tree, Harold, like his namesake, would get an arrow in his eye.)

Royal Arches doesn't have immediate appeal. From the foot, without information, it would be hard to guess exactly where the line will find its way out. A sea of slabs runs upward for hundreds of feet until blocked by swept overlaps. Breaking leftward through these, the climb finishes as a long rising traverse. However, once embarked upon, the intricacy of line becomes intriguing as detail unseen from the ground unfolds, weaknesses are revealed, and the thread of necessity sews the expedition together.

There was a party halfway up the wall and another some rope-lengths above them as I started up the first pitch. The climbing was pleasant and presented little difficulty. But it was hot! The ledges sometimes supported trees or shrubs, almost of a desert vegetation character, and we found ourselves taking anchors where we could keep our feet, in tight rock boots, in shadow. We were making good progress, though, and eventually we found ourselves at the pendulum or tension traverse where the route begins to work leftward. This would be the obvious conclusion to our probe.

Wouldn't it make sense, though, to climb up to the bolts to check whether this passage might present any problem? We'd time enough to get down. On reaching the bolts I was intrigued, so I made the manoeuvre anyway. From here a simple ledge system ran leftward. I could pull Maureen across, we could go to the far end of the ledges easily, and we could return in a few minutes with one extra abseil and without committing ourselves. Soon we were at the next obstacle, another rope move.

As we'd gained height we'd become aware that the two parties above us were moving slowly. The second party had drawn closer to the first and we'd been closing rapidly on the second. It was getting late, yes. But unless we had problems with the next two passages we'd catch both pairs before the rim. Why be too proud to ask strangers for advice? For that matter, we could simply follow them down discreetly.

The short second rope move proved to be harder than the first, the last reach safe enough but feeling a little precarious. And now we arrived at as curious a situation as I've come across but one of which we'd already heard amusing accounts. We were on the right wall of a Cyclopean corner, which fell downward for hundreds of feet. A tall conifer on our ledge had toppled and now spanned the corner wall to wall at a steep angle, giving access to a clear exit at its top. It was the thickness of a telegraph pole and must have been dead for decades but it was still quite sound. The bark had been worn away by generations of climbers, the wood itself polished and repolished. "It is a palimpsest," Michael Tobias had told us, and as usual he had a core of meaning. Unnervingly, the climber faces away from the cliff, embraces this greased pole, and closing his eyes or staring straight down into the abyss he shins rapidly upward.

We caught up the second party, two young Americans, just before the top. They were now being held up by the first older team, a German and an American, on the last pitch. Only minutes of daylight remained. Shortly we were coiling ropes on the rim. Getting out my small torch I asked about the descent. The second party had no torch and no idea of the way off. And the first pair, we now saw, were pulling out sleeping bags and lighting a small stove. They'd only a rough idea of the way off anyway, though they thought it would be obvious by daylight. The younger team expressed a wish to follow us down but there was no moon and a few minutes' exploration in a tangle of shrub convinced me that one small torch between four persons wouldn't get us anywhere. Within a quarter hour the three groups had dispersed for privacy well out of earshot of each other.

The spacious uplands above the Yosemite walls are mainly cloaked in forest, an unfamiliar conclusion for a climb to the eyes of a European. On the edge of the escarpment we found a huge boulder with a considerable overhang forming a sandy cave. This shelter had a little rough walling already and in a crude hearth of stones against the back wall there lay the ashes of an old fire. We sat down for a moment. Through the afternoon the temperature had been in the mid-eighties and we'd been in full sunlight. We shared our remaining canned drink and still felt de-hydrated and drythroated. Saving two biscuits for breakfast, we each ate a hard-boiled egg, shared on orange, and began to feel hungry.

We weren't equipped for a night out. We'd been climbing in shirts and carrying a light sweater each. In contrast with the heat of the day, night temperatures were already low. Every morning curtains of ice had made broad margins down the splashed rock either side of the fourteen-hundred-foot Upper Yosemite Fall. But someone had lit a fire here only weeks or days ago. Down below I'd read that that was an offence, carrying a statutory penalty. Up here it was a precedent. My anxiety was that everything was tinder-dry. And wasn't the Mariposa Stand somewhere in the Park? Imagine burning down America's sacred grove on a first visit. We'd get into the history books and probably into jail. Well, Thoreau himself had once cleared a hundred acres of trees on the Concord River with a picnic camp-fire. "Burnt-the-Woods" Thoreau.

We were shivering already. We organised things with the greatest care. First, remove every single piece of tree litter from the floor of our shelter. Already we had more than we'd need for a while. Stack the rest of it carefully round the corner of the boulder. Keep the fire small at first. Immediately, the task became a ceremony, a celebration, as each twig, each cone, each spray of needles was handled for itself. Systematically we cleared the area of debris, working outward inch by inch and foot by foot. The night was windless and as the semi-circle of cleaned sand enlarged, six feet, ten, fifteen, we began to build a comforting blaze. In spite of its heat, no sparks rose any distance, the flames lapping nicely against the perfectly angled natural hearth-stone. Now we dared to make deep and comfortable beds of pine needles. And so we spent the night, one side toasted, one side iced, stirring at intervals to tend the fire.

Before we'd settled ourselves I'd found myself gazing down again and again into the valley. I'd missed my first Saturday night. I could see the lights of vehicles arriving, cars and bikes from San Francisco, Los Angeles perhaps. The girls would be serving beer in the Mountain Bar.

I could hear music rising with perfect clarity from the Ahwahnee Hotel. Finally I was able to smile at myself and to savour our situation. We spent, all things considered, a reasonable night. Shortly after dawn, as we waited the sun's first warmth and carefully checked that no hot ember remained, we watched two hang-gliders launch from Glacier Point, directly opposite. One white, one rainbow, they sank in easy spirals the near mile down to the meadows.

The other parties were nowhere to be seen but we had our own plan. On arriving in Yosemite we'd chanced to meet Mark Vallance who'd recommended Royal Arches as a starter. But don't take the climbers' descent, he'd said, and he'd declined even to describe it; take the scenic route, it's beautiful. He'd marked it for us, a crude biro scrawl on a little free handout of the valley. I have it still. Campsites, hotels, roads, services and the principal summits and streams are shown, but no details of topography. The idea was simply to walk north through the forest to intercept the track to North Dome and to follow it west to descend by Yosemite Creek. We were hungry and suffering raging thirsts but the route would be mainly downhill.

What a day. After a single initial glimpse of North Dome we were enclosed by the trees with only filtered sunlight to give direction. The gigantic Ponderosas of the valley floor assemble in dark and majestic stands, possibly cleared of castings in some areas to offer tourist walking. On the tops, through Silver Fir and deciduous trees, more light is admitted and the ground is varied underfoot, boulders, small screes, shrubs, windfalls. It seemed as magical as Arden as we wandered onward, feeling like Adam and Eve. Trees: "the best, the most revealing messengers to us from all nature, the nearest its heart," Fowles said. The forest warps time, he said, and in this terrain it was hard to estimate distance travelled with any precision. In some areas we met an understorey amongst which we saw and avoided juniper. Rashly, at one point, I persevered with a direct attack through a thicket of what I later learned to be manzanita. Despite the canopy it was now extremely hot and hours seemed to pass before I caught the sound of dripping water and we were able to collect a palmful or two. Later we reached a small stream. Puzzlingly, Maureen would hardly drink.

We never found the North Dome Trail. Perhaps we didn't quite reach it. Perhaps we crossed it on a rock pavement showing little trace. Perhaps, somehow, we crossed it twice. Finally we gave up on it and turned to the west. Later, on a proper map, we looked at the features we'd passed over: an unnamed stream; Royal Arches Creek; Lehamite Creek; Indian Canyon Creek. It was afternoon before we came on a track and I was sure of our position. Surprising me, Maureen, an easy and tireless walker, had called for a halt two or three times. Now I left her to rest while I followed it down to the rim to confirm. Yes, we were at Yosemite Point and I descended a little further to have a close look at Lost Arrow before returning. Then, the hot dusty descent down Yosemite Creek.

It was to be a year or two before we understood this day completely. Maureen was feeling the first intimations of a serious and chronic illness which, between complete and lengthy remissions, was to cause her great suffering and to circumscribe her activities, mine too, from time to time in years to come. Finally she had to sit down and rest for twenty minutes in cool shadow on a pleasant balcony of the trail while we looked down on our tent, only ten minutes below us and containing the food and drink we were craving. We'd done six hours of climbing and we were returning more than twenty-four hours after leaving. I couldn't regret it. It had passed like a slow delicious dream. And for the moment Maureen was able to believe that her debilitation was simply due to the heat and lack of food.

The bivouac. In anticipation, the very idea divides us. After a spell in the west of Ireland our party of four returned for a last day's climbing in Dalkey Quarry near Dublin. This would avoid a long overnight drive for the morning ferry. The tract of land embracing the quarry is or was then owned by the Church Commissioners, whose curious byelaws, I subsequently learned, prohibited "walking on the boundary wall, throwing stones, begging or preaching." The Church's thinking on the bivouac is not made clear. In fact we were equipped with tents and after we'd finished climbing I began to set mine up. Eric Langmuir was shocked. For a single fine night like this, how could anyone not wish to sleep beneath the stars? He teased me gently but persistently.

I've read somewhere that below a surprisingly mild temperature — fifty Fahrenheit or so — human beings don't, in fact, expose their faces whilst sleeping. They bury them, surfacing for air when asphyxiation threatens, which depending on the nature of the sleeping bag or coverings may be every few minutes. That gives a bad night. Further, breathing through the cheap feather-filled bags of that time left a peculiarly unpleasant taste in the mouth. I made these points to Eric as I crawled into my cosy little tent but his amusement at my unmanly behaviour remained unmoderated. I woke refreshed to a cool clear sunny morning and inspected the dew-sodden bundle in the grass at my feet. The bag was drawn tightly around the top of his skull. All I could see of the star-gazer was his rather long, perhaps already somewhat thinning hair, in which three lustrous four-inch black slugs were rooting listlessly around. I flipped them out with a twig.

I've mentioned the use of benzedrine to keep going. Some alpinists of the sixties, notably Tom Patey, took narcotics for a good bivouac followed by stimulants for a busy day. For myself, I've never deliberately taken anything to help me along but I have to admit to one night out for the most traditional of causes. Staying at the Cave and Crag Club's cottage above the Tremadog cliffs one Christmas we spent a very long evening in one of the village pubs. We raced back up the path at midnight, fuelled by drink, but somewhere in the fields on the top my legs collapsed. Delighted, my companions staggered on to Pant Ifan, each wanting to be the first to report my loss in action to the others at the cottage and to lead out witnesses. On getting there, however, they also felt unwell and obliged to lie down. My night began wildly. I balanced carefully on the spinning globe, clinging dizzily to grass and bracken each time it turned upside down. Eventually I passed out. But amongst those staying at the house was A.B. Afford, elder statesman and guru of this club, a philosopher with a strong interest in the sorts and conditions of men. Alone, he went out to locate and to examine me. When I awoke in the morning I found to my bewilderment that a heap of blankets had been laid over me and very carefully tucked in.

Jarringly, in situations of extreme seriousness, quite unexpected responses may be felt. Early in 1950 I accompanied Pete Thomson and Gerry Hartley to Glen Coe. Deep snow lay everywhere. At the Youth Hostel we found a single visitor, a strong and enterprising merchant seaman, 'Ken' Kennedy. On every shore leave, wherever in the world it was possible, this New Zealander would head straight for the nearest hills. These three were better informed about the glen than I was, this being my first visit.

One day, descending from the summit of Buachaille Etive Mor, Gerry set out to glissade a steep snow gully. As it turned out, this had been misidentified and would have taken him and anyone who'd followed over Waterslide Wall. Losing control, he fell, disappearing round a bend in the gully and passing over a small rock step. We found him wedged providentially into a melt-crevasse against a boulder not far above the top of the wall. He was unconscious and in thick winter clothing so that it was hard to guess the extent of his injuries. At that time mountain first-aid had hardly been systematised. We'd have to seek help immediately.

Kennedy went back up to the summit to take the easiest way down the mountain. Gerry was in an insecure position but was now regaining consciousness at intervals and the visible bleeding seemed to be stopping. Explorations showed that rescue would have to be from above but there'd be serious danger from stonefall if we left him where he lay. With labour, anchored on long lines up the gully, we shifted him slowly and delicately across the snowslope to a dry rock ledge beneath an overhanging wall. After wrapping him in all our spare clothes we began to settle down for a long vigil as the sky darkened. While we were beginning to feel more optimistic about his condition we had the unease of not knowing whether Kennedy had descended safely.

It was a very cold evening but clear and windless. After some hours the moon came up and laid out the huge extent of Rannoch Moor, revealing the numerous gleaming lochans clearly. And further, at some time in the night, an unforgettable phenomenon was shown to us. From every one of these bodies of water an ectoplasmic stratum of mist arose. Each of these dead level emanations, wafer-thin, halted above its host at some slight but indeterminable height, mirroring every complexity of shape with absolute fidelity. These spirits didn't move upon the face of the waters. They simply hung there hour after hour as the night went on, a surreal manifestation.

In the earlier hours of darkness only two or three vehicles had crossed the moor and since then nothing. Startling and impressing us, Kennedy reappeared around midnight with a big sack of blankets and hot flasks. Finally, at about five in the morning, a small convoy of lights showed, drew slowly closer, disappeared briefly from our field of vision and reappeared on the Glen Etive road. Gerry was holding on. Five hours later, a warm sunny morning, we made contact with the Rescue Team from R.A.F. Kinloss.

At that time mountain rescue operations hadn't achieved the degree of professionalism reached today and this occasion was the most carefree major rescue I've seen. The team comprised all levels of experience and all grades of fitness. Of the dozen or so members one had volunteered only that week and was on his first hill. Two were wearing thin black leather shoes. Another had a severe attack of vertigo and declined to come down to the gully. Two were sick from time to time; after an evening of steady drinking they'd been called out for the freezing, boneshaking, 150-mile ride in a canvas-backed lorry through the long winter night. Few had any real experience of ropework. But there was plenty of muscle and willingness, the day was beautiful, and the lift to the summit was finally accomplished.

Rescues sometimes discharge strong overflows of temperament in both rescuers and rescued. Emotion spills out, self-images are made clear, deep preconceptions are exposed, aggressive and defensive stances are assumed. Experienced rescuers learn to control these indulgences but they still have to act out the roles in which they're cast. Sometimes there's a sense that the casualty is the prisoner of the team, a prize only to be handed over to the proper authority of doctor or ambulance crew. Some members of a small civilian party which had made an independent effort to find us during the night were permitted to assist the carry along the ridge but, though the three of us were at least as fit as anyone present, our own offers were flatly refused. Fortunately for our self-regard the team now began to weaken so that the leader, reluctantly, was forced to call on us. Immediately the remaining reserves disappeared and the unspelled descent to Glen Etive allowed us to feel we'd done something. In the end the occasion had the cheerfulness of all survivor rescues and the casualty, with head injuries, bruised ribs and broken collar-bone, lived to glissade more cautiously. He'd been using a borrowed hostel card and the exposure of false identity drew a milder rebuke from the hostel warden than we'd been expecting. A Leeds climber I didn't know must have learnt that you can't believe everything it says in newspapers.

It seems surprising that in a situation involving drama and discomfort the strongest memory retained should be a haunting image, not thrown out of focus in forty years, of the moonlit Rannoch Moor and those milky screens hanging over pools and lochans. Perhaps the sheer length of time spent scanning the moor served to fix the scene. Yet I find a similarity in another clear memory from a more serious chain of events a few years later in the Alps.

There was an Englishman, an Irishman and a Scotsman. And there was a Pole, but the Pole died. His name was André Kopczinski. The Irishman was Peter Kenny, the Scotsman was Jimmy Marshall, and I was the Englishman. We'd met by chance. Through changing circumstances I'd lost touch with earlier friends and I'd come to Chamonix at short notice in hope of finding someone in a similar position. Marshall, who was working as an architect in Geneva and perhaps concurrently dodging the draft, was also without a companion. Kenny and Kopczinski were already a team. Kenny was one of the enterprising Irish climbers I'd already encountered but the other two were strangers to me. Marshall had met none of us before.

We were perhaps known to each other by name, however, in the small world of that time. André had, I assume, travelled westward by the mysterious routes of the displaced person. He'd spent a spell in England where he'd climbed with the Cromlech Club. Then he'd moved to Ireland. At some point he'd paired up with a legendary German girl, Ruth Ohrtmann, a long-haired blonde who was said to have accomplished some very hard rock climbs in bare feet. What I'd heard of him hadn't prepared me for his vivacity and charm. He had an old-fashioned courtesy, a candour and directness of sympathy and attention I've sometimes seen in eastern Europeans. He was excellent company. At the same time he was charged with such a volatile enthusiasm that legends of Polish cavalry officers charging sabre in hand through squadrons of German tanks rose irresistibly to mind.

By contrast Jimmy Marshall was as solid as a rock, so judicious that he wasn't easy to read, secure in himself and perfectly at home in the mountains. Though Scottish climbers hadn't yet ventured onto the most serious Alpine climbs, the winter climbing of Marshall and his circle was already giving them an experience of atrocious weather and variability in snow and ice conditions matched perhaps by few Continental alpinists. I'd noticed with amusement the refusal of the Scots to be intimidated by scale. One Scotsman, setting off alone up the vast ice-flow of the Mer de Glace, explained to me that he'd arranged to meet someone at the top of the glen. A party about to ascend Mont Blanc said that they felt like a hill walk as a break from rock-climbing.

The weather at the time was unsettled. With Hamish Nicol, Jimmy and I set off for the Bionnassay Arête of Mont Blanc but we were drenched by rain by the time we reached the refuge and we were told that worse was promised. We returned, Nicol went home, and we met the Irish party. Then the four of us managed to snatch an early British and first Irish ascent of the short but steep West Face of the Pointe Albert. A couple of days later another brief improvement offered itself and we fixed on the Grütter Arête of the Aiguille des Pélerins. As on the earlier route Jimmy and I would climb as a pair, followed by André and Peter.

I've sometimes wondered whether what followed was related to the fact that we'd no idea who were Chiefs and who were Indians. We were extremely polite and kept agreeing with each other. The climb, taking the hardest options, went very smoothly though I'm not sure we improved on guidebook time. At the summit the sky was overcast but unexpectedly a short debate began. The normal descent seemed to André an anti-climax and without much discussion his proposal was accepted: just for the hell of it we'd abseil down the north-west face into the top of the Peigne couloir. As it happened, Jimmy already knew the couloir. It was then regarded as a standard descent but has since been abandoned as unacceptably dangerous.

The system adopted was for each pair to fix alternate abseils. Jimmy and I would set one up and we'd see down André and Peter, who'd immediately prepare the following abseil. We'd rope down, retrieve our ropes, descend theirs and fix ours. The face was exposed and consisted of steep smooth slabs with narrow snow-covered ledges at good rope-length intervals. The cloud had closed in further, the wind rose a little from time to time, and the situation seemed impressive. But within a quite short time Jimmy and I were retrieving our ropes from the last of perhaps a half dozen rappels, while Peter and André were hurrying across easy ground to the trifurcation at the head of the couloir.

Here, a barrier of rock, split by an easy but very wet chimney, sug-gested a final abseil. This was the old way off the Col du Peigne and an anchor bollard held a mess of slings, mostly ancient and half-rotted. On the face we'd cut new cord for abseil loops. Now, André had simply passed the ropes through a single, apparently substantial existing loop. In retrospect it seems probable that this was simply cotton rope, in use for abseil anchors until about that time and tending to bleach to the glossy appearance of the full-weight laid nylon ropes we were now using.

My sense of certainty wavers. Had we exhausted our supply of abseil cord? Surely I asked aloud why the rope shouldn't be passed through the whole bunch? Did I only think the thought and say nothing? Did the idea come by hindsight, 'the most exact of sciences'? Was it pointed out that André, who'd be descending last, was the lightest of the four of us? And does it matter now?

Jimmy went first and, on familiar ground, set off rapidly down the couloir, easy here. It was getting late and it was important to locate the point where the descent used a fixed rope to climb the right bank, avoid-ing the lower outfall. I followed and was some hundreds of feet down when I heard cries, a confusion of sounds, Peter shouting that André had fallen. The loop had broken. I relayed the news to Jimmy, almost out of earshot, and went back up. Trailing the ropes, André had come down the wall and tumbled a further distance down the slope beneath. Hunched up and groaning, bleeding through his anorak, he was tightly bound in a daunting net of rope. We freed him with difficulty and tried to make him as comfortable as possible. Again, Jimmy and I set off hastily down as darkness was falling.

Finally we had to halt for fear of overshooting the exit. We could find only a narrow chimney for shelter, a tight slot into the base of which we wedged ourselves one behind the other. A little waterslide was splash-ing down the back. We'd left our few spare bits of clothing with André. I was wearing a string vest, a threadbare second-hand track suit and a thin unlined cotton anorak. Jimmy had no more garments than I, though he was in much more robust mountain gear. During the night, at just above freezing point, it began to rain and quickly we were wet to the skin. We crouched back to back for warmth, changing places at intervals Jimmy timed. The inside position seemed, by contrast, a bath of comfort. On the outside we called on what stoicism we could muster and the night seemed endurable. But every so often, closing a still period, a wind, not strong, would move gently up the couloir and from the moment of its first slight touch the body shook uncontrollably with cold. Overriding our discomfort was our anxiety about André, who had in fact already died.

First light came very slowly and our surroundings, unseen in the last of the evening's gloom, started to reveal themselves as presences rather than as detail. Banks of cloud would hang immobile, obscuring large quarters of the scene and then, unexpectedly, would be driven at high speed hundreds of feet up the huge ravine as the wind rose. Just as suddenly they'd halt, having unveiled new features and cloaked the ones already glimpsed. Snow had fallen to just above our height and on slabby flanks below us. Great sheets of wet rock, towers, jagged arêtes and subsidiary gullies seemed to advance and withdraw, a slow dramatic circling dance of Titans.

The power of this dawn was tremendous. As I took it in the thought came to me that it was an artist's vision of hell, the tiny world of human consciousness observing one aspect of a vast indifferent universe in which it has no permanent place. And yet I looked at it with eager curiosity, as primitive men must have looked at strange new landscapes. And these impressions were quickly flooded in a surprising and apparently inappropriate emotion. What I felt developing in clarity and certainty through a few minutes was — awe? wonder? — no, it was something like delight. The whole scene was immensely, stupefyingly rewarding. But while I was gaping at the magnificence of the place, and as we began to exercise our stiffened limbs, Jimmy was judging whether it was light enough to move. The night hadn't slowed his wits and he was thinking ahead. This was the sort of crisis for which Scotland had schooled him. Flesh chilled, hands and feet numb, we set off to find the fixed rope.

Whatever the situation, it seems to me, when we sleep without shelter the coming of the day has new dimensions. To watch the dawn through a house window, to waken and crawl out of a tent to inspect it, robs it of some final intimacy. In the bivouac there's no moment of preparation. Eyes and skin are the only interface. We know our animal natures, stir, ease residual aches, stretch our limbs, and see everything around us as fresh and real.

Lliwedd

ON WRITING GUIDEBOOKS

A climbing novel of the seventies, Roger Hubank's *North Wall*, restricted itself entirely to the second ascent of an alpine climb. The climb and the mountain, as well as the action, were fictions. Boldly, the author prefaced his story with a formal guidebook description of the route and he even supplied a topo. That might seem a reckless relinquishment of a narrator's advantages but I found it effective. I can't guess what sense of power the note might hold for a non-climbing reader but I imagine that anyone who's climbed in the Alps must have felt a response similar to mine. Even in the armchair, perhaps more so there since energy can't be released, the taut coded language sets up muscular and nervous tensions. The italicised stonefall warning will be at the back of our minds all the way up. For hours before we get there we'll be ready for the critical rightward pendule where the line of weakness closes. Higher, a misleading piton will be visible on a false line. We know all about that, the dismaying expense of time and energy. After the preliminary assessment the description, a flawless imitation, is entirely referential but it's loaded with the emotive and physical connotations of all the remembered climbs through which we make it real.

If, anthologies excluded, an older climber were asked to name, say, the dozen classics of British climbing writing, the miscellany he'd come up with might include novels, reminiscences, expedition accounts and one or two less easily categorised works. And, yet: these would probably be books he'd read twice, at twenty-year intervals perhaps, maybe three times. By contrast it's the case that a number of guidebooks have been read again and again not just for their informative content, as research for future ambitions or to relive old adventures, but also for their liveliness.

There were two determining influences on the earlier rock climbing guidebooks. The first was that of the Victorian alpinists in whose writings a full range of attitudes to climbing was explored and an appropriate vocabulary developed. Essentially, with *The Playground of Europe*, Sir Leslie Stephen introduced into mountain writing the highest external standards of ease, discrimination and style. Edward Whymper's *Scrambles Amongst the Alps* was the work of an artist, an engraver; yet he tried for a scientist's precision in his structural descriptions, estimating inclinations, heights and distances with a careful eye. Alfred Mummery's *My Climbs in the Alps and Caucasus* drew attention to a bizarre discrepancy between the terminal risks of the enterprises and the gleeful impetuosity with which they're often approached.

Importantly, this literary heritage was modified by a domestic source. Almost from their beginnings the inns which were to become the bases of the enthusiasts had provided Visitors' Books and as exploration developed these came to be used for notes on excursions. Eventually, at such centres as Wasdale Head and Pen-y-Pass, they developed into or were supplemented by New Climbs Books. By their nature, however, these books were open to anyone and every entry risked the anonymous annotation or the initialled retort. From them we get a sense of a dialogue of rejoinder characterised by scepticism and wit.

The elements we see in these Victorian writings persist through nearly a century of guidebooks. Above all there's the problem of how to handle difficulty and, to a lesser degree, hazard and route-finding. Many writers are excited into what will be seen by later climbers as overstatement (though some have used it to entertain): "this route is reserved for the expert in perfect training on a warm dry windless day in glove-fitting rubbers." Within a few years or a few months these claims have to be withdrawn for reapplication to a more recent horror. Yet it's a fact that climbers enjoy sensationalism and Paul Williams' *Llanberis* in 1987 gave at least as much pleasure as Peter Harding's *Llanberis Pass* in 1950.

Other writers have taken care to protect their work from what may later be seen as exaggeration and this caution is evident even in the preliminary notes to the first of all our pocket guides, Archer Thomson's *The Climbs on Lliwedd* in 1909: "Vertical is not used as a synonym for steep, but describes rocks actually or apparently at an angle of ninety degrees. Overhanging is not used as a synonym for vertical, but describes rocks actually or apparently impending. Angles of inclination have in most cases been measured with a clinometer."

The use of deliberate understatement is most pronounced and most engaging in the guides of Menlove Edwards in the late thirties. Here it's always subtly qualified. Edwards on difficulty: "a fine open climb which tends to be slippery when wet. Then, one may well feel insecure." On route-finding: "between the three harder parts there are undistinguished grass slopes on which it is not altogether impossible to lose the way." On the anxious search for safe anchorage on unstable ledges: "a tall spike rises above the fernery on the left. It is fairly firm..." The Edwards guides rest undamaged by time but understatement or defensive undergrading, even when used consistently, will draw protest from the unprepared. Perhaps there's a certain immodesty, too, in demanding that the newcomer acquaint himself with the guide-writer's cast of mind.

The easy solution to the overstatement and understatement dilemma is to try to eliminate subjective comment and personal style. This was the approach attempted under the editorship by H.M. Kelly of the Second and Third Series Lakeland guides. Rejecting the discursiveness of Archer Thomson and the enthusiasm of George Bower these guides were intended to be entirely factual and squeaky clean. At the time they seemed to be setting a style for all future work. But in 1937 the new Scafell guide was given to Edwards for review and the result was an influential polemic, brilliant, amusing and unfair. "So I may as well say straight off that I think it is excellent, a very great improvement on the previous edition...; and that I wish to attack it." The Method guides, Edwards said, were competent and boring. "You can read it, the dry print, but only with headache."

It would be interesting to see a comprehensive study of climbing humour, which keeps resurfacing in guidebooks. Is it, in the main, just a special class of gallows humour? In the general literature it often notices interpersonal transactions ("with characteristic generosity he offered me the lead") but in guidebooks it plays most on the risk of falling and on the absurd (Lockwood's awkwardly constricted chimney is "most entertaining when done with a large number of large climbers in heavy rain"). Condensed into a dry wit it's occasionally visible even in Archer Thomson. With George Bower it's a central feature: "the hyacinths grow sixty feet below the traverse and great care is required to keep them at this distance." It will be seen that the simplest jokes are recycled from time to time to be enjoyed by each fresh generation.

Harding remarks of one climb at Llanberis that "the groove is climbed with a piton, or difficulty, or both." Paul Williams advises for which routes it may be prudent to reserve a bed in Bangor Hospital. Such remarks as these have conditioned our attitudes to climbing.

The writing of my own two guidebooks gave me experiences wildly different in character. The first was the Eastern Crags volume for what's now counted as the Third Series of Lakeland guides. (The Eighth Series is at present in progress.) This was in 1957.

It would be the last guide to be edited by H.M. Kelly. Neither initials nor surname were negotiable. To his climbing companions he was Harry Kelly, a charismatic leader and the life and soul of the party, but to my generation he came from so far away that he wasn't even Mr. Kelly, he was just H.M. Kelly. Apart from Sid Cross I'd only recently begun to meet such survivors from the twenties and thirties as A.B. Hargreaves, permissibly and affectionately just A.B., and J.L. Longland, usually Jack or, later, teasingly, Sir Jack. H.M. Kelly, however, had started climbing before the First World War, too long a stretch for comprehension or familiarities.

I was summoned to his home at Old Trafford for inspection and briefing. It seemed strange that a man who'd lived for mountains should choose to spend his retirement in a big city and I questioned him. He lived for other things as well. He was there for the cricket and for the Hallé Concerts. Well, alright. He was a mystery, I learned later. He declared his views on politics and religion readily enough (socialist, agnostic) but it's said that he never declared either his occupation or how he'd sidestepped the First War, questions still unresolved. Some faint memory trace suggests that I asked him his profession directly and that he may have mentioned civil engineering.

Kelly was in some anxiety about this guide. He'd written the Pillar guide of 1923 and he'd served as guidebook editor since the thirties. With this final volume the current Series would be complete. Unhappily, the two older climbers who'd been assigned the area had made slow progress and had finally asked to be relieved.

When I said that I'd start afresh, would check everything, and would complete it within a year, Kelly was startled and I could see that hope warred in him with disbelief. I had no choice. Now a qualified teacher I was working at Buxton at the first of the countless Outdoor Activities Centres shortly to be established by Local Education Authorities. By what was called a gentleman's agreement my post had been offered for not less than one year, not more than three, it being felt then that work in outdoor education could only be regarded as a short and privileged sabbatical from real teaching. I was beginning my second year, I intended to leave at the end of it, and I might find myself inconveniently placed. However, I'd already done a fair proportion of the harder routes in the area and one or two new routes within the past year. I'd enjoy repeating these and racing through the easier climbs, which would mostly be fresh to me. The area was geographically large and I'd have the pleasure of entering enticing valleys I'd never seen. Swindale already had a number of recorded climbs, and the map showed crags in Mardale, Rydale, Kentmere, Threshthwaite Cove. Ought I to trust the surveyors of Fusedale, Bannerdale, Boardale, Wet Sleddale? There were climbs on Carrock Fell and Arthur's Pike to be checked so I'd be able take in little hills I didn't know.

There were a few uncertainties. I had the equivalent of teaching holidays but I worked at weekends. With my free time mainly in midweek blocks I'd have problems in finding companions. I couldn't yet afford to buy an old car or van and I was disinclined to go back to a motor-bike so I'd have to get up to the Lakes by bus or hitch-hiking. It would be awkward to get from valley to valley and I'd have to be careful to avoid leaving single climbs on widely spaced crags unchecked. Convenient accommodation wouldn't be easy to find.

The collecting of information might also be a problem since this would be the first full guide to the area. A number of routes had been gathered together under "Outlying Crags" in a prewar Langdale guide. The Sheffield University Mountaineering Club, which had acquired a base at Ruthwaite Lodge in Grisedale, had just published an invaluable little booklet covering climbs within walking distance. A search of several runs of journals would be necessary. I'd have to contact past and present explorers. I'd have to follow up reports, rumours and legends. It would be fun.

It was fun. The area had more history than I'd guessed. I found myself corresponding with George Abraham, born 1872, one of the inventors of Lakeland rock climbing. He'd climbed the first route in the eastern fells in 1890. And with Col. Westmorland, who'd also started climbing here in the nineties and who'd found the first route on Dove Crag in 1910. This climb had been rediscovered in 1937 and with an extended start had been described and named in innocence by the later party. Dare I say it? The colonel had been heard to think aloud that the climb ought properly to bear his name. Archer Thomson wouldn't have approved, as he made clear in Lliwedd: "To distinguish the climbs and features of the face, descriptive epithets have been used, that no personal names should suggest a lien on Nature's freehold." (Just a smack at Mallory?) But everybody bowed, including H.M. Kelly, and the guide-writer was instructed to make a note.

A literary history was linked with the climbing history. Lonely as a cloud, Wordsworth had wandered over all these hills. Dickens had puffed up Carrock Fell. Harry Griffin drew my attention to an account of an ascent of Helvellyn in 1844 by a party including Matthew Arnold and Arthur Hugh Clough. During this excursion two aspirant clerics in the party had detached themselves, and the Men of God had attacked "the Eagle's Crag" in Grisedale, let's say Eagle Crag. At a critical moment the crux was overcome by pulling up on a walking stick, "a Kendal hazel". I take this to be the first recorded use of aid in a Lakeland first ascent.

The year passed like a dream. A year of walking into miraculous valleys, utterly strange yet entirely familiar in that they simply recombined motifs of Lakeland landscapes I knew like the back of my hand. A year of secret purpose: I wondered what speculations the remaining passengers on the Manchester-Keswick express might be entertaining when, on a few occasions, the driver made an unscheduled halt at the summit of Dunmail Raise and, alone, night falling, consulting no map, I set off rapidly up the bare hillside. A year of long approach walks and of camping. Of staying in Youth Hostels where once or twice I found myself recruiting fell-walkers to the sport and using them to tick off easier routes that would have bored experienced companions.

I had some bad days. The worst, I think, a day of perfect weather and bone-dry crags with no-one available. I used it to check out an easy gully on remote Harter Fell. I wondered whether anyone had revisited it in the thirty years since its ascent. The entry to a steep and narrow section was blocked by a wedged and rotting sheep, awkward and unpleasant to pass. Here the walls were smooth and the bed consisted of small scree which collapsed as I was twenty feet up. It was a descending escalator and I just managed to step off and bridge a second before plunging into the wreck. I set off again more cautiously. That evening I joined friends as the weather broke and I was given news of several new routes on two crags at opposite corners of the area.

Old friends rallied round and new friendships were made. Geoff Roberts, Andrew Maxfield and Terry Parker spared me time and my brother arrived for two or three critical ascents. Crucially I had the assistance of some Sheffield University climbers, Mike James, George Leaver and, especially, Jack Soper.

Within a couple of years Jack would be climbing the hardest routes in the Lakes and Wales. He was amongst the first of a new generation which would discover that all the routes of Brown and Whillans were within its powers and which began to fill in gaps they'd left. He was some years younger than me but his confidence and independence of mind impressed me immediately. Whilst the avant-garde was starting to drop knowing hints about cannabis he'd upstaged all that by choosing to take snuff and he was correctly equipped with a small silver box.

I completed my project narrowly. While I was working through old climbs new climbs were being made and I had to take in these as well. One of them appeared over the name of Allan Austin. I knew who he was. My first memory of him is as a tiny bespectacled Wolf Cub. He lived then in what seemed to me a substantial mansion about a mile from our back-to-back terrace house. He followed Neville and myself, perhaps a year behind Nev, to the same school where for reasons I don't know he was called Pussy Austin. Quite recently he'd arrived in Ilkley Quarry where he was a beginner for two or three days and then the local expert. We'd reintroduced ourselves. He had a van and I climbed with him for a couple of days in Derbyshire and a week or so in the Lakes.

Allan was to become the central figure in Lakeland climbing for more than a decade. He was also, and famously, the firmest spokesman for clean climbing we've seen in forty years. His few longer written pieces are in a traditional vein of self-deprecating humour but in odd polemical letters and in later interviews a different voice came out, plain, strong and forthright, unlike any climbing has heard, reminding me at times of William Cobbett. Always presenting himself as a no-nonsense York-shireman he entered his occupation as Rag Merchant in applying for membership of a senior climbing club. In fact his father owned some sort of woollen reprocessing mill. This trade description was misunder-stood by one of the club's more ancient members and the committee received a letter of angry protest. Once, the complainant said, the club had been "an association of gentlemen walking the hills." He regretted that it should consider admitting a rag-and-bone man. This comment was received with amusement and was apparently leaked to its subject who quickly produced a climb named Ragman's Trumpet.

Happily for me, Allan's attention first concentrated itself on Langdale. By the end of August 1958 I'd abandoned the idea of checking all the uninspected valleys. I'd had no time to test twenty possible lines. I'd failed to find two old routes and I'd missed out on leading three or four modern routes, though I had partial or a second's acquaintance with all but one of these. The exception was Dovedale Groove. I'd made a brief attempt at it before its first ascent and I'd been up twice in this year only to find it greasy. I might have failed had it been dry. It was time to give in and to enter it, as was the practice then, by printing and attributing Whillans' own description.

I presented my manuscript to Kelly. It was written, of course, within his own format. He was delighted, the Series was complete. I was to meet him only once more by a cruel trick of fate. Years later I was called out of the bar of a Lakeland hotel. One of the residents had been taken ill and an extra pair of hands was needed to help manoeuvre the stretcher down to the ambulance. I went up to be told that the sick man was Kelly. The head of the stretcher was waiting for me in a tight corridor so that I could only bend to see him upside down. He looked up, recognised me, said hello, and closed his eyes on the rotten indignities of life. It was an awkward moment but he was to recover and to live into his nineties.

So it was done, the war was over. And, yes, I'd thoroughly enjoyed it though the feeling that I'd like to write another guide never entered my mind. I went to live in Derby, then Ilkeston, then Nottingham, and in 1964 I came to North Wales, re-encountering people I hadn't seen for years. Amongst these was John Neill, then editing the Welsh guidebooks. Neill has a disarming urbanity of manner and can turn a paralysing charm onto his listener. He bought me a few drinks, he made me feel needed, and before I'd thought much about it I'd agreed to write a new Lliwedd guide. Did vanity betray me? I'd be the first climber ever to write standard series guidebooks to both the Lakes and Snowdonia.

Neill had a huge advantage over me. He'd discovered that I hadn't yet done a single climb on the cliff. He talked about it with affection, respect, and considerable subtlety. Certainly it wasn't popular nowadays, it didn't have hard modern routes. Yet the odd thing was that modern experts kept having setbacks on it. Purgatory wasn't getting any softer. Central Gully Direct had only had a handful of ascents in nearly thirty years. It was a place where experience counted. It was a noble cliff, it was the biggest precipice in England and Wales, it was steeped in history. It wouldn't be easy to follow the Archer Thomson 1909 guide, the Menlove Edwards 1939 guide, the two most famous guidebooks ever written. But he thought, just possibly, I might be the man for the job. I agreed with everything he said.

It didn't look like a daunting task. None of the problems attending the Lakeland guide obtained here. Instead of countless crags disposed over four hundred square miles I'd be confronting a single big cliff. I was living ten miles from that cliff. I had the time and the money. I had more transport than I could use. I could pick and choose companions. The information was more or less all there. Nobody would be chasing, all exploration seemed to have come to an end. Since there were so few hard routes I'd save them for perfect weather and I'd knock off the easy things in the winter.

Before starting, I asked around. "How many routes up Lliwedd could you get through in a day?" I asked Joe Brown, "you" meaning me or anyone. He thought hard. Was it a trap? The famous can't afford to get judgements wrong. "Four", he said. I was taken aback. "Only four?" "Well, that adds up to about the height of the Walker," he said. We were talking at cross purposes; a lot of climbs finish at or start from interrupting terraces. It's possible to string together three named routes in a single base to summit ascent. The cautiousness of this reply began to impress the scale of the place onto me.

I talked to surviving members of the last generation to fall in love with Lliwedd. Dick Morsley, for instance. In the years I've lived in Wales we've recognised the ascendancies of a succession of five-year heroes; but through most of those years we acknowledged Al Harris and Mo Anthoine as the central movers in the scene, as creators of the style of the times. It seems wrong to diminish them by putting them in a perspective but Morsley, many years older than either, certainly exceeded either in his need and capacity to produce social shock. He was the actor in incidents which might get through in a modern novel but which would give huge offence in a book about real people.

Morsley had been forced by illness to give up climbing before I started on the guide. Yet he hadn't quite finished with Lliwedd. At funerals an irrepressible cheerfulness finally overcomes most of the mourners. At Morsley's funeral this cheerfulness didn't extend to my own friend Len Baggott. Len had first climbed with Morsley in the thirties (and was yet to climb Soap Gut with me in the nineties). He'd been set a task. Morsley had made it known that he wished his ashes to be scattered on Lliwedd, not from the summit but, quite specifically, from a stance high on Central Chimney.

Len was uneasy. He'd severely damaged a leg in a forestry accident since making the promise. It was October, the cliff was out of condition. He knew Central Chimney, steep, not really a chimney, a V Diff that stopped VS men in poor conditions. Ordinarily he could have relied on Dai Rowlands to lead. But just now Rowlands had badly bruised his ribs and was impeded by a corset of strapping. A younger climber, Chris Harper, was impressed into the party as leader.

There'd been heavy rain during the night. The wind quartered Cwm Dyli and beat at Llyn Llydaw. Cloud rolled though Bwlch y Saethau. The cliff was a shocking sight. The three roped together and struggled bravely upwards, intimidated by occasion, climb and scene. While Harper was leading from the ledge known as the Summer House there was a tremendous explosion from hundreds of feet higher, announcing a substantial rockfall. The party stared up in terror, then shrank into the wall. All three were hit by debris. Rucksacks and clothing were torn. They felt hunted. They imagined Morsley above them on the Big Wall in the Sky, jeering and crowing in delight. As they cast down the ashes the wind blew a scattering back so that their wet clothing was pasted. The summit felt like an escape. Regaining the slopes beneath they saw that the cloud was lifting and a long thin clean grey stripe divided the whole lower wall, Morsley's last joke.

Len died in 1995 and his own ashes were deposited at a specified point in Slanting Gully, a little higher than the legendary resting place of King Arthur's knights. The two old comrades occupy the twin peaks on equal terms. I have to say, though, that in my view this practice has gone quite far enough already.

What is it with this cliff that overcomes us? In the Introduction to my guide I said that it takes thirty years and a World War to produce a new Lliwedd guide. I might have added: "and the suicide of the previous writer." Archer Thomson wrote the book, took carbolic acid, and died. (Carbolic acid, two pints!) Menlove Edwards wrote the book, took prussic acid, and died. (Hydrocyanic acid, that's what they said then; later they said potassium cyanide.) I wrote the book, took lysergic acid, and survived. Maybe Kelvin Neal, whose new guide should beat the deadline, has been watching the late news anxiously and listening for gossip on my state of mind?

(Lysergic acid diethylamide. I think that's probably right. LSD 5, LSD 26, I couldn't work it out. I was travelling up from London on a crowded train. Sitting nearby were two girls, crazy, laughing, screaming, unaware of other passengers. After Chester the compartment had emptied except for the three of us. They'd calmed down a little. I had a couple of cans of beer on my table and left one open and unattended while visiting another part of the train. On returning I saw that their attention now included me and that they seemed to be trying to conceal a huge but private joke at my expense. Before I got off at Llandudno Junction I had strange winding aches in my stomach, powerful, yet gone in twenty minutes.

(Driving up the valley things began to happen. The effect was of stained-glass church windows, say five matched lancets of minuscule jewelled fragments, each panel continuously welling up centrally and descending like a slow-moving fountain. This screen filled my entire field of vision yet, despite its brilliance, my view of the road behind was unobstructed. I'd no idea what was happening and felt divided between a happy-hour contentment and a sub-stratum of strong anxiety. I was aware that I was gripping the wheel as if to crush it and was steering the car with the whole of my strength. I kept wondering whether I could actually stop. Then, checking and re-checking, I found that I was moving at a conspicuous eighteen miles an hour. Curiously, the road was almost clear of traffic. All the time I remained spellbound by the display which was spectacularly pretty. Slowly the intensity diminished and by the time I reached home hardly a trace of sensation remained. An obvious explanation occurred to me but the timescale was hopelessly wrong. A couple of years later I read a note on the new short acids which had become available at that time and the experience made sense.)

The two distinguished lunatics who'd gone before me had led sad and desperate lives. James Merriman Archer Thomson, who never married, was the Headmaster of the John Bright School at Llandudno. His tendency to silence was so strong that it gave rise to an Archer Thomson joke, technically an addition to the world's known forms of joke in that the punch-line is a non-verbal response to something a companion has said. Alan Hankinson retells a classic example. A professor from Bangor, also notoriously incommunicative, has a day out on the hills with Thomson. Neither speaks. As they're parting the professor cracks and gasps out, "I have a brother who is even more silent than myself." Thomson gives him a sharp look and says nothing. (In recent years Clint Eastwood has successfully revived the Archer Thomson joke. The possibility occurs to me, once a teacher myself, that Thomson was conserving his voice for Monday mornings.) No scandal emerged after Thomson's death. At the inquest the coroner remarked that nervous breakdowns were noticeably on the increase and said that he could explain everything. "It is a sign of the times. We are all going at express speed." This was in 1912.

John Menlove Edwards, who never married, was a physician who could not heal himself. A practising psychiatrist who couldn't keep his head on straight. A peerless essayist who completed six pages a year. A diligent guide-writer who admitted that he hadn't the faintest idea of the standard of anything he'd ever climbed. A latent homosexual who couldn't face the physical crudity of the taking off of trousers, only wanted a cuddle really. A man of impressive physical, moral and intellectual strength who made a battle of the simplest things. His account of his final month on Lliwedd is entitled "Up Against It".

For me it took five years, two editors, thirty companions. For some of those companions a single visit in bad conditions was enough. Others, not even dedicated climbers, proved highly resistant to storm and stress. Maris Purenins, what do you remember of Lliwedd? What entertains you nowadays, Bob Holroyd?

In some years this cliff takes over two hundred inches of rain. Let's say the best part of a hundred feet of rain fell while I tried to mop up. It tumbled down grooves, it swilled down slabs, it ran off overhangs. In winter it blackened the rock, it turned lichens and mosses an intenser green, it lined the interiors of cracks with a dark and lubricating emulsion. It called up in me a strange, exuberant, unflagging energy as, in stiff old waterproofs and heavy mountain boots, I fought for Diffs.

That's not the whole truth. There were those gorgeous days when the midsummer sun gets round onto the cliff and the dry warm buttresses stand up from gulfs of shadow. Evenings when, descending to the lake, I had to stop again and again for a backward glance. We went there and across there and up there.

I traced the footsteps of ghosts. Not just the Victorians. This is Birch Tree Terrace Climb. I.A. Richards and Dorothy Pilley had climbed it nearly fifty years before me. The quartz string led across the wall and the continuity, delicacy and interest of the moves astonished me. That pair never missed a trick. On Richards' lecture-tours, from North America to China, they'd kept slipping away to the hills.

That's the Direct Finish to Yellow Slab. It seemed too wild and committing for 1932, but then, it was Maurice Linnell who'd been in the lead. He'd died on Nevis two years later. Here's Mallory's Slab. Last seen on Everest in 1924. (His daughters, Clare and Beridge, were both accomplished climbers. One son-in-law died in an accident in the Eastern States, rappel, stonefall. On a glorious summer day a few years into the future I'd climb the route again with a young American visitor, Mallory's grandson.) That's Cracks Rib, 1937. Noyce had led, Edwards seconding. I'd taken the middle-aged Noyce round Stanage once, only his second day on grit; yet he'd picked a couple of straight VSs for himself and he'd led without pause. He'd died in the Pamirs in 1962.

This thing here is the Yellow Slab — Purgatory Connection, 1937 again, J.H. Buzzard. He hadn't found an exit and he'd had to rope off. While I was reworking the young Buzzard's moves, perhaps the old Buzzard was scratching his wig. He'd made some smart moves since then. But had they been tough enough on the two bad girls, Christine Keeler, Paula Hamilton-Marshall, who'd been made to stand up in front of him? Pity that that other one, Mandy Rice-Davies, hadn't been there that night. She'd been impertinent, said she thought sex was fun. She'd made his colleagues look foolish, she'd played the court like a barrister. (Was she aware that Lord Astor denied having had intercourse with her? "Well, he would, wouldn't he.") At least he'd got Keeler put inside for nine months, Hamilton-Marshall for six. They should have hit them harder. How about a couple of years of Community Service each, helping whoever Neill could manage to con into taking on Lliwedd? That would have made the mascara run.

It went on and on. Again and again I had to remind myself: when these old-timers did these old routes they were younger than you are now. I never succeeded in improving on four consecutive days. I started taking breaks on other cliffs. As I staggered towards the finishing line Tony Moulam and Hugh Banner had to take turns at supporting me. I crossed. John Neill had handed over. Trevor Jones caught me, shook me, and the manuscript fell out.

"So how does it feel to be the author of the slowest-selling guidebook in the Western World?" That's not fair, that's not the point. Yes, of course I asked myself the question, ten, fifteen years later, but no-one ever thought that this cliff would pull the New Wave. It was just that the full climbing record had to be kept in print, our history must never be forgotten, the Climbers' Club had willed it. They'd told me to fix it and I'd done the job. But something strange has happened. Amazingly, beyond a barren old age, Lliwedd has grown a late crop of Extremes. Every day I climbed there I finished on the summit. Now, climbers are working on single-pitch desperates and roping down. And every time they do that they exchange some scrambling for some climbing. Perhaps this ancient chapel of remembrance has a future?

Does the traditional guidebook have a future? In the sixties Marshall McLuhan argued (in a printed book, *The Gutenberg Galaxy*) that the printed word is on its way out: new means of transmitting information and encoding culture — aural, pictorial, electronic — are destined, he said, to marginalise the text. The announcement outraged and terrified the literary mafia. Backing the hunch the topo guide arrived, starting a parallel debate.

The individual topo, sometimes loose-leaf, takes three characteristic forms: If the start of a climb is properly located it can be an abstract route map, a linear arrangement of symbols, without any background at all; or it can be a photo-topo, the line superimposed with coding added and perhaps with supplementary symbols ('icons', from Computerese) against route name and details in the key; or it can be a drawn topo, the traditional crag sketch, with the same treatment. Some topo guides call themselves Rockfaxes or Faxsheets though in what sense they're fac-similes is unclear.

In fact the topo is nothing new in climbing. Archer Thomson used some embryonic topos to amplify his text. A Chamonix guide of the late forties even had a choreo for the Knubel Crack. And since McLuhan, pushed by photographers and Sunday Supplement addicts, the traditional guide has itself gone further in augmenting the word with action shots, with stars for quality, and with codings for technical difficulty. It would be possible to produce usable guidebooks entirely without illustration or (almost) entirely without words. The guides we have are compromises, the traditional guide saying as much as possible in words, the topo guide showing as much as possible by illustration.

The arguments for the topo are as follows. Its compression of mean-ing can make it cheaper than the written guide and it can be loose-leaf, easy to carry. When it uses an international code of symbols, and often in any case, it dispenses not just with English words but with all lan-guages, making it invaluable for foreign visitors and backward readers. For outcrop climbing where the whole line, the type of climbing and the likely crux can be seen from the ground, it's all that's needed by the man on the spot. It can work for climbs of any length if there's little opportu-nity for divergence and if unmistakable features are visible once estab-lished on the route. Topos and crag drawings can be appealing, they're the visual art-form of climbing. Our experience supplies appropriate responses and we examine them as the afficionado reads a reported strat-egy in chess.

The traditional guide can handle any situation but its main virtue is as follows. Up to the present it's been the repository of the spirit of British rock-climbing which, unlike Alpinism and Greater Mountaineering, has only recently begun to produce a respectable bookshelf. Our club jour-nals have actually transmitted sub-cultures for a hundred years but they've had restricted readerships. The magazines now extending their grasp are rejected by some as commercially driven and are classed by others as throwaway reading. The traditional guides, on the other hand, have been the sacred books unifying us, storing and handing down our his-tory and culture. They linked armchair and crag. Climbers read them insatiably, searching for purposes, learning legends, picking up phrases and passages by heart.

The question at issue is whether the topo guide can bear this responsi-bility. It may have problems with internal contradictions and with the facts of human nature. This is seen when we look at its handling of humour and history.

Of course, wit and interest are stored even in the titles of climbs. Reset Portion of Galley Thirty-Seven; Good Afternoon, Constable; Bored Daughter Meets the Power Bulge Boys. Sometimes we know the story, sometimes we have to use our imaginations. Certainly some amusing climb names continue to appear and the topo wouldn't dare attempt to replace them with numbers. But the names alone can't carry climbing humour. The correct McLuhanite response is to replace written humour with the cartoon or the comic strip. However, the theoretical and the economic drives are towards compression and the drawn joke actually needs more space than the printed word. It doesn't have the same reach anyway.

Similarly the topo guide can compress itself further by deleting the List of First Ascents and the Historical Notes, perhaps recording party and date in the topo key. That's not a popular move. The principal recent explorers into whose hands production is likely to fall are anxious to see their own contributions handsomely acknowledged and to be shown as an advance from an earlier history where this exists.

Attention to some simple points would improve most guidebooks. (At this good distance I see that my own weren't quite so neat as I thought them at the time.) Even if the fieldwork is cross-checked by large teams, all draft manuscripts ought to be tested on unaccompanied first-time visitors so that sloppy location and description is exposed. All earlier routes should be rechecked, since many guides continue to reprint corrupt descriptions and unsafe gradings of the easier climbs. This work is best done by a sub-group sharing knowledge of middle-grade routes with the main team but operating at a lower standard.

It's certainly time to start demanding a degree of modesty in guidebook writers. In the Historical for the 1950 Langdale guide Arthur Dolphin allowed his numerous recent ascents, some of which passed a new threshhold of difficulty, a single aside of less than two lines. Now, shockingly, we see histories in which the events of the last year or two get more space than those of the first fifty; or the guide-writer ghostwrites his own story, describing his achievements with unconcealed admiration in the third person. This has to stop. His gradings ought to make the point and even these will be provisional, always needing reassessment when seen in a longer view.

Traditional guides reached, on the whole, a high standard because the guide-writer was selected by a guidebook editor, himself appointed for his competence from a large club. The independent commercial topo guides now appearing don't have any such checks and the producers wouldn't lose anything by inviting outside comment on their drafts.

However, these guides also allow experiment and authorial freedom. While this is likely to produce some of the worst guides ever written it might, by chance, also throw up a few of the best.

In the end the guide-writer has a hard decision to make. Is he writing a state-of-the-art guide with a shelf life of three years? Or is he writing a guide which might serve and read well for the rest of the lifetime of the climber whose standard has levelled off? If it's the first, he'll write in the compelling new idiom of the moment. But he has to understand that those youngsters just now arriving at the foot of his crag will quickly reject that argot, inventing a new language for their own generation.

SERMONS IN STONES

Sweet are the uses of adversity...
And this our life, exempt from public haunt,
Finds tongues in trees, books in the running brooks,
Sermons in stones, and good in everything.

Shakespeare, As You Like It

Domes north of Gebel Musa with the El Tih plateau beyond

GEBEL MUSA

In deep dejection I trudged with Maureen up the dusty, badly lit road
into Ophira, on the hill above Sharm-el-Sheikh. The stout little Egyptian who'd befriended us puffed along beside us. Suddenly he began to
chuckle and without any warning he thumped me hard on the back and
halted. He wiped his streaming eyes. "In our country we have a
saying," he gasped. "Perhaps it is All for the Best."

I explained our predicament to the Scandinavian girl traveller, a long-
haired blonde with dirty bare feet, harem trousers, skimpy blouse over
bare breasts, bracelets on wrists and ankles. Nice tan. She spoke good
English and listened gravely and attentively, eyes on the ground, until I
reached the end of my tale. Then she looked me straight in the face. "So
now you're free," she said.

The Wall Enders had proverbs too. "A watched pot always boils over,"
Parker and Shotton would say. Despite unceasing vigilance we'd lost
our luggage. We had our passports, our travellers' cheques and the light
tourist clothing we were wearing. We had no sleeping bags, no walking
or swimming gear, no toothbrush, no Egyptian and hardly any British
currency. And the bank, it appeared, would be closed for the next two
days. The Egyptian's thoughts were chiefly concentrated upon what
Maureen would wear to go to bed. Repeatedly, he offered her the use of

his spare djellaba and the offer was politely declined as not addressing our real problems. It was a very nice djellaba, he said wistfully.

I'd wanted to get to Sharm-el-Sheikh so badly. Look at an atlas. In the context of the Red Sea or the Middle East it draws the eye, the settlement at the tip of the Sinai peninsula, the point dividing the Gulf of Suez and the Gulf of Aqaba. Look at it on the most detailed map you can get, which won't be much good. Its isolation remains unthreatened. Off it lie the coral reefs of Ras Muhammad, amongst the richest in the world. A few miles up the coast the earth's most northerly mangroves are found. Inland, the rock peaks of the desert underwrite the sky. And here we were, both of us holding Maureen's handbag now.

We'd been staying at Eilat, Israel's seven-mile beachhead at the top of the Gulf of Aqaba. Forty years earlier a single mud hut had stood on that shore. Now, huge hotels had risen amongst plots of still undeveloped scrub. Around the main street we'd found lively bars and cafes, supermarkets, an excellent secondhand paperback shop. The place had an electrifying frontier town atmosphere, as well it might. Israeli girl soldiers in the briefest khaki shorts sauntered along, the automatic rifles slung on their shoulders dragging at half-buttoned shirts. The surrounding mountains seemed hardly distinguishable from gigantic spoil heaps, except that at dawn and at sunset they assumed apocalyptic colours.

We'd settled in at the Caravan Club, which was caravanless and the cheapest establishment we could find. At first glance a rather squalid assortment of concrete and breeze block structures, it had proved endlessly entertaining. Three miles out of town it stood almost opposite the reef which had occupied most of our time. Before swimming we'd made the mistake of visiting the underwater observatory and we'd cast dubious eyes on the captive sharks and rays in the pools in the compound. There and everywhere we'd studied a poster alerting visitors to the hazards of the sea. The creatures illustrated were divided into three classes: marine animals that bite; marine animals that sting; poisonous marine animals. More than forty species were shown. On learning the simple rules of prudence our fears had been allayed. Underwater visibility in the Gulf can approach a hundred feet and a snorkel and mask will offer most of the rewards of diving. From what, in the flat lighting, seemed as ordinary a beach and sea as I've ever looked on we broke the dull surface to enter an unimaginable world. Dense clouds of brilliant fish changed formation to allow us passage or to admit us to accompany them. We followed the extraordinary hour-long nature trails indicated by marker blocks on the sea bed: the Japanese Gardens, the Winding Trail, Moses's Rock. Still, I was always slightly relieved to get back inside the reef, within which only one species of shark ("not known to attack humans") is recorded.

On an inland excursion we walked for some miles up a broad wadi, resting occasionally in the cool shade of an occasional tamarisk or acacia. At the end, high above us, stood the craggy summit of Mount Jehoshaphat. By our route it gave a pleasant scramble, never quite demanding the use of a rope. At the summit there was no scrap of litter and we'd seen no trace of a path. Vaguely, I wondered how often this little hill had been climbed and who might last have stood here. And then, glancing at my feet, I noticed that small stones had been arranged to form a word: Charlie. On a hazefree day this modest eminence offers a remarkable view. To the north we looked back into Israel; to the east into Jordan; to the south-east into Saudi Arabia; and to the south-west into Egypt, more particularly into Sinai. Within a compass of thirty miles these four countries border on the Gulf.

For two or three days we swam from Taba. Sovereignty of this small beach, with its strategic quarter-mile headland commanding a view of Eilat, was now the chief cause of dispute between Israel and Egypt. A few yards to the south stood the barbed-wire fence and the tall wooden watchtowers from which, alert for signs of an invasion, the Egyptian soldiery was focussing its binoculars on topless and sometimes bottomless girl sunbathers. Each day small groups of sun-crazed hippies crawled out of primitive shelters at the back of the beach and fell inert upon the sand. Amongst these one group of mixed nationality sometimes struggled into sitting positions and with guitar accompaniment delivered a few songs. One lyric was in English, perhaps a reworking of some current ballad, and the chorus came over distinctly: "Next week, maybe, we'll cross over into Egypt / Or maybe we'll just stay here, on Taba Beach." The last three words were repeated rousingly three times with emphatic backing. But on conclusion the party fell exhausted on its backs and I remained convinced that the effort of packing up would prove too daunting.

Israeli vehicles, even if hired by foreigners, weren't allowed through the frontier and few Israelis would have cared to risk the excursion anyway. As a result, the east coast of Sinai was almost empty of tourists. For us there was no problem. All we had to do was to walk through the wire, negotiate the one-week restricted visa, and take the daily bus to Sharm-el-Sheikh. The cost of the ticket would be three pounds sterling. So one morning, having got through the formalities within an hour and carrying in our rucksacks only those essential items we were immediately to lose, we found ourselves sitting in the only civilian building, a small hut serving as the bus terminus snack bar. Outside, a big clearly-lettered sign addressed us: "This is a Muslim country. Respect local custom. Do not appear knacked." In fact I felt keyed up with excitement.

The hundred and fifty mile coastline now has a modern highway, built by the Israelis during the occupation. However, with a rainfall of only an inch a year, delivered often in single three or four year instalments, it's almost waterless. Before Sharm-el-Sheikh, aside from seasonal Bedouin encampments, there are only two settlements, the oases of Nuweiba and Dahab spaced at fifty-mile intervals. At each there's been a little peripheral development: an Israeli-built hotel or holiday camp; a shanty town of displaced Bedouin; a small attempt at modern agriculture; a clinic, and army and police establishments. The bus halts at only these two places, there being almost no other habitations.

Our fellow passengers comprised a few local people and a mixed bunch of young European travellers. On boarding the bus all luggage was seized by the conductor and stowed quite carefully in the outside compartments. It was a beautiful day and the road ran close by the sea's edge. We saw hardly another vehicle and the whole journey was marvellous for its ambience rather than its particulars. The Crusader island fortress of Gezirat Fara'un held the eyes for a while. A few stands of palms fringed empty sandy beaches. A few files of camels wandered by the sea. Below a tight bend we saw the new but burned-out remains of a German tour coach in which half the passengers had died; without the resources to deal with a disaster of this magnitude the Egyptians had opened the frontier to the Israeli army and Red Cross for a day. We were puzzled to see that an occasional distant tamarisk sometimes had a huge black bundle hanging from its lower boughs; later we learned that these held the tents of the Bedouin who would be camping there during their seasonal journeys. Less engagingly, large notices intermittently announced that in the interests of safety foreigners were not permitted to leave the road. A tempting wasteland of hills looked over us most of the way. Opposite lay the haunting roadless coast of Saudi Arabia, virtually uninhabited.

At Nuweiba most of the young travellers got off. Having taken a careful look at the men as well as the girls I got off too and made sure that our rucksacks weren't thrown out by accident or design. At Dahab there was another twenty-minute break and the remainder of the Europeans left us. Again I watched the unloading, saw that only our gear was left, and waited until the conductor lowered the doors. Now the road left the coast and climbed a long pass into desert mountains. Throughout the journey the driver had kept his foot down but here, after discussion with the conductor and the remaining half dozen Egyptians, he drove more slowly whilst everyone scanned the roadsides and slopes. Suddenly there were shouts, he pulled in, and everybody scrambled out and began to break off the foliage of a nondescript desert shrub. A sympathetic little man who'd struck up a conversation with us told us that the leaves could be used to make a refreshing tea which reduces blood pressure and cures countless other complaints. At his insistence, we gathered some ourselves. Back on board, the driver now set out to show us what his vehicle would do on the downgrades.

At Sharm-el-Sheikh the sun was setting. The conductor lifted the flap. There was a theatrical scene in which everyone took part. Theories were advanced. Translations were offered. Advice was given. The excited gathering exercised itself with fantastic ideas, each earning the same consideration as the simple truth: the conductor had forgotten to lock the flaps, the latch-springs were broken, the compartment floor had no lip. As the bus lifted its wings in flying round and down the now distant bends our rucksacks had been flung out into the desert.

Over the next week, in each township, I had a series of frustrating interviews with officers of the Tourist Police. It was hard to distinguish these functionaries from the military and though they'd be introduced as captain or major they all seemed to be wearing the uniforms of generals or field-marshals. All I wanted was a three-line note to say that the bus company had lost our luggage, as on the first evening the conductor and two or three passengers had testified. Something in writing for the travel insurance people. Every time the story had to be told through an interpreter from the beginning, with the promise that a senior officer would be informed. During this year an English girl, sleeping on the beach, had been killed. Seven Israelis, bold enough to cross the frontier, had been slaughtered on another beach by a demented soldier, drawing an eventual apology from Cairo. If I couldn't get a simple note, how on earth had these affairs been handled? Encouragingly, at the end of each lengthy interview, I was thanked and a simple declaration was made: "Now we will find your bag."

Within an hour of losing the sacks a plan had come to me. The answer to what we were to do was clear. We'd do what we'd come here to do: that is, we'd still try to get to St. Catherine's Monastery to climb Gebel Musa. Our visas gave special permission for this inland journey but the resolution proved simpler than its implementation. We wasted a first day taking the bus back to Dahab and back to Sharm-el-Sheikh again, scanning the roadside without result. Then we spent another idle day there, waiting for the bank to reopen so that we could buy some necessaries. I sat for a hot uncomfortable hour outside Ophira police station, waiting for my man to arrive. There was a wide view over the baking plain and not a soul was stirring. Amplified to drown the world's loudest pop concert, a huge voice from some unseen minaret — a mile away? three miles away? but in which direction? — raving, hectoring, hysterical, filled the sky and the land for the whole hour. In the afternoon we swam at Naama Bay. Grotesque hotel constructions. And someone had had the brilliant idea of beheading at twelve feet every one of the long line of palm trees that had recently graced this once attractive beach. The remaining stumps had then been used as the centre-posts and the timber and leaves as the material and thatch to produce a beach hut on the site of each tree. These neat shelters now provided the shade lost through the cutting of the beautiful date-palms.

For a month I'd been poring over the best map of Sinai we'd been able to find. Already I was conscious of a strong sense of regret that the monastery and the mountain were now degraded by ease of approach. For fifteen hundred years pilgrims had devoted months and years of their lives to this journey. In the Middle Ages two brothers, pardoned murderers, chained together, had walked from Brittany to expiate their crime. Now a good road ran the fifty miles up from the Aqaba coast to the area. A second road approached from the Suez coast. A small airstrip had been constructed a few miles away. One or two hotels were beginning to form a village nucleus nearby.

A perfect approach, perhaps the best walk in the world to my taste, stands out on the map. From the Mediterranean the Wadi El Arish winds southward for two hundred miles, working up onto the El Tih plateau to reach a final maze of granite peaks. But our map marked only two or three waterholes along the whole route through this furnace of sand and rock. I've no idea whether this journey has been made on foot in modern times. Today it may still offer uncleared minefields and political considerations will probably forbid an attempt in the foreseeable future. I'd wondered, before the loss of our gear, whether we might walk in from near Dahab in the time available. Clearly that was now impossible and shortly I was to see that the idea had been unrealistic.

At Sharm-el-Sheikh we discovered that an ancient little bus was running two days a week all the way to the monastery. Then it turned out that it took the western approach and our visas wouldn't permit this. We met a couple of young travellers who'd bought tickets and tried to bluff a way through but had been taken off the bus at the first army checkpoint and had had to trudge the five miles back to town. By the third night we'd settled into the hotel at Dahab but were still no nearer finding a means of approach. During the Israeli occupation the practice of making up parties of six or seven to share the cost of a hire car had arisen. Now there were hardly any visitors except the few vagabonds on the beach and none of these had money or inclination for this trip. Finally we met a young American, Kay McDivitt, a doctor who'd spent a year working in refugee camps in Lebanon and had been travelling alone through Syria and Jordan, en route for Egypt before returning home. She spoke a little Arabic and was anxious to visit the monastery if not the mountain. It was agreed that the following morning we'd go to the Bedouin village and she'd try to bargain for the cheapest transport we could find.

As I got into bed at midnight I felt a cautious optimism. I'd hardly been lying down a full minute when there was a furious banging on the door. I opened it to see a very handsome young man in Arab dress. "I am sorry," he said, in good English. "You must come to the office immediately. There is a problem." I pulled on some clothes and walked over with considerable misgivings to find the hotel manager, various others, and two policeman lined up, all looking grave and important. "Now we have found your bag," the senior policeman announced. "It was discovered by the Chief of the Bedouin. He has found it by the side of the road." He swept an arm out and there stood my sack, though unaccompanied by Maureen's.

In our room we emptied it out. It had been rifled and an inexplicably odd selection of items was missing. Some objects of use and value had been removed, others ignored. A collection of Seamus Heaney's poems had been taken. Who in Sinai would want that? After careful repacking in the original order our single bottle of spirits had apparently been deliberately broken so that every shard of glass remained on the sleeping bag at the top. A demonstration of Muslim purity? Nothing was stained or damp. At any rate, we now owned one sleeping bag, one sheet liner, one light cotton jacket and various smaller items. And I had a pair of boots.

With Kay, next morning, we walked a mile and a half along a fine sandy beach to a picturesque little group of thatched fishermens' huts. A crude sign marked "Garage" stood outside one of these shanties. There were neither mechanics nor vehicles to be seen, though a single patient camel was tethered to the door-post. We discovered shortly a small cool café-bar, also serving as a store. It had hardly any goods on display except that the entire stand of shelving behind the counter, from the floor to a height of eight feet or so, was filled with a wall of cans of corned beef. These bore, in English, the inappropriate trade-name "Lucky Cow". Kay sent out messengers through the proprietor and for two or three hours tried to negotiate the hire of a car and driver, foreigners not being permitted to drive themselves. But today, apparently, it was impossible, though tomorrow it might perhaps be possible. Hopes dashed, we walked back along the sands, uncomfortably hot now and pursued by clouds of flies. We'd almost reached the hotel when a jeep, hooting furiously, caught up with us. The driver would take us today for sixty pounds if he could get clearance from the army.

No hesitation, we piled in. First we called in at the driver's mother's house in the middle of a large scrap and plywood shanty town of dispossessed Bedouin. It was impossible to guess at the population of this unexpected settlement. Yet the shack itself had a high-fenced yard, a tree, a garden almost, and a sense of ease, privacy, even graciousness about it. The mother, a strong and smiling woman, seated us hospitably in the shade and offered us tea. We'd have accepted this with pleasure but her son said we hadn't time and in a few minutes we were parked outside an army building. A quarter of an hour of loud shouting and angry argument was heard from within before he came out scowling with his documents.

We were on our way at last. Soon we were bowling up into the hills and the surrounding landscapes became ever more interesting with distant little encampments and increasingly attractive rock peaks. The gullies and couloirs of these peaks spilled out not as screes but as cones of the finest golden-white sand, hourglasses. A half dozen times we were halted at army road-blocks. The driver and the companion he had with him were interrogated, our passports were studied, our faces searched. As we gained altitude it grew cooler and then cold in the seatless back of the jeep. We wrapped what scraps of clothing we had around us. I couldn't relate our route to anything on my crude map. On reaching the small final settlement it was already dark, the driver hastily put us out, and declining to answer questions about our surroundings he turned and drove rapidly back down the road.

We were short of information. How far away and in which direction might the monastery lie, and the mountain? Beyond the dim lights of a few ramshackle buildings we found an incongruously modern hotel. All the beds were occupied by a German tour group and the only possibility, the helpful receptionist told us, would be at the monastery itself. She gave us rough directions. Kay had a small flashlamp and using this sparingly, after various false starts, we found ourselves on a roughly cobbled road. Intermittently, up above us, we glimpsed a single light and after perhaps two miles of gradual ascent we saw the massive buildings outlined against the night sky. The ancient barrack-like hospice stands outside the monastery wall. Here we found a few Europeans who told us that beds were probably available. First, though, we'd have to introduce ourselves. And after a half-hour the Arab janitor appeared and led us, lamp in hand, towards the wall.

St. Catherine's is fortress as well as monastery. A gantry on the forty-foot wall still stands, a means of accepting provisions without opening the door. Our guide conducted us to a small eye in the wall, one of the world's great gates, a door that tells the traveller conclusively that he's arrived. Wooden, hardly head-high but wide enough to take a laden mule, it's two feet thick, clad in battered metal sheeting and studded with heavy iron boltheads. The dark tunnel beyond led us into a warren of alleys with electric lighting and shortly we found ourselves sitting in an elegant and fascinating reception room.

The long high-ceilinged chamber was sparsely but comfortably furnished with old armchairs and couches. Clean lace curtains covered the tall narrow windows. A large photogravure of some former King of Greece hung upon one wall. Incongruously, an enormous new red-enam-elled electric coffee-grinder stood on an ancient armoire at one end. Three monks, thickly bearded and clad in the black gown and the tall fez-like hat of the Greek Orthodox Church, were seated about the room. The apparent senior amongst them, tall, dark, with a pale composed face, was at a central table engaged in fluent conversation with two thirty-year-old Frenchmen. This unhurried and courteous dialogue continued for perhaps twenty minutes while we sat at ease and in a state of great contentment awaiting our audition. Finally the others left, we asked permission to stay the night and were asked in turn the purpose of our visit. After we had signed the book and surrendered our passports the janitor was recalled and led us back to the hospice. Here we were conducted to a door and handed a heavy old iron key.

It was a cell really, with concrete floor, roughly plastered walls, and a small iron-barred window. There was no lighting or water and the room was empty save for three or four old iron double bunks, each with a lumpy, indescribably dirty mattress. The blankets in a substantial pile on one bunk were heavy and stiff, unwashed for decades. We had a few candles, bought at Sharm-el-Sheikh in a power failure, and by their light we shared some of the little food we had with Kay whilst debating our plans. My chief wish was to climb the mountain but I'd no idea where it might be. All I knew was that we were in a tight valley with very high walls. I'd read somewhere that it was usual to leave very early in order to avoid the heat of the day and to see the dawn from the summit. All I could settle for was to rise at first light and hope to find someone with local knowledge quickly. If we couldn't get up it tomorrow we'd be pressed for time. We sorted out the cleaner-looking blankets and arranged ourselves for the night. At over five thousand feet and well inland it was very cold even indoors.

I was aroused in the middle of the night by soft gasps of terror. Maureen. As I collected myself and reached across to her bunk I realised that she was having a nightmare. I reassured her as she jerked out her story. She'd been in a tiny room, the ceiling was moving down on her, she was being crushed. As she was explaining the effect I was removing the cause. Heavy as flagstones, I heaved off one folded blanket after another. While she was calming herself and beginning to understand my amusement I saw through the dirty little window that it seemed to be almost light outside. Unlocking the door I found that a full moon had risen and the valley was now brilliantly lit. I walked round to the portico. Granite walls like those of Yosemite hung above us, every detail sharp. Opposite was an impenetrable darkness but a high tormented skyline suggested similar formations.

It was a ravishing scene. I paced around, not wanting to return to my bed. And suddenly, surprisingly, I caught the faintest sound of singing. Surely monastic offices weren't performed at this hour of the night? The sound died for a moment or two and then I caught it again. It was outside the monastery. I walked across the terrace. Now it seemed a little closer but from somewhere down the valley. Finally, on the other side of the ravine, I picked out a file of torches about to bypass the monastery, the singing not quite loud enough to fix the language. It could mean only one thing, a party setting off for the mountain. Where else could they be going?

I went back inside and, speaking very quietly to avoid waking Kay, told Maureen what I'd seen. Thinking aloud, I said that if we'd been ready we could simply have followed them. Might it still be possible? We'd have to cast around a bit to pick up the track and we wouldn't see the torches from behind. But on this still night we might hear voices at two or three miles. Outside the shadow it was as clear as day. If we could get ourselves moving within five minutes we'd probably find out roughly which way the route went at the least. "I'm game if you are," said Kay from the darkness, startling me.

We scrambled into action. Frustratingly, we had to go down-valley for some distance in order to cross to the track the walkers had used. It was in shadow and restricted our pace. Above the monastery it crossed a level area of bare ground and soon afterwards became less obvious until it lost itself in boulders. Patiently we returned to the clear area and using Kay's torch sparingly I traced its perimeter until I found the true track. We'd had neither sight nor sound of the party ahead since starting but now we emerged into strong moonlight and the way was clear. Presently the path steepened considerably. We began to hear voices ahead and sensed that we were closing the gap. Shortly we started to overtake small groups of stragglers and realised that there were a number of groups on the mountain. Turning around for the first time we saw chains of lights at intervals behind us.

Having not yet eaten, we paused for a small snack. In the valley bottom, walking very briskly, we'd stayed quite warm. Standing in a slight breeze now, we began to feel the cold. We had spare stockings on our hands. Occasionally, we swapped our two overgarments around. At this point I had the thin cotton jacket and Maureen had the sleeping bag draped around her shoulders. She was also wearing wedge-heeled rope-soled sandals with crossover ankle straps, a full mid-calf-length cotton skirt, and a large headscarf. In the moonlight this somewhat Biblical outfit seemed powerfully resonant and appropriate.

Pushing on again, we overtook the larger party at a strange little cleft or man-made cutting through the toe of a great rock buttress. This track, we were to learn later, was the route developed to give access by camel or mule to the final steep ascent. Turning the flank of the mountain we lost the moonlight again but found ourselves climbing a narrow man-made stairway of rock slabs. It was already clear that we'd be up in time to see the dawn and we realised now that no-one was in front of us. As we began to feel that we were approaching the summit we started to notice hoar frost on the rocks and soon we found that the polished steps were progressively becoming glazed with ice. Ice in Sinai. Just a few miles away, in just a few hours' time, the heat would be debilitating. Finally we were standing alone at the top.

Gebel Musa, Moses' Mountain, the Mountain of God, Mount Horeb, Mount Sinai. In fact, the route taken by the Israelites has been strongly disputed. The title of Mount Sinai is claimed by at least two other summits and the Northern Route for the Wanderings has logic on its side. Two hundred miles to the north, the long narrow insecure sandspit dividing the Mediterranean from the great Bardawil lagoon is proposed instead of the dividing of the Red Sea. The annual series of eastbound autumn thunderstorms following the coastline in that area provides the pillar of cloud by day and the pillar of fire by night. The manna and the quail are available too. After their migration the birds still fall exhausted on that shore. The sweet deposit of the tamarisk offers the manna. And the northernmost Mount Sinai isn't far away. But these intriguing suggestions stand no chance against the entire weight of the religious tradition. The mountain on which we were standing, incomparably the more inaccessible in ancient times, has somehow been sanctified as the place where Moses received the Ten Commandments.

We'd got it marginally wrong. It was still an hour at least before first light, a long time to wait in our inadequate clothing. However, it felt exciting to be alone at the summit for ten minutes or so before the first group from what proved to be a numerous procession was to join us. The top of Gebel Musa is crowned by a small Greek Orthodox chapel, perhaps seldom if ever used nowadays. A tiny mosque stands close by and a number of primitive chambers and meditation cells are walled in the clefts and corners amongst the wind-sculpted boulders. We moved from one to the other seeking better shelter from the wind. Maureen took off her sandals and settled into the sleeping bag. Towards dawn something like a hundred people representing many nationalities had joined us.

In the east the sky paled slowly and we saw that the sunrise was not to be perfectly clear. Over the Gulf of Aqaba a confusion of low cloud of varying opacity was spread. From behind the mountains of Arabia the sun came up, first back-lighting and then freeing itself of this encumbrance. Everyone looked out in that direction and as the first warm rays struck us the preponderant German element in the congregation began to sing the words of Schiller's Ode to Joy. Clearly they'd been rehearsed and they sang well.

Many British hill-walkers, for whom the presence of another human being on a mountain will spoil the day, would have felt scorn and fury at this scene. The weatherbeaten buildings, the heterogeneous crowd, the odd bits of litter referred back to the summit of Snowdon on a summer Bank Holiday. I felt no such aversion. Having company on the hill doesn't bother me and I experienced this gathering as a rare moment of pure community. *Freude trinken alle Wesen an den Brusten der Natur.* For fifteen hundred years at least — since before the Dark Ages, since the Romans left Britain — without intermission, despite appalling risks and discomforts, huge multitudes of people have travelled colossal distances to climb this hill for no material purpose. *Seid unschlungen Millionen!*

As the sun began to reveal the land we turned to look at the prospect to other sides. To the south the Red Sea was still obscured and to the west Mount St. Catherine curtained off a part of the view into Africa. But it was on the north anyway, on the interior of Sinai, that the eyes fastened. Bright red in the low lighting the tightly massed granite domes and pyramids showed no clear avenues. Without a good map, how many days to find a way through? Beyond these summits we could see a hundred miles of the El Tih plateau, hostile to human life. Yet, all through recorded history, nomads have lived in this waste and invaders have crossed and recrossed it, "that great and terrible wilderness", the land bridge between Africa and Asia.

It seemed madness, almost unbearable, to leave this summit which we might hardly expect to visit again. But we had to go sooner or later and the cold breeze still resisted the sun. We hurried back down the steps and now to our delight we saw below us what had been hidden in the darkness, the miraculous sanctuary of Elijah's Hollow. This perfect bowl was filled with warmth. The narrow exit from the fine amphitheatre of rounded cliffs and eroded boulders is perfectly concealed. On the level floor the shrine and the thousand-year-old cypresses are faultlessly composed. Lifting a wooden cover we looked down to see well water and we were amazed at the coolness of its breath. In this serene and beautiful place the summit gathering had dispersed itself widely and even the Germans had fallen silent.

Tobias and a handful of his followers had rested for some time in a cave here. It's recorded that he spoke for five days while a disciple wrote down his words. That would be about ten years before our visit. Perhaps the manuscript is that from which a page is reproduced on the back cover of *Tsa*, the twentieth century's most ambitious attempt to communicate without exposition. I entered a little rock-backed hermitage I recognised from one of his photographs. Empty. Where the hell was Michael now? He'd come to see me, he'd asked me what I knew, he'd talked and talked and talked. We'd put together *The Mountain Spirit*, our crazy beautiful book, and he'd disappeared. He was somewhere out there in the big world — Alaska? Bhutan? Hawaii? — fighting for the recognition he feels to be his due. I thought of my young friend with amusement and affection. He'd entertained me, he'd widened my horizons.

It was clear that we'd taken the mountain the right way round. The gentle approach of the camel track had been easy walking in the dark and its presumably less dramatic setting had seemed amply mysterious. The descent we were now making kept producing theatrical surprises. We passed through a hidden cleft, the steps resuming down the narrow gully, and arrived at the archway at which Stephanos had questioned each pilgrim. Now we found ourselves looking down a steep and magnificent ravine. To either side the continuous cliffs rose vertically for four to eight hundred feet in a smooth firm granite, rough in texture, warm in colour. Each wall was split by innumerable continuous cracks of all widths threading through and around great overhangs. There were no easy lines but hundreds of feasible lines. It was a climber's paradise as perfect as any I've seen. Yet I felt immediately that to work out routes here, over the pilgrims' heads, would be an act of the grossest insensitivity. At our leisure we descended the several thousand steps of Stephanos' stairway. The monastery now came into view beneath us. Towards the foot of the ravine we came across two marvellous springs, the first natural running water we'd seen in Sinai. "Water, the ace of elements."

In the afternoon we walked around the monastery. A notice in English asked that lady visitors should show respect for the monks and not display naked arms. It seemed curious to think of the arm as an erogenous zone but I recalled that a hundred and fifty years ago De Quincy's specification for perfect happiness had required a girl with beautiful arms in a Lakeland cottage. The arms of my companions being veiled I was able to concentrate my attention upon our surroundings. Here was the Burning Bush, still unconsumed. The tiny church was an Aladdin's Cave, heaped with treasures, a grotto from the sea bed. It offered seating for less than twenty monks in individual carved and canopied thrones along either side wall. I noticed, beneath the skirts of the young monk guarding the relics, jeans and trainers. We gave the ossuary a miss and wandered through the alleys of this extraordinary maze, the random achieving a perfection planning couldn't hope to equal. No buildings on earth have been in longer continuous occupation than those of St. Catherines's Monastery.

Here was the Library. Beyond it lay the restricted area of the Rare Books Room, the second greatest collection of ancient manuscripts on earth. In the nineteenth century a German scholar had borrowed the *Codex Sinaiticus* on the authority of the Czar of Russia. The Czar had decided on reflection that it would be safer if he kept it in St. Petersburg. It had passed into Stalin's hands. Hard up, he'd flogged it to the British Museum. Ignoring a century of appeals we're going to keep it, like we're going to keep the Elgin Marbles and the rest of our loot.

Great scholars have travelled here, have produced their letters of accreditation, and have been refused access to the Rare Books Room. For Michael the doors had swung open. He'd have turned his charm on. The Abbot would have known a Desert Father when he saw one. Michael would have examined the monks in dead languages they ought really to have known, he'd have addressed them in living languages they just couldn't quite recognise, he'd have thought aloud in future languages he'd only just invented. How had he spent his time here? He'd have known exactly what to look for. Had they counted the leaves of the *Codex Syriacus* since his visit? No, no, I'm joking. He'd have handled the ancient books with reverence, knowing that it was a privilege to be here. Most likely he'd have donated to the library a codex of his own, knocked off some dull afternoon. The Book of Tobias.

Kay's travel schedule demanded that she get back to the coast immediately, pack her belongings, and resume her journey in the morning. Her full visa permitted the onward journey to Cairo. We still had one day in hand and Mount St. Catherine, without the significance of Mount Sinai but slightly higher and a rather more difficult ascent, presented a strong temptation. Unhappily it seemed unlikely that we could fit it in on foot within the day and if we weren't back at the frontier on time we'd face unknown consequences. The journey up had been expensive. Now we were in a seller's market. Any driver we might find could hold out for every penny we'd got if we left it to the eleventh hour. We decided to leave with Kay and the three of us started to enquire about lifts amongst the several groups gathered in the courtyard.

Nearly all of these parties were returning to the Suez coast but within an hour, to our great relief, we were invited to share a pre-booked taxi with four young Americans bound in our direction. The Bedouin driver didn't even adjust his charge which divided to allow a cheap journey. The soldiers at the road-blocks still seemed hostile, one still-unforgotten face dangerous, seething with fury, psychotic. He prowled around the car as our passports were examined, peering in again and again at each of us. We kept our faces expressionless and passed through. "Which do you prefer, the Israelis or the Egyptians?" one girl asked the driver, a handsome young man with a disconcerting full set of glittering chromium-steel dentures. "For the Bedouin exactly the same, both bad," he said. They were experiencing the weight of government. But these reminders of the political world couldn't suppress our delight in the wide desert landscapes as we cruised on down towards the coast. Soon, and with real regret, we were saying our farewells to Kay, bound for Cairo and then a new post in Boulder, Colorado.

St. Catherine's Monastery. Everyone who's been there feels elected. One writer says that there are Santa Katerina freaks, people who try to get there again and again, others who never return in order to keep the memory unsullied but who can't stop remembering and talking about the place. She tries to distance herself but she's one of them. So am I. It was true, we hadn't bought the experience at a fair price as earlier travellers had. Months or years of travel; passing from one local guide to another, seeking security in numbers where possible, enduring heat, thirst, cold, hunger, fatigue, illness and danger. Yet the accidents of recent political change, the loss of our gear, the lack of information, the limits of our time and money — all these combined to make me feel that we'd slept at the monastery and climbed the holy mountain only by precarious interventions of chance.

I've enjoyed no mountain excursion more than this trip. At the same time my delight was troubled, the fix I was caught in bothered me. I'd travelled up to St. Catherine's in a jeep when it was right and proper to have walked in from the sea, and to walk out again. As things stood, though, I've no idea how a pedestrian would have been received by the army: arrested or detained on some pretext or other?

And the situation was surely destined to get worse. I tried to put it into perspective. Travellers have the sanction of an immemorial tradition here. Now the road was being upgraded to expressway standard, the airstrip would soon re-open and charter flights from Cairo would be wheeling in. During the occupation tourism had been encouraged and at one point the dozen remaining monks, overwhelmed, had shut the doors and closed the hospice. That seemed like a good idea. Egypt would soon be promoting the place as a major tourist attraction but the offer of a slog up a big mountain rather than a stroll around the monastery might thin recruitment out.

On the other hand the monks were selling a lot of art and history books and could impose a whacking admission charge. Some amongst them might even enjoy wrestling temptation, the torture of the turn of a delicate ankle or the shocking glimpse of an upper arm. My own impulse, anyway, is clear. During the lunacy of the Gulf War I drew great pleasure from the recurrent thought that the mountain must be empty of visitors. And here I find myself in agreement with the ecoteurs. Not just to keep things the way they are: to put them back the way they were. Destroy the roads and airstrip. Forget about the needs of the very young, the very old, the crippled and the fat rich. Let them ride camels.

At Nuweiba the following evening we walked along the lonely shore to an abandoned fisherman's hut on a headland. Here we saw rotted boats of archaic design and noticed also heaps of castaway syringes, relics of the hippie invasion which followed the Israeli occupation. We'd spent the afternoon swimming in the lagoon. In the morning I'd had my final interview with the tourist police.

I was expected. The Chief of the Bedouin would also be attending the hearing to give his account of his discovery of my bag. I was conducted into a cool empty spacious hall and seated on a carefully placed upright chair facing but fifteen feet distant from an enormous desk. No-one appeared, the voices outside died away, and I sat there alone for an hour. Then an old Arab came in, smiled at me, and signalled me to rise. He picked up the chair, led me out onto a wide terrace at the back and reseated me, indicating the sun with a gesture of approval. Another hour passed and I began to feel uncomfortably hot. He appeared again and reversed the procedure. Twenty minutes later, followed by an interpreter, an immaculately groomed officer walked in and seated himself behind the desk.

I recited my story again. The Chief of the Bedouin, it turned out, had not been able to make it and had sent his apologies. Yes, a note that the police had been informed of my loss could be provided. The interpreter was dismissed and now a scribe in Arab dress entered with a pen and a bottle of ink. Gravely, weighing each word carefully, stroking his moustaches, the officer dictated and I watched the pen of the calligrapher dance graceful arabesques across the sheet of paper. From time to time he was asked to read back what he'd written. Corrections were made. A clean copy was written out. And finally an impressive rubber stamp was produced and thumped down upon the paper. I have the document here now. I've often wondered what it says but perhaps it's best not to know. I doubt whether, for this small claim, the insurers secured a translation. The blurred stamp, the seal of Egypt, incorporates an eagle but otherwise only a single detail has meaning. With slight variants the numbers the Arabs gave us, and upon which all our Western science rests, are recognisable at the foot: 1984/11/11. An odd juxtaposition. 1984, Orwell's nightmare of the maturity of the nation state. November eleventh, Armistice Day.

BON ECHO ROCK

I've done a fair number of beautiful climbs on sea-cliffs but can't pretend to be an afficionado of the genre. Nearly always it's the scene or the incidental image that comes to mind rather than the particularities of the route. Climbing on clean white limestone above a sparkling Mediterranean, the glare so fierce that my brother, who had no sun-glasses, developed first-degree snow-blindness. Climbing on firm dry granite in West Penwith, the sun shining through a periodic curtain of water, a hundred-foot explosion of rainbowed wave and spray only thirty feet out but as vertical as the subwall that built it so that not a drop fell on us. Finding the descent, for the first time, to the foot of Pen-las Rock or into Mother Carey's Kitchen in Pembroke, even into Pigeon Cave on the Great Orme. Standing on a narrow ledge, only six feet above deep and rising water, while for half an hour and at a distance of twenty feet a puzzled seal bobbed up and down, watching us with unblinking eyes, trying to understand what we were about. Miscalculating the swell on a sea-level traverse at Gogarth so that, poised on small holds on a bottomless wall, it seemed safer not to risk some hasty moves and to freeze as the sea rose smoothly up to my thighs and sank away.

The ancient Chinese word for landscape is shan-shui, Japanese following with san-sui. The two ideograms actually mean mountain and water and represent in themselves oppositions, vertical and horizontal, solid and fluid. To watch heavy seas breaking against cliffs is to see a plausible illustration of irresistible force meeting immovable object. Yet in the end, as if in a Zen parable, the hard and upright is overcome by the soft and supine.

It's easy to see the ancillary attractions of sea-cliff climbing. It generally takes place in areas where there's much less rainfall and much more sunshine than we meet on the mountain crags. Time and effort aren't wasted in walking and often the only ascent is the rock climb itself. The surroundings may offer pleasant coastal paths, beaches for sunbathing and swimming, cafés, pubs, and sometimes cultural possibilities, so that hardcore enthusiasts are able to deploy lovers, wives, husbands, children and dogs with little fear of an ultimatum. The climber may even, if he wishes, use the alleged needs of a domestic entourage to allow him to take a break and to divert himself with fishing, swimming or people-watching for the odd day. Around him is a landscape and a wildlife arrestingly different from that of the mountains. And then there's the sea itself, continually drawing the eye whatever its state of activity or quiescence.

There are other arguments to be put for sea-cliff climbing though they're often double-edged. Some will say that to the entirely adequate difficulties and hazards of inland crags the sea adds gratuitous increments of peril. It's entertaining and arousing to play Last Across, skipping from one islanded boulder to another as the swell reaches for the ankles; but though the seventh wave theory might average out it's clear that the sea can't count. There's a real feeling of commitment in attempting a route only accessible at low tide; but in the event of failure the patience to sit still for many hours to make a safe retreat seems to be lacking in most climbers and parties are sometimes forced into desperate alternatives. The more remote and atmospheric routes, hiding themselves from inspection from the land, offer a concentrated sense of exploration in approach; yet these approaches by unseen abseil, down appallingly exposed grass slopes or on shockingly insecure vegetation and rock may alarm the most experienced mountain climber. The restless action of the sea ("the water's wrench and thud," Trypanis; "the water's heave and suck," owner mislaid, any offers?), so hypnotic to the eye, may be found subtly disturbing to the sense of balance, as unsettling in its way as a strongly gusting wind.

As it happens, one of the most memorable days I ever spent climbing above water was five hundred miles from the ocean on a lakeside cliff. In theory, this situation ought to have offered the best of both worlds with the hazards of the sea removed and with any fall from the unprotected start of a climb to be fielded by the forgiving element of still water. In the event I made two small mistakes: one might have cost us money, discomfort and effort; the other might have killed us.

We'd come to Toronto on a family reunion. Maureen and her cousin John, with myself and Monica in attendance, were paying a return visit to their expatriate cousin Joan, who'd been living in Canada for many years. This would be a holiday with a difference. A very comfortable house to stay in. Amiable hosts. A big and lively city to explore. And the possibility of excursions into wild country. This, if it matters, was in 1976.

We'd had one surprise already. A year or two earlier the Director of Toronto's Boyne River Natural Science School had called in at my own establishment in North Wales during a tour of Outdoor Education Centres in Britain. Some time later we'd learned that he was the godfather of two of Joan's children. How could that be? The family had no commitment to the outdoors beyond obligatory skiing and fishing trips. Well, it was just that the world is so small. He happened to be their neighbour, they'd known him for years.

With specialist advice and the offer of the loan of equipment the possibilities were suddenly extended. Before we knew what was happening a canoe trip had been prescribed and equipment was being assembled. Aside from two open fibreglass Canadian doubles this included such items as felling axe and bowsaw. We faced the embarrassing problem that none of us had stepped into a Canadian canoe before and my three companions hadn't handled any canoe, so that a little preparation for the wilderness seemed advisable. As it happened, the house had a large swimming pool with a Canadian double lying by it. Our training began with a few minutes in this pool. It concluded with a hair-raising half-hour, the four of us jammed in together, on an attractive little lake a quarter-mile from the house, Grenadier Pond. The two-hundred-mile reach of Lake Ontario was just as close at hand but a heavy sea was running and time wouldn't permit us to await calmer weather in order to practise from that shore.

The project recommended to us was an excursion into the roadless area of the Killarney Lakes. These lie to the north of Georgian Bay, itself a hundred and fifty mile annex of Lake Huron defended by a peninsula and a chain of islands. A station wagon had been provided and on a very hot day we drove the heavily loaded vehicle northward through the stark landscape of the Laurentian Shield. Conifers. Bogs. Smoothly planed hummocks of pre-Cambrian rock. It was already dark when we left the highway to follow the forty miles of dirt road to the little settlement of Killarney. Transient frogs were crossing the track in thousands. A fox leapt across. Owls hooted in the woods. Nothing we couldn't have seen at home but a big sense of space. We saw no other vehicle on this road.

Killarney had a new and grossly modernistic hotel, an older motel, a few houses, a number of neat little float planes moored at the small jetty, and a splendid establishment called the Sportsman's Inn. This last consisted of an outfitters for canoeing, hunting and fishing and a large, rough and ready bar in which I felt instantaneously at home. A notice offered food and a messenger went through to the kitchen with our enquiry. He returned to tell us that Vera had a headache and didn't feel like cooking. This easiness delighted me. We went back to our motel room to cook some camp food and returned as quickly as possible.

In a long evening there were never more than six or seven other customers, all locals. Confusingly, at one point, a well-lit, nicely-curtained house slid by just outside the window. Peering out I realised that we were facing onto the bay and saw that this neat wooden two-storey building occupied the whole deck of a strange raft-like vessel. It was bringing home a half-dozen quarrymen from their shift at a small-scale excavation somewhere along the shore. John, with some knowledge of the industry, was appalled at the idea of quarrying in darkness. In fact one of the work-force had already attached himself to us, a survivor of the previous shift, now overtaken. From time to time the barmaid relayed phone calls from his wife, announcing the progress, the availability, and the wreck of his dinner, and finally appealing for an estimated time of arrival. What do you get through? I asked him. A case a night, he said. Later, two optimistic drunks tried to land punches on each other. The attractive young barmaid opened the door, caught each in turn by a sleeve, and flung them out into the darkness. I was impressed. How long had she been working there? I asked. Three days. But she'd been brought up in Killarney. She could handle the local men.

The expedition began propitiously. The four of us had shared a motel room. We'd finished packing when Maureen asked me to look under the bed to check that we'd left nothing. I'd already glanced beneath its skirts but I made a gesture of resignation and got down on my back. From this position I was now able to see a glossy black cylinder and I guessed its contents immediately. A bottle of whisky and, yes, unopened. It was off-season and we decided that the last occupants would have written it off by now. The pleasures of our first night by a campfire were completed by this find.

The first two hours of the trip presented the only difficulties. George Lake, our entry point, was extensive and a steady wind was bringing up sizable waves. The canoes were quite well laden leaving little freeboard and the idea of lashing them didn't occur to me. Instead we kept fairly close inshore until it was possible to cross by a shorter traverse. John and Monica, we soon found, paddled much more strongly than Maureen and myself but with incomplete control of direction so that we kept perfect pace and they revisited us from time to time. By the afternoon we'd made the first of several portages and were on calmer waters. The rest of the trip was an idyll, following a chain of lakes through low hills densely covered with birch, maple and conifers. The occasional untrodden cliff could be admired, the fall colours were just beginning to appear, the blackfly season had just ended, the sun was warm and the days windless. At each camp we found within a few paces huge slabs of cast-off birch bark, thick and heavy, and these burned almost as if resinous.

It had come to light that our advisors, with vast experience of difficult canoe trips, hadn't actually visited this area. Possibly lake canoeing wasn't serious enough. You may come across wolves, bears, moose and deer, they'd told us. Perhaps that was a joke. The wilderness seemed empty of creatures except squirrels and wildfowl, though well out in one lake I came across a small snake swimming easily, head high above water. All in all, though, it was a marvellous trip. In Britain I'd always had mixed feelings about canoeing since the onset of an occasional back problem, quickly reactivated or exacerbated by a few hours in a kayak. By contrast I found the kneeling position in the open Canadian more restful than sitting in a chair and in these placid waters I felt I could paddle for ever.

Very good, though it wasn't climbing. The Boyne River people had taken me out to sample two or three small limestone crags they were working on. The best place to climb, they said, was a hundred miles away, Bon Echo Rock, a three-hundred-foot volcanic wall rising from the waters of Mazinaw Lake in Eastern Ontario. Information was obtained, a car was provided, and Maureen and I made a leisurely drive to the lake one beautiful day. Having booked into a motel we were able to walk out just before dark to examine the cliff.

Mazinaw Lake is shaped like an hour-glass, aligned north and south. From memory it may be fifteen or twenty miles long, though we never visited the northern end. It's surrounded by gentle wooded hills. The road follows the western shores whilst the cliff stands on the trackless eastern side opposite and north of the constriction. I looked at the small strait with care. It was no more than a rope-length across and it was wadeable except for a deep channel in the middle. Through this channel, on this evening, a quite strong current was running, even though the two lobes of the lake were apparently of equal height. The trees on each bank were set just too far back to allow any fancy tricks with ropes. If we were to swim it we'd have the problem of keeping our gear dry. In any case, most of the more attractive climbs started from deep water. All right, we'd hire a canoe, though since we had no roof-rack we'd have to approach from somewhere up or down the lake. We had the time and now we had the expertise as well.

In the morning we found a little marina on the southern lake and hired an aluminium Canadian double. It was three or four miles to the cliff but the weather remained perfect and there wasn't another boat on the water. In an hour or so we'd passed through the bottleneck and were drifting in beneath the crag. Impressive. We inspected the base of the main precipice which rises vertically from the depths. Pictographs painted, we were told, from the canoes of Algonquin Indians show at intervals along the rock face.

I looked at these with interest. They appeared at a consistent height somewhat beyond a man's reach, perhaps through a seasonal variation in water level, perhaps through erosion of the lake outlet. Beavers can back up rivers for astonishing distances, we'd noticed areas of half-drowned trees at Killarney, but surely not a lake of this extent. It occurred to me that it might have been simpler to have made these notations whilst standing on the winter ice but perhaps the Indian inks or paints would have needed anti-freeze.

The designs are geometric and abstract and their significance isn't known. They should be called petrograms really, though some I examined suggested a binary code, assemblies of dots and dashes. (I ask myself now, did NASCII precede ASCII? Native American Standard Code for Information Interchange.) Unhappily, in the large task of tidying up the sub-continent we'd lost, along with the passenger pigeon and effectively the American bison, some two-thirds of the three hundred Indian languages. (We'd lost a lot of Indians too.) North American Indians had no writing and with the single exception of Cherokee even the surviving languages weren't transcribed until comparatively recently. We couldn't now ask the Algonquins what the pictographs meant. We'd armed the Iroquois with weapons good enough to allow them to exterminate these particular Algonquin tribes, whose land we needed badly; but not with weapons good enough to give us any problems when, stage two, we needed the land of the Iroquois. Perhaps I oversimplify? Nobody thought to write down the last words of the last Algonquin or to ask what the symbols meant. Here they remain, sermons in stone perhaps, which no-one now can read.

We paddled along, identifying the main features. The earliest exploration had taken place in the late fifties and had been initiated by a small group from the Wild Geese Section of the Irish Mountaineering Club. I hadn't met those climbers but I'd been, through those years, a member of that section and perhaps the only Sasanach it had admitted. These expatriates had then recruited John Turner, a pushing English climber who was setting formidable new standards in eastern Canada and the New England states. He'd had an eventful first visit. I recalled that Irish climbing had a long case history of misadventures on water, this ancestry stretching back to H.C. Hart's explorations of the cliffs of Lambay before the turn of the century. In the fifties a small armada of grossly unseaworthy craft had made an evening assault on Ireland's Eye, off Dublin. On the return a violent squall had dispersed the fleet widely, scattering or wrecking it over several miles of the Wicklow coast.

At Bon Echo, that weekend, Brian Rothery had judged it impossible to abseil back into the leaky rowing boat serving several parties and had opted for the swim from the end of the cliff. Weakening, he'd pulled out onto a ledge to warm up and to recover strength. From that perch he'd tried to hitch a lift from the blazored and yacht-cap-hatted captain of a passing motor cruiser. The captain, with humanitarian instinct and Maritime Law in mind, had changed course towards the seaman in distress. But, on closer inspection, to Rothery's thumb up the captain's wife had given a decisive thumbs-down and the boat had veered away. Any respectable hitch-hiker would at least have kept his underpants on. There'd been nothing for it but to plunge in again for the second leg.

We looked at the intimidating line Turner had been applied against on the following day. Already named by the Irish as The Joke, it had been no laughing matter for Turner. Nevertheless, he'd made more than two hundred feet before taking a big fall in front of the spellbound audience on a flotilla of weekend pleasure craft. Striking rock before he was held, his trousers were stripped to his ankles, one of which was broken, and he was obliged to kick the garment off into the lake. His spectacles had already preceded it. But he was a determined man and he returned to crack The Joke.

We settled for a less serious undertaking. This gave us the unusual experience of getting into our harnesses and roping up in a gently swaying canoe. I pulled onto the rock and belayed the boat to three or four chocks with the utmost care. The route, of which, unusually, I can't remember the name, gave about four pitches of steep balancy climbing reminiscent in some elusive way of Tremadog. It was a very pleasant ascent but my strongest memory is of looking down at one point to see a

sudden wild disturbance in the water. I followed the track of this creature, surely not a fish, as it quartered beneath me. Would an otter or
beaver, if found here, produce so much turbulence? Tantalisingly, the
monster wouldn't quite break surface and the water was impenetrable to
the eye. After a couple of minutes it sank to the depths leaving me
anguished with disappointment.

We sat on the cliff top for a long time, enjoying the sun and the wide
views of lake and forest. Until, finally, we had to go, two or three
abseils, all from trees. I set up the first with care, went to the edge to
cast the coils and, just at that moment, noticed a big loose block above
me, close to the line of the rope. The retrieval might bring it down on us.
I moved a little distance to one side and, keeping the rope clear, asked
Maureen to kick it over. As it trundled slowly towards the edge I remembered the canoe.

An image from many years earlier flashed into my mind. We were
climbing in the Calanques, the half-drowned limestone gorges between
Cassis and Marseilles. With Geoff Roberts I was out on the west wall of
En Vau, three hundred feet above the sea. I'd been struggling with the
hard pitch, my attention concentrated entirely on each move for the past
few minutes, when, pulling out at the top, I disturbed a small loose rock.
It was hardly the size of my fist. I half-turned to watch it fall and saw
directly below me, making a lazy breast-stroke, a girl who'd swum out
the two or three hundred yards from the beach. Floating on the skin of
the clear blue water, the depth of which I couldn't guess, she looked
graceful, fragile, vulnerable. I didn't even manage to call out. The stone
pierced the surface, a small splash at that distance, just a few feet from
her and she apparently didn't hear or understand it. For a moment I'd
been paralysed with horror.

At Bon Echo I hung out from a small sapling to see the position of the
canoe. For three or four long seconds I watched the block home onto it.
The only alternative to swimming would be a trek without food through
pathless woods, a day at least if the terrain were difficult. Then the
block hit the water like a bomb, two or three feet out. Terrified, the boat
leaped up into the air and fell back. It had no flotation, might the waves
swamp it? It bucked and rolled wildly, gathering water, jerking at the
long slings before slowly calming itself.

Our final abseil dropped us into it. We paddled very carefully to the
narrows where we were able to beach and empty out water before
resuming. We'd realised that we'd be returning in darkness but we
couldn't see a problem in that. The hire form said that the canoe must be
booked in by eight o'clock but we'd manage that alright, provided we

took a direct line rather than hop from cape to cape of the little bays. As we set off the sky darkened but we could see the lights of the marina in the far distance. Soon we were over deep water, skimming along in a moonless blackness, an exquisite pleasure. The forested slopes were just a sensed presence and we could judge our headway only by the rate at which, passing some distant promontory, the skylined trees eclipsed the stars.

We hadn't noticed a boat on the lake all day. Now, to our surprise, we heard the sound of a high-powered engine and saw a light crossing from the marina towards the eastern shore. A few minutes later another appeared on a different course, and then another. An explanation came to us quickly. We knew that the east shore held a number of holiday cabins, hidden in the woods. It was a Friday night. We were seeing some sort of rush hour as the weekenders arrived. It wasn't until one launch swung round in a long curve and headed in our direction that we realised the hazard of our situation. We could see them but they couldn't see us. We could hear them but they couldn't hear us.

A frantic half-hour followed. We'd abandoned our course and were paddling hard for the west bank, intending to creep along the shore, when a big cruiser swung inside, intercepting us. It passed close by and just in time I remembered to set the canoe up correctly for the huge wake and then the counter-wake. The length of the preliminary curves made it difficult to judge the eventual directions of the launches and two or three appeared to take slalom courses just for the hell of it. Some had powerful searchlights on the bows, others just boomed off into the blackness, cutting engines and showing lights as they neared the far shore. Weren't they afraid of floating logs? We'd cut in half more easily than a log. If it seemed we were going to be run down, would it be best to dive in and swim deep? If the canoe wasn't hit or swamped, how to find it again in the darkness?

After several attempts, aborted as launches headed for the northern end, an interval allowed us to get across. At risk of hitting underwater rocks we followed a line close inshore. But it had been in fact commuter hour, activity was slowing down. By the time we reached the marina there wasn't a soul in sight, not even an employee to fine us for late return. We tied the canoe up and now, by a slipway, I saw a notice I'd missed in the morning: all craft must show lights after dark. The English traveller abroad. It had been a careless little adventure in which we might have died. We resolved to manage things better the following day.

The Poisoned Glen

BEARNAS BUTTRESS DIRECT

When my brother first set foot in Ireland in 1953, he and his companion
were removed from the queue at the Aliens' barrier by a port official and
were led into a concrete-floored warehouse. Without explanation they
were told to stand still. A moment of wild confusion followed as, from
behind their backs, an assistant hosed down their boots and much of
their bodies with a chemical spray. From their ragged clothing it had
been assumed that they were returning cattlemen and precautions were
in force against a Foot and Mouth outbreak somewhere in the United
Kingdom. They entered the land of the unexpected with their trousers
wet.

   This excursion had been inspired by an article in the occasional journal then published by the British Mountaineering Council. Neville had
recruited friends from Wall End and he'd made prior contact with the
Dublin climbers. He came back with tales of impressive routes, unforgettable country people, the warm hospitality of the Irish climbers and
the embarrassing gaffes of his own team. As it happened, in that same
year in the Alps I chanced to meet the three leading Irish pioneers of the
time, Frank Winder, Peter Kenny and Sean Rothery. They talked on and
on about their hills and cliffs.

   I've spent as much time climbing in Ireland as in Scotland, and spread
over a similar number of mountain regions. My vote goes for Ireland

though it's not easy to explain this partiality since there's nothing over there to compare with Nevis, the Cairngorms or the Cuillin. Perhaps it's that in Scotland we often travel through range on range of inland hills, diminishing the impact and individuality of those of our destination: in Ireland, after the rite of passage of the ferry crossing, we reach hills standing like groups of sentinels, watching over the sea, ringing and guarding the inland plain, usually unrivalled by close neighbours and with character enhanced by free space. Or perhaps it's that in Scotland we inevitably first visited the famous centres with long and unbroken histories of exploration: whereas in 1953 the Irish Mountaineering Club wasn't yet five years old, and outside Dublin and Wicklow probably only the Mournes in the north and the Twelve Bens in the west had lists of more than a dozen climbs. The hills were robed in mystery.

Or perhaps it's something more personal: that we're attracted by what's strange and there are polar oppositions, phonetic and temperamental, between the beautifully cadenced speech of the far west, articulate and candid, and the brusque observations of the Yorkshireman, sceptical and unforthcoming. Or that when I reached Ireland I was already familiar with much of the literature of the Irish Literary Renaissance and already had, and still have, thousands of lines from Yeats stored in my head. So that I arrived there with a coherent, if romantic, sense of culture and landscape. "We dreamed that a great painter had been born / To cold Clare rock and Galway rock and thorn..."

Anyway, Nev's attention had now fastened on one brief note in the article. There it was, the magical act of naming had been performed: the Poisoned Glen, the Derryveagh Mountains, Donegal. Was it the draw of this strange name? Someone mentioned a garbled legend of a clan feud; someone referred to the genitive form of an Erse word and claimed that it should properly be called the Heavenly Glen: quite recently I learned that a poisonous plant apparently used to grow there, *Euphorbia Hiberna*, Irish Spurge. Or was it that the valley was said to have granite buttresses up to a thousand feet in height and that only two short climbs had so far been recorded?

Easter 1954 and we were there, accompanied by the two girls who've already appeared as hitch-hikers. The village of Dunlewy stands just outside the mouth of the glen on an old road ascending the flank of Errigal. A string of sorry buildings; a post-office-cum-store; a small hotel; and a half-derelict guest-house, the Poisoned Glen House, bearing an old Cyclists' Touring Club badge. Leaving the village we descend a track past the last cottages and look straight into the glen. Isolated and dead central in the foreground stands a church, burned-out later, best not to ask about that. Beyond, to either side, matched shoulders frame the boggy glacial valley. The skyline shows two passes, flanked by worn domes with rocky epaulettes. Beneath that skyline, walling the head in, the big cliffs stare us out.

We didn't get a lot done. We climbed an obvious rib to the left of the central feature, the Castle, and we made an experimental ascent of the heathery right flank of this buttress. I thought we did a climb on the clean little cliff by Ballahageeha Gap, and perhaps took the girls up it a few days later, but that can't be right because it's not confirmed in the record and we wrote the record. We prowled around the bases of the big cliffs and prodded them cautiously. The four of us walked up Errigal to see where we were: to the south the Blue Stacks centred a wilderness of hills; to the west the Donegal Rosses ran out to Aran Island; turning, we looked down on Bloody Foreland and out to Tory Island, standing ten miles off; beyond it the unbroken ocean stretched westward to the Americas and northward to the Arctic. We fell deeply, blindly, helplessly under the spell of Donegal.

These landscapes need their figures. One of the features of British climbing in the fifties, less evident today, was a strong tie with those people of the hills with whom we came into contact. Ronald MacDonald of Glenbrittle, in whose unseaworthy boat and to whose uncertain navigation the climber's life was sometimes ransomed; Ike Myers of Langdale and Daddy Williams of the Nant Ffrancon, in whose barns we slept or in whose fields we camped: these three and others like them can never have known that in every county in England, in a thousand city pubs, their characters, lives and fortunes were repeatedly discussed. They'd achieved a celebrity and are remembered even now with an affection which would have astonished them.

Even those few whose relationships with climbers were sometimes more difficult shared in this renown. The patience of Chris Briggs at the Pen-y-Gwryd, of Wilson Pharoah at the Wastwater, even of Sid Cross at the Old Dungeon Ghyll, was sometimes tested to destruction by the crazy gangs who invaded their premises. They responded according to their natures. Chris Briggs banned the more wayward and added the problem of enforcement; "And a pint for Ginger Woods" always brought him hurrying around to check the Everest Room. Sid Cross outwitted the rowdies or appealed to their better natures, often successfully. Wilson Pharoah, a noted Cumberland wrestler, tossed them easily through the door or in extreme cases cracked an arm or a rib; the injured parties felt privileged and boasted of these manhandlings, they'd fought the champion himself. These three, again, have been subjects of fond reminiscence in some of the remotest places on earth.

Through the comparative infrequency of our visits we didn't achieve many similar intimacies in Ireland. For Neville and myself only Thomas Bodkin, of Glen Inagh in Connemara, held a comparable stature. When Nev's party had first arrived there the old man, emerging from his house in its wasteland of peat, had welcomed them warmly. He'd recited an adapted version of "The Solitude of Alexander Selkirk": "From the centre right down to the sea / I am lord of the fowl and the brute" he declaimed, his large gestures encompassing the glen, the chickens peeping shyly out of his front door, and his sturdy sons.

When, two years later, I reached the glen with Ted Langley, chance guaranteed us a rapturous welcome. A month earlier we'd watched the Grand National at Aintree, the only racing event I've ever attended. (In the past week, in Kerry, we'd competed against a dozen Irish climbers in a race on hired ponies to the summit of the Gap of Dunloe: the only time I've ever ridden a horse.) Now it turned out that one of the sons, seen at a distance of a quarter-mile propped dazed against his peat-spade, had won first prize in the Irish Sweepstake. Eleven thousand pounds: a huge sum of money at that time. We were pressed again and again to describe both race and horse, tasks for which I had no vocabulary. "A fine horse, a fine horse," the family kept declaring. On the second evening neighbours from miles away were summoned and tea, bread and butter were served while we were questioned again. Then everyone else moved chairs back to the three walls of the bare, concrete-floored room and upright chairs for Langley and myself were placed centrally, facing the fire. Bodkin stood in front of us, back to the fire, and proceeded to put riddles to us. We couldn't solve a single one. We couldn't even understand the answers when they were explained to us. The audience chuckled with delight at the dull-wittedness of the young Englishmen. A few years later I saw that a two-storey concrete house, no fence, no garden, had risen from the bogs a couple of hundred yards from the cottage of Thomas Bodkin.

Donegal gave something else, it was a country of strange encounters, a land of "I met a man on the road who said..." We were hitch-hiking, there seemed to be no tourists, only local people about their business. One night Neville and I camped on a headland outside Dunfanaghy. A voice addressed us from the darkness as we brewed up. We unzipped the door and a policeman poked his head inside, examining us in silence for a long moment. "There is no cause for alarm," he said slowly, "no cause at all. You were seen passing by and some of the villagers were a bit worried." Mysteriously, he added, "They thought you might be the queer people." He looked around the tent in surprise. "And you carry your little house on your back like a snail!" he said. He stared at the roaring primus stove: "And you have your own little fire!"

In the store in Dunlewy, on our first visit, we were told that we'd get dairy produce from the cottagers and for a couple of days we bought milk, eggs and butter wherever they could be spared. Then, one morning, payment was refused. It was Easter, we must take what we needed. To our unease the gifts continued for four days before these poor people would touch money again. Some nights we walked up to the Poisoned Glen House and had a pot of tea, bread and butter, while the aged proprietress, Biddy McClafferty, began to bake us a loaf. Having arranged this on a griddle above the peat fire she'd bring out an accordion and play to us. The girls knew a few of the melodies and they sang well, which greatly pleased her. At intervals she'd break off to examine the progress of the bread. Finally she'd pronounce it ready but would instantly resume playing. At around midnight she'd suddenly fall asleep in her chair and we'd tiptoe out of the lantern-lit room. Can that Ireland and can those people be found today?

Five Aprils later I was still around. Now the valley offered another twenty climbs and the three big buttresses had been breached. We'd approached them with circumspection. When Neville and I climbed Kon-tiki on the five-hundred-foot West Buttress, we'd felt we were into something serious and we'd used alpine tactics. By rope tricks, tension moves, variations on a theme of Dulfer, I'd reached the middle of the cliff and as I brought Nev across I was working out how to get back. If we had an accident or got ourselves cragfast, what next? We'd never seen a single walker in the glen. There were a half dozen climbers in Ireland who could have got to us, given time; they were in Dublin, a full day's drive away, and they didn't know we were in Ireland. There were a fair number of climbers in Britain who could handle a rescue but they were two or three days away and none had climbed in this country.

Allan Austin was amongst those who'd listened to our accounts of Kon-tiki and he'd taken his own team out. They'd forced a brilliant line, Nightshade, straight through the central overhangs of the West Buttress to join the finishing pitches of our route. I noted that the apostle of purity had permitted the placing of at least eight pegs on this ascent. Allan's team had also taken a step into the future by making the first route on Bearnas Buttress, which nears a thousand feet in height. Their line took a natural weakness but it mounted the buttress from its flank and it didn't get round to the final central corners. The challenge rested.

At Easter 1959 I had the company of three strong-minded individualists, Geoff Sutton, Eric Langmuir and Andrew Maxfield. The four of us had been, or were, or would one day be associated with White Hall, Derbyshire's Outdoor Centre at Buxton, Max and myself on the staff, Geoff and Eric as Principals. In passing, the post of Principal at White Hall was for many years restricted to former Presidents of the Cambridge University Mountaineering Club.

For this week Bearnas Buttress was at the top of the agenda. The plan was simply to find the easiest way up the cliff. The foot of the buttress presents a clean and holdless slab two hundred feet high and capped by a long unbroken overlap. It's rather like the aprons of Yosemite. A thin grass-filled crack divides it magnificently but appears to fade out before the overlap. Something for the future. Above the slab there's a region of grassy fields and above these there's a steep headwall showing a couple of weaknesses.

We by-passed the slab barrier on the right. This reduced us, for several pitches, to linking stair-carpets of grass with interruptions of perfect rock. While clawing my way up one of these sections I looked down to see, off my line of ascent but perhaps dislodged by the rope, a nine-inch block of rock tumble out of the grass and bound down towards the others, huddled together on a ledge. As it reached them Eric made a decisive and surprising move, coolly and deliberately shouldering it aside. We continued up and across until we found ourselves at the felt centre of the cliff. Above and to either side the headwall hung over us but an exit offered itself, a fine corner crack which was unfortunately stuffed with grass. It was late in the day and we redescended some distance, avoiding the initial pitches with a long abseil into the flanking gully.

A schism became evident in the party that night. I wanted to get back on the buttress first thing in the morning. Max had found it richly amusing and was equally keen to resume. Eric now admitted that the falling rock had had more mass than he'd anticipated. He was sure that nothing was broken but he was unable to raise his arm above shoulder level. However, he was willing to come along as backup. Geoff, who exercised a benevolent authority over all of us, was ordinarily the most outgoing and cheerful of companions, generous and thoughtful; except that on occasions made unnerving by their rarity he was subject to silent rages at the fecklessness of his assistants and then he scared us. Now he announced that he wouldn't be joining us and offered polite and transparently false excuses. This abstention subsequently drew an impertinent comment ("Achilles sulking in his tents") from Joss Lynam, the doyen of Irish climbing from that day to this and the chronicler to whom all activity in Ireland was reported. What was it? That Geoff didn't care for insecure grass? Or for the generalship of leaders around whom the cliff fell apart? Or for something I was too obtuse to notice?

Laboriously, I cleaned out the corner crack, first with peg protection and then on aid until I felt my time was up. Max took over and continued until an escaping traverse threw him off. I resumed and succeeded, re-entering the main weakness by a steep little slab. Then, by a chimney and a grassy ramp we reached the summit. It had felt like the Mont Blanc of Donegal so we called it Route Major. True, a half of the ascent had been on grass; true, we'd avoided the lower apron of the cliff; but we'd found what was possibly the easiest line of ascent and we'd established a central exit which might well collect a number of subsequent climbs.

The problem with the buttress was clear. The rock itself was superb. It reminded me of the Rosa Pinnacle in Arran and Eric told us that it seemed to be identical with that of the Trilleachan Slabs in Glen Etive, of which he'd been one of the original explorers. Bearnas Buttress, in fact, offered more positive weaknesses but these were often encumbered with vegetation. I didn't see that as a difficulty. I was sure that one day the glen would attract many climbers and that, with traffic, these routes would clean up to give climbs as good as anything in Britain. I overlooked one circumstance. As it happened most of our visits had been or would be at Easter or in the spring. We almost always had good weather, sometimes heatwaves, perhaps just a lucky run. A number of summer visitors came to experience torrential rains or insufferable clouds of midges and retreated in dismay.

Max had clearly enjoyed this ascent. Without permission or notification he was back within ten weeks. Significantly he took as supporter a Derbyshire caver, a man who didn't mind dirt on his hands. Going for the big prize they found a point of attack at the foot of the buttress and to the left of the apron. This line started promisingly but detail then confused them and they arrived at the wrong side of the traverse of Route Major. From there it seemed more logical to escape up the walls of the right flank.

Six weeks later I was back with Neville. This time we were joined by Vivian Stevenson, one of Nev's original Irish party, now Lt. V.N. Stevenson, R.M. The lieutenant had planned his assault on the Glen with prudence, surrounding himself with an escort of three instructors from the Cliff Assault Wing. Two of these were competent and the third was the more than competent Zeke Deacon. For most of this week civilians and military operated independently. Perhaps the civilians were rather more successful though the military were to win significant victories in Wicklow after fighting rearguard actions out of the west. We came down from one of our climbs to find the little patrol hopelessly bogged down in the swamps of the glen. Vivian had fallen in attempting Nightshade and had abseiled off but found himself unable to walk. Putting his hat on, Lt. Stevenson had ordered his NCOs to carry him back to headquarters but they'd gone about this ineptly and were temporarily exhausted. We showed them how to handle their thirteen-stone leader.

The problem stood: the Direct. The solution was simple, link the start of the Maxfield-Fryer Route with the finish of Route Major. Recovering, Vivian joined us for this attempt. We were interested to see that Max had cleaned out the lower pitches of his climb, revealing clean cracks in perfect granite. We continued, taking what seemed a logical line. And finally, in the evening, we realised that we were too far to the left. To our anguish we saw that we were standing beneath the crux of Allan's original route, four pitches still to go. The Roundheads had placed pegs while cleaning up this pitch and at this point a crisis and a shambles ensued. Quite suddenly the sky darkened and fell upon us and our skins were black with midges. I simply couldn't spare my hands long enough to concentrate on the hard moves. After two brief attempts I had to place a couple of aid pegs, finishing driving them with one hand while brushing my face in the crook of the other elbow.

It was still very warm. We ran down the glen in torment, slapping and smearing at faces, necks, wrists and shins, suffering more intense attacks whenever we slackened pace. Without pausing to eat we locked ourselves into the Marines' car and drove hastily to the nearest pub at Bunbeg. Now if you don't know this, the area around Dublin where English Law had once been imposed with comparative success was known as The Pale. The rest of Ireland was and perhaps still is Beyond the Pale and in 1959 the licensed hours for drinking were ten in the morning to ten at night; however, bona fide travellers might possibly be served until midnight. It was now five to ten and as I hurried through the door I got ready to assert my bona fides. The barman was briefly absent but the bar was supporting a single drinker, or drunk. "What time's closing time?" I asked him with the abruptness of desperation. He considered the question carefully from several sides as if there were a trick in it before offering an opinion: "About September." It was soon made clear that he was right.

A bit of time passed, ten years. And now I was with Maureen and Jo and Jim Williams, and this time Jim and I nearly pulled it off, connecting with the exit of Route Major. The weather broke while we were trying to suppress the feeling that the climb deserved full independence. It took the natural weaknesses, yes. But the arête to the right of the crux promised a brilliant pitch and above that a direct finish was available.

Another two years and the four of us returned. This time Max was to join us. Maureen and I had a tent, Jo and Jim were sleeping in their camper. We awoke the first morning to find that Max had arrived early and on foot: donkey jacket, jeans, old boots, no socks, ragged holdall. Resourceful as always, he'd foraged for fuel and lit a roaring fire. In it he was melting down the bottles thrown aside by previous campers and would later, in his capacity of Art Lecturer, examine and grade the attractive and colourful shapes for aesthetic values. The black thing on top of the fire was the brand-new aluminium kettle Jo had chanced to leave outside their vehicle. I decided to stand clear while that was sorted out. We picked an oddment for the first day and my companions proved once again that disabilities can be overcome; Max was short of a thumb, Jim a finger-joint.

There'd been a welcome change in Dunlewy since our last visit. For some years the settlement had had a youth hostel and now it had a bar as well. We went in to find it packed with a noisy young crowd swallowing Guinness at a rate which would have led to the suicides of English hostel wardens. Also, wedged unrecognised in a corner, incongruously smart and colourful in the immaculate dress uniforms of a recent Himalayan expedition, we discovered the bearded figures of Chris Bonington and Nick Estcourt. They'd been to look at Slieve League, misled by the time-honoured Irish tradition of claiming the huge seaward slope of the mountain as a cliff. They'd no information on the glen and in order to keep them well away from the great lines we offered them a nice possibility.

On the left side of Bearnas Buttress there's a stupendous clean-walled corner in which, unfortunately, we'd never seen the crack dry out. One of the first Irish visitors had named it Obituary Corner. Taking the cue, I'd christened its unclimbed right arête Obituary Column and Max had followed it to a fall a couple of years before. Now we handed it over to Chris and Nick who bypassed the move that had stopped Max. In the meantime, close by, we tried the conspicuous Wiggly Crack, hard to protect, and also decided to outflank it.

It was time to return to the Direct and eventually we found ourselves at the ancient anchor peg I'd placed some twelve years earlier. And now we succeeded in climbing the nose, Max settling it with a series of bold moves. The crack leading into the continuation corner was wet and slimy and it was as late as it always was, so we exited by the final gangway of

Route Major. Through traffic or by avalanche this had now lost its hundred-foot grass strip.

Chris and Nick had planned to stop off at Fairhead on the way home. They'd be returning by a northern ferry, more convenient for Max, and he decided to change sides. I was never to see him again. For that matter, I wouldn't be meeting Nick Estcourt many more times.

The last crack still hung over us. We gave it two days to dry out and in sunshine belayed beneath it, say eight hundred feet up the buttress. It was still oozing, a brief obstacle barring access to an easy grass corner. It offered perfect jams, impossibly lubricated. It was the last day of the holiday and, resolution collapsing, I placed a peg to get onto the grass. It was, in fact, the last day I spent in the glen, though I see it with the inward eye and still hope to return.

In an article in the Irish Mountaineering Club Journal in the late fifties, Brighid Hardiman wrote about an arrival and a farewell in Connemara. "The mountains were quiet and unchanged, affected neither by our coming nor our going and I wished that there were some part of them that would miss us as we would miss them. But they were the ones who laid claim and remained untouched...."

What did I have to show for my years in the glen? Neville and I had three neat clean little climbs on Ballaghageeha Buttress. With various companions I'd done various lines on Creaghnambrack. I'd followed Frank and Betty up a fine route, Ulysses, on the Castle. With others I'd made a number of vegetation-encumbered excursions on the bigger cliffs and some of these followed good natural features. With Nev I'd done Kon-tiki and though this has now been straightened and freed the original line probably remains the easiest way up the West Buttress. With Max and Eric I'd made what may still be the ordinary route on Bearnas Buttress and with Jim and Max I'd worked out the Direct, though this cliff is big enough to offer other Directs or Superdirects. Yet all these climbs were to some extent only a groundwork for the finer, cleaner, more dramatic possibilities with which, at the very first glance, the valley had teased us.

David Roberts concluded an essay on mountaineering in Alaska by describing the disturbing dreams his climbs there had excited. His dream mountains weren't perfect copies of the mountains he knew and his efforts were always frustrated. On a few occasions in recent years I had curiously similar dreams. The valley of those dreams bore a confused resemblance to the Poisoned Glen but from the structure and material of the cliffs, from the haunting sense of unrealised possibilities, and from the strong affirmation the place aroused in me, I understood clearly that it stood for the glen. And beyond that valley, in those dreams, in a west impossibly displaced, there was another area we hadn't yet looked at. And beyond that ...

PANTHEON

What is tourism? Serious mountaineering — in passion, in risk, in rewards, in its colossal calls on body, nerve and judgement — seems a class apart. Yet it's nowhere possible to draw a clear line between the more and the less serious forms of the enterprise. Nor, I think, can we distinguish the activity in kind from some forms of special interest travel; or claim, where it involves substantial journeys, that it causes less environmental damage; or assert that it never contributes to cultural degradation. Joe Simpson has described himself, and by extension the high-altitude mountaineer, as a credit card adventurer. The popularisation of the eight-thousand-metre peaks has kept perfect pace with the development of Mediterranean resorts. Retrospectively, then, I'm proposing Reinhold Messner as the world's top tourist for the nineteen-eighties.

I'm certainly a tourist. If the roads are quiet I find shameless enjoyment in driving a car through interesting landscapes. (Thinking of the car as an agent of liberty, ignoring its absolute destructiveness of town and country.) I find some cities as fascinating as mountains. It's not just the nightlife or the foreign food, I like streets and atmosphere. Buildings always catch my attention though I'm usually drawn more by the domestic and vernacular than by the public or monumental. (I never return from a journey unattended by impatience to resume work on the New Jerusalem on a hillside near Llanrwst.) I've nothing against wild beaches,

162

even if modestly popular. I'm captivated by the music of other languages. I'm a student of appearances with a special interest in the women of other nations and races. (Sometimes my companion kicks my ankle.) And in memory every long journey has a distinct emotional resonance.

One year the idea came to me that I'd like to visit Istanbul. Let's say this might be 1970. Stamboul, Constantinople, Byzantium: through recorded history its various names have held exotic promises. And in fact the Blue Mosque alone was worth the journey, the memory of its interior still soothes me, its miraculous spaces, shafts of light and caves of shadow, structures and patterns, as restful as a clearing in a great forest. Of course, we were lucky, the place was almost empty, all voices hushed in a velvet silence.

In making an extended journey by road, one of the tricks is to pay particular attention to the homeward route. A holiday is diminished if so much time is spent at the main objective that the drive back becomes a gruelling race, an endurance test needing a day or two of convalescence afterwards. Important, then, to fix on a novelty fairly close to the end of the return so that a mood of anticipation is conserved. It might even be a so-far-unvisited part of the south of England.

Similarly one has to find a number of good overnight stops on a long drive. Some will stand out as obvious but others must be left to chance. These may turn out badly on occasion but in retrospect they'll put the rest of the trip into better perspective. I recall a disenchanting night exploring soiled roadside lay-byes with Maureen and the Mansells in search of a clean bivouac site. This was somewhere north-west of Geneva in those rolling mysterious wooded hills known ever since as the Forest of Durex. Frustratingly, I've never kept records of routes across Europe and can't fill in some gaps with any certainty now. However, I think it was on the road to Istanbul that we struck lucky the first night by pulling in at Limburg; stepping in a few strides straight into the Middle Ages, narrow half-lit streets of timber-framed buildings carved with ferocious grotesques.

I always try to combine business with pleasure so our route had to take in mountain areas and the first of these would be the Kaisergebirge. I knew that Tony Moulam would be out there with Nick Longland. At that time I was climbing with Tony fairly regularly, each assisting the other with guidebook work. The previous summer we'd had a fortnight in the Bregaglia. That holiday had been rather unproductive for reasons outside our control, though we'd visited secondary summits almost every day. Our final ascent had been of a route on Piz Morteratsch, giving us a tantalising head-on view of the Biancograt, one of the most beautiful snow ridges in the Alps: and nothing we could do about it. Now, I hoped, I'd join the Moulam and Longland party for something more satisfying in these mountains I knew only by reputation.

We located our friends at a campsite in St. Johann. The weather hadn't been good, rain was now driving down, and having been there for some time already they'd decided to cut their losses and use this bad day to get back to the Western Alps. In twenty-four hours we were on our own again and the following morning woke to unclouded skies. Maureen had no inclination for serious routes in the Alps so I looked at map and guidebook for an attractive hill walk. Immediately the Goinger Halt proposed itself, actually the second highest summit in the group but accessible to the scrambler by an intriguing approach.

The next day found us walking the long road up the Kaiserbachtal. Traffic was restricted to residents but without solicitation a pleasant old lady stopped and insisted in wedging our rucksacks into a car already bulging with provisions. She'd drop them off at the Gasthof at Griesener Alp, not far short of the steep path zig-zagging up to the col. Unladen, the road free of vehicles and walkers, we enjoyed the approach. On the final ascent we met only a path restorer attended by what proved to be a polar-bear-sized St. Bernard. This beast had been baying dolefully in our direction for the half hour since it had noticed our approach but proved on acquaintance to be without the slightest malice. I studied the work of the very old man with interest and admiration since some of the most insensitive path restoration work in the world was beginning to appear at that time in the Snowdonia National Park.

The Stripsenjochhütte proved to be the biggest alpine refuge I'd ever visited, having the appearance of a large hotel. Surprisingly, it was thronged with walkers who'd presumably approached this famous saddle by the long route through the Kaisertal from Kufstein. There was little space to spare on the long shelves of matratzenlager. Where to lie became increasingly difficult as the night wore on since the dormitory happened to contain the loudest snorer in my experience. Some people just sat up and listened open-mouthed or laughing. Some threw pillows, some threw boots, and others, I think, put on boots and kicked him; after an apology, within a few minutes he'd nod off and resume. Mostly, people moved to the further corners of the room and sat huddled in promiscuous heaps, aiming simply to see out the night. One party, by torchlight, began to play cards. When morning came most of us moved out and sat haggard-eyed in chairs on the terrace, warming ourselves in the first rays of the sun. It had felt like a bad bivouac.

Our route to the Ellmauer Tor and Goinger Halt summits lay up the

Steinerne Rinne: the stony gully; the rocky gutter, runnel, rift. After redescending some distance from the col the steep cliff barring access is easily overcome. The natural route up this obstruction has been pedestrianised with hacked steps and steel cables linking the ledge systems and weaknesses. A via ferrata, almost, a little outside the limits of its natural range. This access behind us we found ourselves in an impressive canyon inclined at an angle of thirty degrees or so. Huge towers of limestone, the Fleischbank, the Predigstuhl, stood in continuous walls, not a quarter-mile apart. The floor, often planed bedrock with a boilerplate appearance, was littered with debris ranging up to colossal blocks. A few grass carpets lay scattered about. The whole feature seemed to be sculpted by ice rather than water, lifting to either side of the fall-line in concave slopes to grade smoothly into the walls. It brought to mind the swept valley of the English craftsman slater.

We'd barely moved up three or four hundred feet when I heard, striking a half-mile further up the ravine, the sound of heavy stonefall. Once this signal has been heard for real in the Alps, the synapses are organised for the rest of one's life. Doubting that anything would funnel so far down we nevertheless moved hastily into the shelter of a convenient boulder. Silence. Another twenty seconds and the air around us was dense with projectiles following precisely the angle of the bed to glide out, like flocks of birds, over the cliff beneath us. The place was a death trap. I had a helmet in my sack, Maureen had nothing. She wouldn't wear it, I won't say why, so I left it packed and we advanced alertly up the couloir like infantrymen, plotting a route from cover to cover, ears straining, eyes roving.

At the foot of the subwall we'd noticed a number of memorial plaques but I'd hardly glanced at these. Now, on the side of a giant boulder, another caught my eye. It remembered Walter Glass, a twenty-year-old student from Munich. Beneath these particulars was a curt inscription which still sounds in my head. In part this is because I'd forgotten most of the German I once knew and on that day I misread it: "Unlucky in the Stony Gully."

Verunglückt in Steinerne Rinne. This epitaph, so laconic, so fatalistic, haunted me for years. But in the back of my mind the word for unlucky kept coming up: unglücklich. Finally I checked and saw that the expression simply meant "met with an accident". Still, it had a Teutonic terseness and finality.

From one of the twin Goinger Halt summits, in the warm sunshine, we were able to admire the huge towers at our leisure. It was fairly unusual for me to find myself in mountains to which my brother had preceded me. But then he'd been to Skye first, while I was in Greece, and he'd been to Ireland before me. More recently he'd visited these mountains.

My thoughts went back to that year and to the Western Alps. A year of epic, comedy and tragedy. I'd joined Nev and Graham Sadler on the traverse of the Grépon. After passing the North Summit I'd abseiled first from the Grande Gendarme, leaving my sack in case the unseen swing to the gap were to prove awkward. Nev had then clipped two of our three sacks together and had started to lower them; but in the meantime another party had arrived and they'd cast their rappel ropes inside ours. As I hauled the sacks round from the far side of the nose these ropes somehow fouled our sleeveless snaplink and, as sudden and shocking as the fall of a climber, I saw the two sacks, still clipped together, sail out over the Mer de Glace face. I leaned out. They struck the rock once, at four hundred feet, then shot out again for a further long fall, leaving my field of view.

It had been hard to accommodate ourselves instantly to this startling change of fortune. At one moment we'd been on the top, well equipped, making good time for a party of three; at the next, two of us were without anoraks, gloves, food, axes or crampons. Beneath the south ridge there was the whole of the Nantillons glacier to descend.

After that climb I'd had to return home. Nev and Graham were out for a longer spell and their thoughts turned to recovering the sacks. Almost immediately they chanced to meet Nat Allen who'd just climbed the classic East Face route and had noticed an object jammed in a chimney some hundreds of feet to the right of the climb. Their first attempt had been foiled in a bad storm and a desperate retreat had ended in pure farce. In the morning, on descending the cliff on which the Refuge d'Envers des Aiguilles is perched, they'd been obliged to jump down across the schrund onto the ice. Returning in darkness and torrential rain, wet to the skin, they couldn't reverse this leap. But Nev had discovered a narrow tongue of ice running up the cliff straight towards the refuge. On climbing this thin sliver he'd found that it terminated against the actual wall of the building with the terrace still several feet to one side. He'd had no alternative but to traverse by pegging across the masonry itself. During this operation the caped guardien had emerged, shone a light from the terrace, and with a cry of terminal despair ("Aaaah! les Anglais!"), had hurried back inside.

On a second attempt they'd succeeded in making the traverse from the East Face Route to the gear. They'd been amazed to find the two quite heavy sacks suspended from my wooden-shafted axe, which was bridged across the chimney wall to wall. After a fall of seven or eight hundred feet it was only slightly sprung and I use it still. Retracing the traverse they'd continued up the East Face to reach the summit a second time and there they encountered a French party in difficulties through having had to abandon a jammed rope. Nev and Graham were able to spare them one and had continued down the normal descent. After some hundreds of feet they heard rockfall and unintelligible shouts. A long way down the glacier they were appalled to come across the unroped body of one of the men they'd been talking to only two hours earlier. He'd fallen nearly two thousand feet. Having seen enough of Chamonix for one year they'd moved on to the Wilde Kaiser. A year or so later Graham and a companion had disappeared on an attempt on Rondoy in the Peruvian Andes.

From the Goinger Halt, on this pacific afternoon, I could see one of the lines they'd climbed, the Südöstweg on the Fleishbank. The Butcher's Shop, the Shambles. My feelings about being here as walker rather than as climber were confused. The great towers sang like sirens, my eye traced and linked weaknesses, my muscles cried out to wrestle rock. I tried to count the compensations. I wasn't going to die on this trip. I'd be spared the day-long drain on vigilance high mountain routes always impose. And we were headed further, for the warm south.

Twenty years ago the autoput of Yugoslavia was surely the worst arterial road in Europe. It called itself a motorway but was simply an undivided, deeply cratered two-lane concrete highway, extending several hundred miles. It was open to horsedrawn traffic and sometimes two convoys fifty strong, each led by a horse and cart, the vehicles in danger of boiling in the hot sun, would pass each other at funereal pace. The drivers couldn't meet each other's eyes. Most of the tourists on this road were Germans and in this land of bandits and veteran partisans they seemed fearful of their safety at night. They slept in their cars on roadside waste ground and, prior to locking selves and possessions in, formed up the vehicles tightly nose to tail in disciplined laagers of fifteen to twenty wagons. This endurance test over, we were in Northern Greece.

Pantheon, also known as Mytikas, is the principal summit of Olympos, Mt. Olympus if you like. The second summit is Skolio. The third is Stefani, also known as Thronos Dios. The three tops, standing at about ten thousand feet, differ in height by less than thirty feet. Chains of subsidiary summits run out generally to the north-east, this aspect offering scrambling approaches. To the west the mountain presents high limestone escarpments giving lengthy rock climbs.

We camped by the sea somewhere near Katerini and on our second evening found ourselves watching a double volta in Litochoron at the mouth of the Mavrolongos valley. I'd overdosed on sun after swimming and I was shivering violently over my drinks at a pavement cafe as the strange ritual proceeded. I'd never seen anything quite like it in Athens. The drumbeat in my head seemed to echo the suppressed excitement of the parade as the groups marched and countermarched, the young men and the chaperoned girls exchanging information in split-second flashes of the eyes.

As with other high hills near warm seas, it's best to climb Olympos with a very early start in order to get the dawn views before the haze builds up. It was our plan to do it directly from the roadhead but it seemed sensible to check the beginning of the approach in case the path through the forest were to prove confusing in darkness. The next day then, about midday, we drove to Litochoron again and continued to the road terminus. There were no buildings here and we wondered a little about the security of the car as we set off up the only obvious track.

From the very first steps this route, revealing itself only a little at a time, was unremitting in its invitation. It led us upward through a deliciously cool broad-leaved forest. In my memory this was, or somehow became, a beechwood. Now I'm in confusion; consulting a guidebook I see chestnuts and planes listed as dominant in the lower woodlands of these mountain valleys. The path led enticingly left and right until, quite suddenly, an altitude zonation substituted conifers. Above these again, beyond a well-defined timberline, the mountain opened out. (And here we experienced that manumission of the spirit Arne Naess describes in his remarkable essay, "Metaphysics of the Tree Line".) Yet even here the slopes were strewn with monstrous fallen pines. We were at the scene of some natural catastrophe of which the cause was no longer obvious. For every theory I was able to produce, an unassailable objection offered itself. With the way upward clear we paused to consider the route ahead.

We were using the most interesting map I've ever consulted, a small photocopy supplied by Mike Dixon, who'd been here some years previously. The topography was shown by a hachuring so crude that the impression given was that of a Rorschach ink blot test, open to wild interpretations. A very few features were named in badly printed lower case Cyrillic script. However, the path was plain enough. We were moving quickly. The afternoon was so pleasant, the slopes above so attractive. that we decided to go as far as the Hellenic Alpine Club refuge, where with luck we could buy a drink.

The building, a perfect replica of the smaller refuge of the Western

Alps, surprised me. Somehow I'd expected something more ethnic. The guardian lived up to Mike's description. Tall, striking in appearance, assured and amiable in manner, it was a pleasure to talk to him. He was a professional climbing guide and he asked our plans. We explained that we'd been reconnoitring and would make the ascent from the valley very early next morning. "You're halfway there," he said. "Why do it twice? You can stay here." I said that I'd be worried about leaving the car unattended overnight. "Your car will be okay. No-one would think of touching it." I said that we had no food. "We can provide simple dishes. We have beer and wine. It is not expensive." I said that we had no sleeping bags or warm clothing. "We have blankets. Take a look at the fire inside." All this encouragement was delivered with amused and teasing smiles and with an irresistible charm.

Refuge A on Olympus — there are five or more huts serving different approaches — seemed a cosy place. When we entered, the most impressive wood fire I've ever seen was already burning in the open hearth of the common room. It consisted simply of three great rounds of wood, obviously cut from one of the thousands of stricken trees. Two of these extended drums lay side to side, the third was nested in the groove between them. In a wide range of intense pure colours, long steady jets of flame, resin-fuelled, stood out in all directions. At this altitude it was already becoming cold in the late afternoon but through a long evening no-one was able to sit near the conflagration. When we left, the following afternoon, the same three logs, now shrunken to greying ghosts, were still balanced in the same position and still emitting warmth.

In the closed society of the alpine refuge we look at other visitors with interest. What manner of man is this? The stage is a small one and national characteristics seem exaggerated. We had a party of Greeks and a party of Germans for company. Each gave a small problem. A highly compatible Greek with whom we had a long and sympathetic conversation changed his tune abruptly and reprimanded me angrily when I chanced to reveal when and why I'd last been in his country. I explained and excused myself — I was nineteen, I was a conscript, I knew nothing — and he was mollified so that our talk recovered its friendly tone.

The Germans, mostly harmless young people, included a tiresome middle-aged man. Back turned to us, he made loud interjections from time to time in the most impeccable upper-class English. He said that what he would most enjoy at this moment would be a cup of tea. Extending his little finger as he raised his glass of wine he said that everyone simply has to agree that tea is the most refreshing of all drinks.

He said that our dear Queen drank very little else. Between these and similar remarks he continued in German, raising gales of laughter from his younger friends. They were all quite drunk. Some brief retorts in German came into my head but, knowing I couldn't sustain a conversation, I had to adopt the manner of my English ancestors and treat foreigners as invisible.

Years earlier, I'd looked at Olympos from a troopship, its snows obscurely visible behind Turneresque amassments of cloud. Years later, I was to see it from a charter flight, detailed spiny ridges rising again from cloud and looking more substantial and particular than mountains often appear from jet cruising height. Each time it projected a strong air of mystery and hauteur. On the morning of our ascent it held no such reserve. It gave us, simply, a perfect hill walk. At eight o'clock or so we were on the summit, which we had to ourselves, with no sign that the Greeks and Germans had even risen yet. The first ascent of the mountain wasn't claimed until 1913 but perhaps it has the longest climbing history of any peak on earth. Opposite us, within shouting distance almost, stood Thronos Dios. Before the first man was born the Titans had sieged that summit, the first expedition in written record. On the Matterhorn, Whymper had thrown down rocks to advertise his victory to Carrel's team; on Thronos Dios, Zeus had cast thunderbolts to turn the usurpers back.

Looking at that companion summit now, I was surprised to notice a figure descending from it and heading rapidly towards a distant ridge. We weren't quite alone after all. In a tin box I found a summit book and opened it to write our names. Now I saw that we weren't even the first on the top that day. Someone had been here before us and he'd even logged the time, an hour earlier. His home town was a surprise, Abergavenny. It seemed incongruous and entertaining. We relaxed in the sun and a half-hour later, dishevelled, sweating and gasping, from an unexpected direction another Welshman arrived. On establishing our nationality he asked if we'd seen a solo walker. We're supposed to be meeting here, he said, there are some others coming up but we all took different ways. I pointed out the man from Abergavenny, a distant speck travelling at high speed towards Profitis Ilias. Nobody was going to catch him that day.

We resumed our journey. We by-passed Mount Athos, since the monks still exclude all women from the promontory. We stopped at Kavalla. At that time a group of young Nottingham climbers were making trips to mountains in North Africa and Asia Minor on the slenderest resources. Every year we have a Poor Man's Grand Tour, Ray Gilles had told me, and Doug Scott had mentioned an intriguing feature of these enterprises. An attractive assembly point towards the further end of the journey would be agreed upon and each participant would make his way there independently by whatever means he could afford. Several days were set aside for this assembly and with half the journey over people would have stories to tell already. Good psychology. Doug had mentioned Kavalla and above our camp site there, on some small overhanging rocks, I noticed a couple of old slings dangling from a roof crack. Probably there's hardly an outcrop beside any main route through Europe that hasn't been bouldered at some time by passing British climbers.

At the Turkish border the man in front of us produced a Nepalese passport. "Nepal, Nepal, where the fuck Nepal?" the obstreperous border guard roared out in English. "Napoli, you from Napoli?" "No Napoli, I Nepali," the traveller replied stiffly, with wounded dignity. Then we were in Turkey, a golden oriole flashed across the road and we overtook our first camel. I stole a pebble from the shore of the Sea of Marmara. The belly dancers of Istanbul were unsettling, though not quite so transfixing as those of Tangier.

The voyage home was full of interest too. At the Bulgarian frontier post the photographs of a hundred wanted men were on display. Nearly all of these moustachioed dissidents or villains bore a startling resemblance to my associate Dave Nicol. A dozen or so had been crossed out with a red felt pen. Yet we saw great murals in the style of Diego Rivera on some of the factories and larger buildings, several proclaiming in English "No More War". We ignored a tempting sign for the Vale of Attar but spent an unplanned night in the country; the Bulgars were imposing, on those Philistines who chose to drive straight through, a tariff greater than the cost of a night in a comfortable hotel. In Austria we climbed a lonely and beautiful hill somewhere above the Rosenthal. Without a map then, I'll never now learn its name.

The English speaker abroad has one frustrating problem. Almost everywhere he goes he'll find someone who has perfect English. This gives him a sense of cultural backwardness. It's quite unfair, since the speaker of any other language simply learns English and gains access on equal terms to most of the world. We've no such easy choice. Whatever we learn will probably be useful in only a single linguistic block and we'd need a half dozen languages to open up so wide a field as English.

The only consolation we get is the cheap amusement to be drawn from mistranslation. Once, looking down the menu posted outside a restaurant on Thira, I found Stuffed Boot on offer. I was anxious to try it, for the experience, but Maureen flatly refused and said we ought to look next door. There, at the top of the list, was Smooth Fried Hound. I was puzzled until I looked through the French and German columns and realised that the translators had been most at home in the last. Boot is German for boat and the dish was stuffed aubergines. The fried hound was dogfish. On our return now, through Germany, we pulled into a campsite with a amazing information board from which I recall only the opening sentence: "We greet you wellkom in the lovely place of Murg."

The final drive to Holland finished very late at night and Maureen fell asleep. For hours, it seemed, I found myself following empty secondary roads through a mysterious, slightly undulating countryside. Hardly a house in the villages still showed lights. Somewhat tired, I kept my eyes open for the name-boards of these small settlements, trying to chart our progress against the map in my head. The rivers were also signed, a practice I've always approved. Crossing a named river seems a far more significant moment than passing through a town. On the lower ground all these river crossings were presaged that night by eerie drifts of mist, enforcing modest speeds.

Abruptly, descending a wooded slope, I came into a bank of fog so thick that I was obliged to crawl forward at walking pace. Watching the edge of the road in anticipation of a constriction at the bridge I caught sight of a sign and had to back up and swing the car a little to read it: Neanderthal. I'd never known exactly where it was. The atmosphere had a Gothic chilliness, suggesting endings as well as origins. Cheeringly, an hour or two later, we were on a camp site in brightly lit Amsterdam where, the next morning, I found myself appointed technical advisor to young English flower children who were trying to pitch their newly purchased bivi-tents upside down or inside out. The tour, the holiday, was almost over.

Cavall Bernat from the north-east

EL CAVALL BERNAT

I reached the Cavall Bernat a bit at a time. Years earlier, I'd admired some rocky hills whilst driving down the coast of Spain. On returning home I'd identified them, the Sierra Aitana. At a later date there'd been a far-sighted but premature attempt by a holiday tour operator to promote the area for off-season climbing breaks. At just that time Dave Nicol had joined the staff of the Mountain Centre at which I was working and our superiors, impressed by his Patagonian exploits, had immediately requested that he organise a proper expedition and teach the whole of his skills to a party of West Midland youngsters. They realised this couldn't be done in a week — how about four weeks? Dave, knowing a bit more than our superiors about the hazards of icy mountains and also, maybe, a bit more about both sides of young people, had informed them that some little-known hills in Spain near a place called Benidorm would offer a suitable challenge. At the very last moment I'd found myself conscripted into the party in the capacities of driver, mountain guide, and insurance man.

From the resorts of Benidorm and Villajoyosa the Campana dominates everything, its steep rock sentinel, the Cerro Puig Campana, buttressing it like a poor dry Dru against an arid worn-down Verte. A group of us enjoyed a spaced-out bivouac on the summit of the Campana with sunset separating range beyond range of empty hills to the west, then

Benidorm glittering beneath us like New York while a pale lightning flickered over our heads, then sunrise laying out the placid Mediterranean to the east. We'd climbed a selection of the main summits and ridges in the area. We'd followed Dave on the first ascent of a short but delightful gorge, that of the Rio Bolulla. A couple of our parties had climbed on the Gibraltar-like headland at Calpe which would begin to become a popular venue for British climbers in another ten years or so. I'd glanced at a possibility on the unclimbed south-west face of the Cerro.

In the end the scorching days and late nights had started to prove taxing. And Dave and I both felt that the beach campsite, the cheap sangria and the lifestyle were giving the wrong ideas to our mixed party of fifteen to seventeen-year-olds. They were supposed to be on an improving mountain expedition or to be studying, with our supporting staff, desert and mountain botany and ecology. If we went on like this they'd finish up with characters as bad as our own. We were camping at Villajoyosa, still quite unspoiled, but Benidorm was close by and exerting a strong pull. Looking like the Avenue of the Americas, it had surprised our little convoy as we'd driven in. I'd remembered it as a small attractive resort with some new development in evidence but still quite Spanish in atmosphere. Dave had remembered it, a year or two earlier still, as a tiny fishing village and for the fact that he'd spent his single night there in jail, understudying a Basque dynamiter the Guardia Civil was anxious to lay hands on. On a brilliant impulse he proposed that we shift the party well away from these seductions to a distant isolated mountain I'd never even heard of, Montserrat. He'd read about it in a German climbing magazine.

I hadn't quite finished with the Cerro Puig Campana. Eighteen months later, with Maureen, I joined Frank and Ivy Davies at Benidorm. Friends assure me that whole truths have to incorporate dates. Well, this would be three years before we climbed on Bon Echo Rock, which was the year after we bivouacked on top of Royal Arches; and that was the year in which Dale Bard and party made the fourth ascent of Tangerine Trip on El Cap, we watched them inching upwards for four days. If that is any help? Alright, my second visit to the Sierra Aitana and to Montserrat was in 1973.

With Frank, I used the weakness I'd located to get into the huge shrub-filled basin on the south-west face of the Cerro, finding no evidence of earlier visitors. Two days later we returned and pulled out of it onto the little gap between the huge overhanging headwall and the top of the long, pinnacled south-west arête. We visited that minor summit to discover it already supported a tiny cairn. From the gap we traversed rightward along a narrowing six-hundred-foot ramp I'd looked at from various viewpoints at a mile's distance. Midway along it an old sardine tin surprised us. Just short of the nose the ramp merged into the wall but the limestone gave good holds for the crossing. A steep pitch up the nose took us to a confirmatory peg on the Meldrum and Royle route, which had approached from the other side and which, we were now speculating, might not have taken entirely new ground. Several hundred feet of easy climbing on perfect rock led us to the summit and to the end of an ascent which had offered continuous novelties but on which the satisfaction of pioneering had been steadily undermined.

Frank and Ivy, on a short visit, had to return. Maureen and I set out to retrace my route of the previous year with a brief diversion to the Sierra Nevada. We conquered the Veleta sitting down, taking the car from sea level to eleven thousand feet in an astonishingly short time. We made the pleasant walk up Mulhacen, the highest summit of mainland Spain. The view of the Seven Lagunas and the strange barren landscape must now be known to millions. This windy hill was subsequently made safe for democracy and now offers motor access to rival the Veleta. We admired the Alhambra's Arab Palace and were almost seduced from the purpose of our journey.

Montserrat, the serrated mountain, rises from the plains about forty miles north-west of Barcelona. It's barely four thousand feet high and perhaps three or four miles in length. The rock is an unusually reliable conglomerate. Seen from the south the hill shows as a complex of count-less spectacular pinnacles some hundreds of feet in height; to the north it presents sheer walls of up to fifteen hundred feet, almost without weak-nesses. All this rock rises abruptly from a shrub forest, everywhere as dense as a privet hedge.

The mountain is seen as unique by geologists but it's famous mainly for its monastery, fitted impressively into a cirque of pinnacles. The monks have their own logo, a stylization of the primitive cord-tensioned bowsaw, mirroring the mountain's teeth. They're nothing if not enter-prising. The tourists and the faithful come to see the Black Virgin. They're offered ancillary services which include expensive restaurants, cheap cafeterias, food shops, wine shops, bookshops, gift shops, hair-dressers' salons and toilets. I noticed that, as commonly as the logo, the pottery on sale featured the CND symbol, often with the Catalan inscription, Make Love Not War. Vending machines dispense chocolate and cooled beer at any hour of day or night. The monastery itself has published a handsome rock-climbers' guidebook.

We arrived in the early afternoon. In the big tourist carpark an attendant stopped us. On our first visit his predecessor had been helpful. We'd asked if we could camp somewhere in the area. There is a free campsite, courtesy of the monastery, he'd said. We'd told him that we were hoping to do some climbing. The climbing is superb, enquire at the monastery, he'd said. This time it was late in the year and the attendant barred the way. The campsite is closed for the winter, he said. We pointed out a small tent, just visible through the trees. The campsite is closed for the winter, he repeated. Every remark we could think of produced the same response until an emergency called him aside and we were able to continue to the site. It was in fact closed, and the gate locked, but two climbers had persuaded the administration to grant them access. It was a special privilege, not to be extended to anyone else, because they were there to climb on the mountain. So are we, we said, pitching our tent.

Of these two, one was a Swede, working in Czechoslovakia. The other was a Spaniard, working in Switzerland. They communicated in German and apparently comprised a long-standing partnership. The Spaniard recognised me immediately but didn't say so since we'd met on our earlier visit, during which Jean Nicol had surprised him in the act of transferring an armload of food, climbing gear and motor oil from our tents to his own. I recognised the Spaniard immediately but didn't say so since it seemed useful to make friends. Retribution still lay some months into the future and on the other side of the world when Dave was to find himself a day and a half ahead of the Spaniard on the Nose of El Cap.

At night the place changes character. The day trippers disappear and the illuminations and the moonlight emphasise the huge clean facades of the buildings. A serene pleasure to wander around the deserted plazas, arcades and flights of stairs at those hours. There's a touch of de Chirico about it. The monks are nowhere to be seen. Curiously, we'd sometimes hear heavy rock music pounding out from tiny lighted windows five or six floors up and, on a couple of occasions at least, girls screaming. Later I concluded that this must have been in monastery workers' accommodation. However, as if to remind any visitor of the essentially solemn purpose of the place, the monks bang gongs from time to time and they keep this up for most of the night, backed up at regular intervals by strokes and chimes from an orchestra of powerful clocks and bells.

The camp site, perched on attractive narrow terraces above a precipitous slope, looks straight across at the floodlit buildings, a quarter-mile away. On the first night, as I enjoyed this view from my vantage point in pitch darkness, the blast of a trumpet close by my side suddenly shattered the silence. I almost fell over the parapet with shock. Then I made out the Swede, sitting on a camp chair only ten feet away. I stilled my heart, but felt a rush of anxiety as the liquid notes were directed at the monastery. Surely the authorities wouldn't stand for this maniacal attack on their privacy? They'd be up within minutes to turn us all off. Bewilderment followed. The Swede had abruptly suspended play. There was a moment's pause. And then, from the monastery itself, a cool clear voice replied. For a little while I actually assumed that the performance had been set up. Then I realised that I was listening to the most perfect echo I'd ever heard. The squares remained empty and it began to appear that there was to be no immediate and hostile response. I relaxed into listening to this ghostly duet. With impressive authority the Swede played a long and plaintive series of phrases and to each, after a dignified and considered pause, a melancholy answer responded, filling the cirque. It seemed to me the most beautiful melody I'd ever heard and one that would haunt me for the rest of my life. Then the first notes of a second piece erased it absolutely and that too was to slide off my memory, as if by a spell, the moment he rose and walked away.

The climbers' guide to Montserrat is in Catalan. This is good because Catalan resembles a latin attempt at pidgin English, or, perhaps, a climbers' Esperanto. I quote the description of the first climb I did there, on the earlier visit, L'Esquelet by the Xemenia Torras-Nubiola:

> Ruta (Route) actualment utilitzada (actually utilised) com a via Normal (as the Ordinary Route). Aquesta xemenia que solca totalment el monolit (This chimney which completely splits the monolith) es un tipica escalada de tecnica de "ramonage" o xemenia (is a typical chimneying-technique chimney).

Try a bit yourself:

> Molt convenient per a l'escalador montserrati per a completar la seva formacio de roquista. Escalada catalogada en 4t. Al final (sortida) pas de 4t sup. Escalada molt segura. Una mica atletica. 1 hora. Descens en rappel par darrera (via Normal).

Not knowing a word of the language I may have got bits of it wrong but the rock fitted the reading.

I'd been dreaming about the Cavall Bernat. This name appears elsewhere in Spain and if it means Bernat's Horse he must have ridden it hard. Who was Bernat anyway? Out of a pack of St. Bernards I find that one was born in Catalonia and this must surely be our man. The Cavall Bernat is Montserrat's most famous pinnacle and was climbed as long ago as 1935. Constant attempts had preceded this conquest? ("Temptatives constants havien precedit aquesta conquesta.") The successful party consisted of Costa, Boix and Balaguer and a cast-iron plaque placed at the start of the climb twenty-five years later remembers them. Compared with English climbing of the period it seems a notable success and one can't help wondering why we heard so little of the Montserrati climbers. But, of course, only a year later the Civil War began and for three years Barcelona was the focus of one side's hopes. Until, on the twenty-sixth of January, 1939, General Yague broke in. Costa, Boix and Balaguer, what happened to you then?

Immediately, the Second World War was on, restricting the Barcelona climbers to their own mountain. Perhaps they wanted nothing else? Who needs Alps and Pyrenees when he's got Montserrat? They kept on doing what they'd already learned to do. The rock here sets a tantalising problem. In general it's as sound as an excellent concrete and where the pilgrims' stairway runs against it the joint is sometimes hard to distinguish. On the vertical walls the ovoid glassy pebbles are usually bedded horizontally in the firm matrix. As this matrix erodes a stage is promised at which the pebble, of whatever size, ought to offer a positive hold; but this point is no sooner reached than the pebble is released, leaving an equally glassy pocket without the slightest lip. So, one by one, the great walls and pinnacles were bolted. The bolt was an ordinary coach bolt. The hanger was a length of very strong wire twisted into a loop. On these precarious ladders the Montserrati climbers pushed bravely upwards and finally they forced El Paret de L'Aeri, the Wall of the Téléphérique. Allow ten to twenty hours, the guidebook suggested. It's as impressive as Half Dome, Dave Nicol had exclaimed.

We walked up to the Cavall, an hour. It was a warm sunny afternoon. From the north, the long side, the pinnacle is a graceful sweeping spire, an Eiffel Tower. From the south, its height reduced by a half, it is a massive phallic stump. We scrambled up the easy ground onto the shoulder and arranged the ropes. The big pitch starts with a thirty-foot traverse graded at V sup. It went easily to an ancient peg, somehow forced into the back of a pocket. Then a couple of thin moves on pebbles, the wall just easing from vertical. Someone had pecked tiny scars on the surface of the key pebble. There was no option but to step across on it and I persuaded myself to do so and moved into the scoop at the foot of the big chimney-groove. It was more difficult to stand there than I'd guessed and a few awkward moments passed before I was able to fix protection.

Then, slowly up the groove, assisted or impeded by a dozen pegs, bolts, and rotting wooden wedges, these last apparently obstructing perfect hand-jams. At a hundred feet, something novel and disconcerting. To this point, although we couldn't see each other, we'd been in perfect contact. Then, in the upper bulges, I tried to shout down. A long wailing echo from the Paret dels Diables, straight opposite, interrupted and drowned out my words. I tried one word at a time. No chance. I tried clipping each syllable. No chance. Every sound extended into an idiotic howl, ringing like a bell. I continued up the corner, hearing distinctly at one point the sound of a hammer, no echo, close by. Stretching the ropes I reached the small ledge. Two ancient bolts and a peg. I tied on, feeling committed and a bit worried. How would Maureen cope with the traverse? I'd protected it with one rope but there'd be enough stretch to let her into space. I remembered that she'd never prusiked.

I took the ropes in very tight, she understood, and inch by inch she came up. Curiously, a mist had veiled the sun and a cool little breeze started to blow and rapidly grew stronger. At last she came into sight. Don't worry, I said, at least we'll have company for the abseils. I heard a hammer, I said, Pedro must be on the Via Puigmal, the big route on the back. Pegging, she said, no, no, it's that monk! She hung back on a sling and pointed. On the very edge of the mind-blowing wall of the Paret dels Diables a robed and hooded figure was crouched. The mist swirled around him. He was squaring off rock for a shrine or meditation cell on the brink of as fearsome a precipice as I've ever seen.

Maureen joined me and we got ourselves together. I arranged myself hastily for the top pitch which consisted of a short wall, easing into a slab, easing into the perfectly rounded dome of the summit. The steep bit was easy but I came to a halt in the middle of the slab. Reasonable holds but not one of them incut: no protection, great exposure, and suddenly the wind was blowing in powerful cold gusts. Wasn't it oddly dull, too? No, it wasn't dull, it was actually getting dark, and just this frustrating barrier before the top. There was a little vertical flake and I tapped a tiny peg in. I tested it. It moved. I tapped it again. The crack widened. I adjusted a sling to suspend my foot upon the best pebble, waited until the wind abated a little, and made three swift moves to easy ground. Scrambling, then walking up this, a final scare. I was moving up half-turned-round, dragging the ropes, calling to Maureen to untie quickly, when I somehow became aware of a terrifying presence behind my back. I heard myself gasp aloud, I felt the hair on my neck rise as, peripherally, I picked up a silver apparition close behind me. Relax. The Madonna again. I hadn't expected to meet her on this off-beat perch and she hadn't been visible from the approach. I roped her ankles while she gazed serenely into the deepening gloom. Maureen came swiftly up. First British, we said, congratulating ourselves on getting up. A poor thing but our own. What about getting down? I remembered that Maureen had never abseiled. We forced ourselves to rest for three or four precious minutes.

It was the perfect teaching set-up for a first abseil: a descent that graded smoothly from horizontal to vertical; a figure-eight descender; my guarantee on the safety rope; the Madonna looking after the abseil rope; the imminence of darkness. I outlined the idea and Maureen went smoothly down, no problem. I followed, jerked the little peg out, dropped the hammer which stopped providentially on the edge of the ledge, retrieved the hammer, retrieved the abseil rope. Now for the big one. It seemed to take ages to set it up but at last she started down, directly for the shoulder. I composed myself until warbling echoes and the detensioning of the rope suggested she was there. We'd been climbing on a doubled three-hundred foot halfweight and carrying also a similar spare rope. This seemed like overkill but I'd considered the possibility of a single very long abseil. However, I now had the means to protect my own descent whilst attempting to recover a peg I'd placed near the start of the groove. I set off for it but the groove was biased against me and in a moment of carelessness I lost my balance and floated out across and away from the wall. Forget it. I dropped onto the shoulder. Like the prow of a gigantic liner the Cavall reared above us in the obscurity, dividing the driven mist so that she seemed about to run us down. To my delight and pride both ropes fell clean. We descended the shoulder and in five minutes we were on the ground and stuffing the ropes, suddenly inextricably tangled, into the sack. A wild exultation, part relief, was starting to well up in us. But we hadn't quite finished yet.

Deep inside the monastery buildings there was an extraordinary cafeteria. It was the only place open after six, but for one hour only, from eight until nine. Each evening, from the interstices of the monastery, a strange assortment of night people emerged to assemble there. The counters were laden with delicacies and offered every sort of drink. It presented itself to our thoughts now as the essential conclusion to the expedition.

We had no watch and no torch. Our senses led us off the ridge and into a narrow corridor through the forest. Eventually the faint whitish stones of the track disappeared and I had to admit that I'd lost the line, probably five hundred feet higher. The concrete stairway to S. Jeromi could only be a few hundred feet down through the thicket. Our impulses were to crash on down and our bodies were in accord but I recalled the sheer smooth walls terracing the forest at random. We went wearily back up and staggered around, casting about for the path. Finally we found it and felt our way from branch to branch, the trees so dense here that it was impossible to fall out of the tunnel. A half-hour in this lovely magical wood and we stepped abruptly onto the pilgrims' track. Then down and down, counting the features we recognised until a pale glow slowly transformed into the effulgence the floodlights cast on the rocks overhanging the monastery. On and on until the buildings came into view and our way was clearly lit. In five minutes we'd be down. A bell crashed out.

The cafeteria opened at eight and closed at nine. We froze and counted. One, two, three, four. Five and six. And seven. And eight, and an agonising pause. The silence lengthened and became rich and profound. We stared at each other weakly and broke into delighted laughter. Then in a collapsed and aching walk we stumbled down for beer and cinzano, a little food maybe, and a brief but full taste of the absolute contentment that visits us so infrequently, consequent sometimes on such a day as this.

THE VIEW FROM PLATO'S CAVE

Plato unfolds his famous parable on knowledge towards the end of the seventh book of *Republic*. "Imagine a cavern open to the light," he says, "like Doveholes, say, but vast. In the floor of the cavern a pit in which a group of people have spent the whole of their lives. They can't see anything outside but they can see the back wall and they can watch the shadows the sun throws onto it — a tree, birds, a passing fox, Ilam Rock (displacing it a bit), a climber making the ascent. Ignorant of the outer world of substance they give names and attributes to the shadows instead. From this and other considerations I infer that beyond the world we know there must exist an ideal world of which all earthly things are copies or imitations."

There's an odd correlation here with a climber's view. We have the climb as it appears to the remote observer, the climb as the whole body comes to experience it, and the simplified perfect climb of the imagination. Sometimes the three have little in common. The Seen Climb, the Known Climb, the Dream Climb. You can turn it round and round.

Technically, obsession used to mean being molested by a malign spirit outside oneself; possession meant a similar attack from within. Either way, relationships with dream climbs have sometimes been derided but it has to be admitted that they give a purpose to life. However, fifteen years is a long time for a route of less than two hundred feet and that was the period spanned by my attempts on Plato's Cave. During those years I never saw another party on Clogwyn Pen Llechan.

In l972, with Ann Cornwall, I'd made a series of routes on the south-east face of the cliff. We had a perfectly good reason for not writing up these routes (I wasn't able to get hold of a description of a rumoured earlier ascent) and another more selfish reason, in that one of our climbs wouldn't go where it was told and we wanted to get it right ourselves. Promises, Promises was an attempt on the left side of this face which shows a two hundred-foot-long barrier of overhang across its crest. We climbed a good pitch to an impending groove but could make no impression there. We traversed right looking for weaknesses but couldn't get into the most likely one, a niche at the end of the barrier. The slab beyond seemed flawless and eventually we found ourselves rounding the blunt nose of the face and using a known exit a hundred feet displaced.

Ann went to work in America, came back, moved off again. But the idea wouldn't leave me and everything was on my side. The cliff, though nicely shaped, is hung with Persian carpets of a velvety black moss, unappealing to the young climber with an imperfect knowledge of rock types. When wet the place takes on a horrendous appearance and it needs a few days to dry out. The easy routes of our predecessors were unlikely to tempt the new generation. To get into the carpark at Pen-y-Pass you have to queue for hours and if you do get inside they impose a stinging fine. The myopic vision of an earlier guidebook writer added literature's strongest disincentives to a visit. Finally, changes in guide-book coverage left the crag off the map for twenty years.

All this was very good. I could drive up there on a fine summer evening, timing my arrival to allow a courteous salute to the departing attendant. Then a civilised, almost level, twenty-minute stroll. The top of the crag is the most accessible and least frequented summit in the area, giving an exceptional view into Cwm Dyli. Across Llyn Teyrn, at a decent distance, the final crippled conquerors of Snowdon may be seen hobbling down the Miners' Track, hallooing back at the stragglers in their parties. And the rock is superb when dry. Any plump cushion of moss may rest on a rough clean marvellous hold. Now, though, I'd had to surrender descriptions to Paul Williams and anyone strong enough to carry his new guidebook might come poking around.

To detail the several probes I made would distend this account. More often, with various companions, I'd been persuaded to repeat my favourite amongst our earlier climbs and for years at a time I tried to ignore the place. Then the difficulty arose that the longer I stayed away the more seductive my image of the possible route became. Until eventually I found myself attempting it again in the company of my brother. An easier way of starting had been found and the niche resolved on as the key. Presently we were belayed beneath it.

The wall defending it was steep, exposed, and offered no protection. Just one precarious move, really, but after three or four experiments the leader stepped back a little and studied the problem. Only a few feet above his head a sheaf of saplings, a few feet in length but pencil-thin, leaned out from the floor of the cave. If a rope could be passed behind these wands there'd be a bit more security. Instructing the second to untie on one rope, he began to gather coils in his hand.

"You seem to be doing this bit on a top rope. If you get up, will it count as a first ascent?"

"Ruses like this fall outside the domain of climbing ethics. They come into the realm of common sense."

I made the move and clawed my way onto the earthy floor of the recess. I was ten feet higher and fourteen years older. Also, my hair had gone grey and I needed spectacles for reading. I was crouching in a structure like a saint's niche. The floor was level, a square of about four feet angled to the cliff, the little tree extending from its outer corner, the inner set into the wall. The alcove wasn't six feet high but its sides were smooth and its roof almost overhung the ledge so that it was impossible to stand in comfort. It was necessary to face half out, one foot braced on the doubtful grass of the edge, and twist around to see what lay above.

A thin crack rose from the apex of the niche. At that very point it accepted two-thirds of a nut. A foot higher it took a rather better one to extend incidentally a small hold adjoining it. Otherwise there were no footholds to launch from and I could see no handholds to aim for. The nuts weren't quite good enough. If I used one for aid my feet would swing in. As I moved up the resultants would change, the nuts might pop and I'd start a slow backward somersault. The sapling would flatten, the tape ripped over its head. Nev would stop me forty to fifty feet down, snapping my neck, or he'd come with me. He was on an awkward stance with a low anchor. A peg was needed.

So I had a few with me, just in case. Twisted awkwardly, more or less one-handed, I managed to lodge one between the nuts and started to hit it. It looked encouraging. I flailed up at it, pausing at intervals to relieve the ache in my side. As it went in its nose lifted and its eye turned down until its body neared the vertical. Useless. No other placement in reach. I felt as if I'd cracked a rib. There was nothing left to do but to sit down and look at the view.

The view from Plato's Cave. The wide flat boggy armchair between

Cwm Dyli and Nant Gwynant. Two mallards on the tiny pool beneath us, all that remains of the shallow lake which must once have occupied this shelf. The huge clean isolated boulders disposed mysteriously about. On the further shore, in line but spaced at some hundreds of yards, four or five small trees, pony-borne indicators of some ancient trackway. And there had been a change. When we had arrived the morning had been sunny and full of promise. Now a thick cloud had descended the far slope, its skirts were already below our level and soon it would engulf us. This transition had taken place by such imperceptible stages that, absorbed in my purpose, I hadn't noticed it.

I'd wanted this climb for so long. When I first came here I'd been full of confidence but the years had wasted me. I'd lost strength and audacity, my central nervous system was shot, certainly I'd been ill for ages with some untraceable energy leak. But the drive had dissipated so slowly that its loss could only be comprehended by a long reach of the memory. And if I gave up on this, what else? I could go back home, buy a glass tit, and settle down in an armchair to live through our century's restaging of Plato's metaphor. And then? Just the slow drift at the unobservable speed of twenty-four hours a day towards what is, they say, 'only a tend-ing-to-zero of behaviour' — only? only! — the event horizon of death. No, but it was time to get off this cliff, find a new hobby, a new occupa-tion, write down what I knew about subjects more important than rock-climbing. I saw now that Nev, who'd left his sweater at the foot of the climb, was shivering. It touched and impressed me that he'd made no complaint. We got ourselves down safely and for four whole days I knew I'd never go there again.

Enter John Salathé, accompanied by an angel. That's right. Or maybe just listening to an angel, I'd have to read up again. Sorry, we are over in California now, just after the end of the war. (Back in Yorkshire now — this is my story — I'm struggling with Ogden Clough, remember?) The angel had indicated three great possibilities in the Yosemite valley to Salathé. None of John's friends actually saw or heard this angel and they slid quick glances at one another when he mentioned the incident. Still, people were seeing UFOs all over California at that time and John seemed to get everything exactly right. Or perhaps it was just another bit of that oddball Central European humour? Well I say, cutting corners, Salathé was simply using a traditional religious iconography as a meta-phor for that strange joyful rising and firming of the spirit. Suddenly we know with certainty exactly what we have to do. And after four days of depression, through a whole long winter, I bored my friends by miming out the problem.

"Just rope down and bang the peg in properly."

"Not allowed. Has to be done from below."

"These kids just abseil and wire-brush and chip out whatever they want."

"They use chalk and camming machines."

"Let's get ourselves some of those fancy tights."

"We'd look ridiculous. People would nudge each other. Kids would throw stones."

"I can see you with an earring. You've got to move with the times. Look at the pictures of the young heroes in the climbing mags."

"The editors never give credits for hair and jewellery."

When the day came I was accompanied by Duncan Boston. He didn't have the case history but must have guessed that something serious was afoot. I'd declared an objective without allowing our customary half-hour of indecision and fantasizing. Walking up the Miners' Track I couldn't speak. In the early years of the Bradford Boys a sub-group known as the Baskers, giving to sunbathing under crags when it was hot and to hiding in sleeping bags when it was wet or cold, used to make fun of the activists, driven to struggle in any conditions. The Baskers said they climbed for pleasure. I said I climbed for satisfaction. They said pleasure included satisfaction. I said satisfaction included pleasure. This discussion would be interrupted when Peter Greenwood, not a philosopher, would start growling. Finally he'd announce that he climbed for recognition. That was honesty. I wasn't getting much of anything from this project, it had gone on too long. We ate a snack and drank coffee. Duncan produced, inspected and set fire to a long cigar. I smoked a few cigarettes and we began to reminisce about old times. All this without talking about or looking at the cliff, three feet behind our backs. I felt too oppressed to start. Something was needed to lighten the atmosphere. Jokes? I couldn't think of any. I produced a limerick which I here suppress.

Thirty feet up and I found I was enjoying myself. The mood had lifted, the rock was marvellous, the sun was shining. Up the little semi-layback, across the neat hand-traverse, then the false mantelshelf. Back into the corner and over the bulge. The foot-traverse right, eased by a palm-up jam in a low slot. Then, with the assurance of familiarity, up the wedged blocks of the short open corner. I was at the stiff bleached tape and solid Moac from which Neville and I had abseiled.

Halfway up, Duncan called out in surprise and pleasure. He was enjoying it too. Soon we'd made the smart move round the rib across to the second stance and eventually I was back in the cave with neither time nor weather against me. I'd been afraid I'd find it occupied by squatters, a kestrel or even a peregrine. It was untenanted.

Disconcertingly, the problem was exactly the same. I replaced the nuts, clipped into them and the useless peg, and stepped cautiously into a sling on the lower nut which promptly half-capsized. I swung back sweating. So run through some substitutes, outside my normal selection and brought specially for this notch, to settle finally for an archaic cube of alloy with no side taper and drilled side to side for a dirty old loop of laid white Viking. It seemed marginally better but it was a long time before, holding my breath, I sat in a sling on it and deliberately took both hands off rock and rope.

This gesture changed the situation. I was facing the cliff and had both hands free. There were still no holds, the nuts might still pop if I moved any higher, the old peg was still unthinkable but the solution was clear. Get a good one in. And only a few inches higher, a long reach to clip from the ledge, an old-fashioned tinny-looking channel sank in nearly six inches before refusal. Standing high from this, a couple of moves and I was going up the upper wall in a very exposed position neutralised by stupendous holds. Duncan sorted out the ropes and slings and came up coolly and methodically, removing the original peg. And that was all. Soon we were on the top, coiling ropes and congratulating ourselves.

"What's the standard?"

"Straight VS. About Hard Severe on the first pitch but the stance to the peg feels serious."

"They'll laugh at us, aid on a VS."

"They'll laugh till the peg's removed. Then it won't seem so funny."

"You think it's possible without?"

"It's a production. It'll probably need rehearsals. I can't guess the method but somebody will manage it. Pull up on that fingerhold by the top nut, heel-hook onto the bulge, layaway on that slanting edge and make a long dive for the first jug. They're doing it all the time."

Walking back to Pen-y-Pass I felt light-headed wzith the weight off my mind. How to manage now for daydreams and nightmares? I'd need new material but it would turn up, in fact I had substitutes already. And it had been so simple really. No reason why Ann and I shouldn't have done it all those years ago. The chief cause for regret was that

Neville wasn't with us. An irregular visitor to Wales now, he'd told me to grab it if weather, inclination and companion were to come together. But his presence would have stretched our partnership on first ascents to a spacious thirty-seven years. Well, there was more where that came from, if no-one got there first.

Zeno said: "Listen, Harold. Just stop worrying. I was thinking about this the other day. The modern rock athlete runs like a hare up routes up which you crept like a tortoise. But while he's repeating your first ten thousand climbs you'll have done another thousand. And while he's doing those you'll have done another hundred. I know it sounds crazy but if you look at it logically you'll see that you'll always be that fraction ahead. You can call that Zeno's Paradox."

Important not to confuse my friend with Zeno of Citium, who also addresses climbers and has many disciples. (Menlove Edwards: "It has been said that the secret of life is in detachment from it, good.") In fact I was once a Stoic myself, accepting cold, hunger, thirst, pain and failure with indifference. My threshold has changed and nowadays I complain.

I seem to have fallen in with the bad showbiz crowd round Zeno of Elea. Ideas, inventiveness, playfulness. However, I've got to admit that there often seems to be something wrong with his theories, though I can never put my finger on it at the time. Still, Zeno's Paradox. Not a bad name for a climb.

Simdde Ddu

TOO COLD FOR CROW

As the crow flies if the crow won't take advice, Arenig Fawr (as we
choose to spell it now) is fifteen miles due south of my house. Driving,
it's more like thirty and it plays hide and seek. Between Nebo and
Pentrevoelas it stands in absolute independence to my right. I lose it
near Ysbyty Ifan after a brief full-frontal flash. As I climb up onto the
Migneint it moves off left, ducking behind its small but shapely consort,
Arenig Fach. Looping down to Pont-yr-Afon-Gam, where the highest
filling station in Wales once stood, it gets behind my back. As I descend
into the Trywerin valley it's straight ahead and then it's off to the right
again. As I park above Llyn Celyn it hides its head behind a massive
shoulder. We've gone in by the back way and by car. It's an approach
light-years apart from that of those earlier travellers who declared an interest in the hill. George Borrow, for instance, in the mid-nineteenth century:

> After a little time, meeting two women, I asked them the
> name of the mountain to the south. "Arennig Vawr," they
> replied, or something like it. Presently meeting four men, I
> put the same question to the foremost, a stout, burly, intel-
> ligent-looking fellow, of about fifty. He gave me the same
> name as the women. I asked him if anybody lived upon it.
> No," said he, "too cold for man."
> Fox?" said I.

189

No! too cold for fox."

Crow?" said I.

No; too cold for crow; crow would be starved upon it."

It's over twenty-five years since first I walked up the big Arenig. It's possible that at that time the only thing I'd heard about it was that there's a memorial tablet at the summit to the eight Americans who died there when a Flying Fortress crashed in 1943. My map didn't show any footpaths on this hill so I took the entry nearly everybody takes, the gated waterworks track serving the old embankment of Llyn Arenig Fawr. On a fine day this embankment is a delightful place to loiter. On a bad day the tiny cabin close beneath, now maintained by the Mountain Bothies Association, is an equally delightful place to loiter.

As I came within sight of the lake on that first visit my attention was taken by the cliff above the far shore. At that distance I judged it about three hundred feet high over a frontage of more than a quarter-mile. Terraced, broken, vegetated, but offering some very steep rock. The half dozen parallel ledges of the lower part extended in striking continuities, like a bedded formation, unusual. Nevertheless, this rock looked attractive and the headwall presented impressive towers. That was the main face, the east face. Round to the left there was a south face of clean-looking slabs. Twenty minutes later, following the stream up to the shoulder, a splendid zigzag crack suddenly opened in the lower wall of the slabs. From higher still I was able to see a continuation weakness leading to a final chimney almost roofed over by a gigantic block. I knew then that sooner or later I'd have to get to grips with the place.

A bit of time went by before I read in *Mountain* that Martin Boysen had made a route here. No details were supplied. I walked up the hill a few times, reminding myself I'd better get onto the cliff. I checked guidebooks and made enquiries. Finally I started to climb there, recruiting in turn my brother, Ken Richards, Duncan Boston and Dave Wrennall. A bit more time had passed. Somehow we'd reached 1994 before I got going. A quarter-century had slipped away while I'd been sitting reading.

I'll call the cliff Simdde Ddu. (Say it: Shim-the Dee, with a short e in the middle; something like that.) That name appears against it on the 1:25000 map but it just means Black Chimney and refers to an obvious feature. I suppose I ought to say Craig Simdde Ddu but I'll use an English climber's neat if illogical contraction.

We learned the relief and detail of the crag, harnessing it with words. The slabs around the zigzag crack are divided into three tiers by two heather ramps. These fine slabs terminate in a squalid chimney. Left of this an undercut buttress holding a central heather field advances. From a distance this buttress seems hardly worth notice but it proved to offer some amenable climbs. The south face, then, has a main slab area and a terminal buttress.

Across to the right from the foot of the zigzag crack a ledge runs up against the ridge dividing the two main faces. This is a strategic position. From here we've watched peregrines making swift passes along the front of the cliff. Curiously, growing from a crack at ground level we discovered raspberry canes, a long way from home, descended perhaps from the survivors of some Edwardian picnic basket. Beneath this ledge, later, we found the carcass of a fox. Too cold for fox? Straight overhead there's an impressive bulging buttress. If we'd climbed it directly we could have written a bizarre description: "Start between a dead fox and a raspberry bush."

Glance around the nose and you find you're already at mid-height on the main face. First there's a broad vegetated depression. Right again, high up, a tower stands out. It is, in fact, a colossal detached pillar balanced on the face and we named it the Trojan Horse. (You could hide under it; it might be moveable; it's beneath the final wall.) The Horse is perched on a clean steep parapet, slanting up leftward.

Beyond this area the headwall shows a skylined tower with a striking arête and beyond this again there's a big amphitheatre. Central in the cirque of vertical rock comprising it is Simdde Ddu itself, a wet vegetated cleft blocked by a huge overhang. It's reminiscent of Twll Du. North of the amphitheatre, high up, there's another band of clean steep rock. But there's rock all over this side of the mountain: the neat dome down by the stream, Craig Bryn Dyfrgi; the dark towers and the impressive arête of Y Castell, the tiered escarpment opposite the south face slabs; small detached overhanging walls offering countless desperate problems; the buttresses of Daear Fawr on the north end of the shoulder.

Climbing on Simdde Ddu in 1994 and the following year, two sensations contended in me. First, a time-warp had shifted me a century back to the beginnings of the sport. The thread of path along the foot of the cliff was simply the work of sheep. We saw no trace of litter, no print of boot. Sitting on a ledge in the amphitheatre on a rainy day, the curtain of water from the overhangs well clear of us, it was easy to imagine Owen Glynne Jones scrambling wetly up to join us. The ledge on the top of the Trojan Horse so delighted us that, idiots, we built a small cairn there. It will have to be dismantled.

Against that there was the certainty that climbers had laid hands on the crag. A peg in the zigzag crack, which we provisionally titled Unknown Soldier, stated a case. That's a Listed Piton until the explorer steps forward. There was something that might be a threaded sling in a difficult position on the little dome. The cliff felt haunted. Surely this groove ought to hold a clump or two of heather; this scar might show where someone removed a loose flake; the holds on this slab come too obviously to hand; these few stones, overgrown by heather, might once have been a cairn.

This is a detective story. We'd had some great days but now I wanted information. In 1960 Pyatt, a careful researcher, had described the main cliffs as untouched; yet in 1962 Poucher had asserted that Simdde Ddu was "the occasional resort of the rock climber." Which rock climber? I couldn't ask Poucher now. There was a legend linking Nat Allen with the hill. When I'd asked him he'd agreed that it offers good climbing and that it hadn't been written up. He'd seemed disinclined to say much more and I'd not pressed him, there being no hurry. Now I couldn't ask Nat. Boysen's climb I could perhaps identify from a verbal. Derek Walker had been mentioned. I'd chase him up later.

Back to the Sumner household. Ten years earlier the Mid-Wales guide-writer hadn't been able to help. Now he listened in silence while I reminded him that guidebook boundaries give him the hill. He seemed less than delighted. A snowstorm of new route descriptions from all over the area was falling onto him. He thought the mountain ought really to go in with the Moelwynion. Finally he came up with a name and address: The Information. At that point I made a time-consuming mistake.

The address to hand was incomplete, no county or postcode and three places of that name in two counties. I was in a hurry anyway, wanting to talk, and I knew the name. I bluffed my way through a string of unlisted numbers (what's all the secrecy about, over there in the ghetto?), got through the cloak of smoke around the movements of the Guides' Mafia ("He might be in the Alps. His wife might be with him." "He might be back this weekend. Or next weekend.") and reached Terry Taylor.

Terry Taylor was puzzled. He hadn't done any climbing on the Arenigs. Then he mentioned that there'd been another Terry Taylor hanging around Llanberis, though he didn't know him. ("You might get him through The Heights. Or through Pete's Eats.") I procured more unlisted numbers, consulted community leaders in the ghetto ("I think I know this guy by sight. I don't know where he hangs out." "I haven't seen him around for a while. He sounded Irish.") and reached more dead ends.

Back to the Sumners. This time I got Jill. She was pretty sure which town to look in and had the impression he worked in some sort of Centre, maybe an instructor. Now there was no need to write because that was a network I still knew something about. My name might even be remembered. Distinguished author of the first of the Ladybird Books on Outdoor Education. In fact there are a lot of Mountain Centres in the area in question and I drew a few blanks. Finally, a lady redirected me to another kind of Centre, a Health Centre. He'd be away for a week but I'd hunted down the ghost of Simdde Ddu, Dr. Terry Taylor.

Taylor came over as a realist, informed and organised. He sounded too fit and energetic to make a sympathetic family doctor. He supplied details of twenty routes made by Jason Cooper and himself from 1990 onward. He also drew my attention to an article about the mountain by John Appleby. It had appeared two years earlier in a climbing magazine but I'd missed it. A nice piece, I had to admit. He'd anticipated me in the writing as well as the climbing. And my feelings about the climbing were copies of Appleby's and he'd done some serious homework on J.D. Innes, on whom I'd consulted shelfloads of books and whom I have to produce as a key witness. Still, I'd been enquiring before he arrived, I knew things he didn't know, this is my story.

I found Appleby with only the obligatory delay. ("John here. Can't talk right now but if you can contain your disappointment leave your number and I'll get back." Then a little melody. Then the pips.) When we spoke I started to introduce myself and he reminded me he'd called me some years earlier about one of my own writings. Appleby came over as a romantic, engaging but hard to pin down. No, he hadn't any written descriptions. He hadn't named all his climbs. He might not be able to mark them exactly on photographs. But he could point them out on the spot and, come to think of it, he'd love to get up there again. He'd done about ten routes, the earliest a little in advance of Terry Taylor's.

I went further back. Derek Walker gave me useful directions allowing me to bypass a Derek Walker who works for a climbing books distributor and to find a Derek Walker who's written a guide to the Pyrenees. No problem here. The routes, from the early eighties were described and named and dated in a hut logbook. Hard evidence. Then, when we got down to detail, we realised that we were on another mountain, Arenig Fach.

I considered my next step. I could convene a symposium at my house or organise a meet at the cliff. However, there remained the tantalising mystery of the Arenig File, in the custody of John Sumner. What did it contain? The Climbers' Club Dinner was imminent. Did I have the muscle to ask the President to instruct the Area Guidebook Editor to tell the Mid-Wales Guidebook Writer to let me see the file? Or, while everyone was tied up in Llanberis, ought I to go housebreaking in Staffordshire? A chilling thought stopped me: suppose I just asked John if I might borrow it and he gave it eagerly but refused to take it back? It was the news I wanted, not the responsibilities.

The Arenig File. In the event it added nothing startling. Investigations, however, are continuing. I found Charles Evans' account of a schoolboy ascent of Daear Fawr, roped and in winter conditions, in the early thirties. John Appleby came up with a photograph of Colin Kirkus in the recent biography. It shows another schoolboy, in full school uniform, captioned as on the Arenig and dating from the middle twenties; this still puzzles us, since we haven't yet sited it, but even on a boulder there's no mistaking the potential in this beginner. Other leads remain to be checked and the file is still open.

Some will say this enquiry defeats our own interests since we're losing the delicious sense of mystery we enjoyed. I, for one, can't accept that. Years ago, when I was working in outdoor education, one of our parties brought back from Tryfan an astonishingly delicate barbed and tanged flint arrowhead, spotted emerging from the eroded bank of the path between Llyn Bochlwyd and Bwlch Tryfan. The County Archaeologist classified and dated it at a glance: Conygar Hill type, about 1800 BC. All I need now is the name of the man who was dropping gear on Tryfan 3800 years ago. Oh, and what hut was he operating from? And what club was he in? Then the mystery thickens.

The great thing about the climbing here is the regal position, as open a view as from any high crag in Wales. Some early visitors made particular note of the hill and the reason is obvious. In central Snowdonia the roadwalker sees a summit for a half hour and then it's shut out by its satellites; without a good map he couldn't say which is the highest. To pass the Arenig, however, on foot or by pony and trap by the normal approaches from east or west must have made a long day: the mountain rising in imposing austerity beyond seas of moorland, drawing closer very slowly, hanging on interminably beyond the traveller's back.

The very first tourists, drawn by Snowdon or Cader Idris, usually bypassed this area. Pennant and Fenton simply name the hill as an event in a distant skyline. In 1798, the year of his alarming adventure on the Eastern Terrace of Clogwyn Du'r Arddu, the Rev. William Bingley remarks on it as seen from the Rhinogion.

Other travellers left testimonials. On a dark night in the autumn of 1910, out of funds and exhausted, James Dickson Innes arrived at the isolated inn then open at Rhyd y Fen. The innkeeper, Washington Davies, fed him and cared for him on trust. Innes saw the mountain next morning and it hit him like a blow. He was only twenty-three but already knew that time wasn't on his side. He had tuberculosis. He returned early next spring and persuaded his friend, Augustus John, already a celebrity, to come up to see what he'd found. As a base they rented a cottage at Nantddu, a mile to the west, for ten pounds a year. An Australian colleague, Derwent Lees, subsequently arrived to strengthen the team. This was a novelty: the Slade's first expedition sieges Arenig Fawr. As was the fashion then, the three painters had been taught that the big scene was the South of France, the colour, the light. Over the next two or three years, each in his own way but collectively soon to be known as the Arenig School, they tried to fix this moody northern hill.

This whole episode is extraordinary but it's mistaken to picture these hard-drinking womanising Bohemians holed up in monastic seclusion. The tide of local economy hadn't yet ebbed from the valley. The long-dismantled railway was still running and there was a halt at Arenig. There was the inn nearby. John had a special interest in gypsies and a craving to paint incompletely dressed gypsy girls. He already spoke Romani, giving the three artists an entrée with the Cwm Trywerin band so that they were able to fraternize with them.

A strange assortment of visitors arrived at Nant-ddu. They included John's companion Dorelia, with some at least of the six young sons with which his ménage a trois had so far provided him. Euphemia Lamb — Lobelia, to her associates in the bisexual squaredance forming up around the early Bloomsbury Group — a beautiful girl with whom Innes had walked from Paris to the Pyrenees, stayed for a while. In 1912 Innes buried her letters in a silver casket in the summit cairn. (Sit still: the Fortress demolished the original cairn; local shepherds found fragments of old writings blowing around near the wreckage.) Derwent Lees competed gallantly in all activities. He was a less gifted artist and must have been cruelly handicapped on this daunting terrain by his wooden leg but it's said that he was just as successful with women, interesting. The cottage itself was demolished quite recently and now there's only a Eurobarn and a long-deserted chalet at this forlorn spot.

For John and for Lees, this was a happy interval in their lives. For Innes it was the last chance. He looked at the hill in all conditions, often completing two paintings a day, oils on tiny wooden panels. I've seen only one of the originals, now well dispersed, but I have a sense of them from reproductions. He admired Constable, the attack of Turner, Japanese mountain prints. He learned something from Cotman and Wilson Steer. And then, surprisingly, he brought to bear on this cool hill very hot colour, as in Derain and Matisse. No central debt emerges. By a route of his own he found a style somewhere between Post-Impressionist and Fauvist, primitive, brilliant, intense, firmly designed. No hill in Britain has had so large a legacy from a single hand. "Mynydd Arenig remained ever his sacred mountain and the slopes of Migneint his spiritual home," John wrote later.

"Ah, Innes," my friend A.K. Richards, former head of an art faculty, murmurs reflectively; "an interesting minor figure." He's forgotten I do revaluations. "Innes's Arenig scenes must be counted among the greatest achievements of Welsh art," a Phaidon Companion states. "This intense working period has been cited as one of the most important in the development of modernism in British painting," another Art Dictionary says. Consider that: Modernism in British painting began on Arenig Fawr. By the winter of 1913 Innes was gravely ill and went to Morocco (where, desperate, he experimented persistently with a startling new tobacco) but returned to die in England. He was twenty-seven. "When Innes died and the focus of John's interest shifted, something went out of English painting that left it colder and more prosaic," Rothenstein wrote.

The elasticity of time defeats me. It can't just be counted in years, it stretches and contracts with change or the absence of change. A quarter-century since I saw the hill and a quarter-century again to the Boeing crash. Go back thirty years more and Innes was here. That's the odd one, an interval spanning a time when few motor vehicles had been seen in these parts and an era of huge aircraft.

Ten years earlier, usually snubbed because he betrays no trace of feeling and no sense of humour, W.G. Fearnsides was examining the hill as closely as any climber, any artist, any shepherd. He saw through the hill. His paper of 1905, "On the Geology of Arenig Fawr and Moel Llyfnant", must have cost months of arduous and solitary work, patiently distinguishing volcanic intrusions from the basic material. That bedrock is so distinctive in type that the earliest in the succession of Ordovician rocks in Wales became known as the Arenig Series.

Go back another half century and George Borrow, the one-man Inquisition, is loping along the road at his customary five miles an hour, interrogating everybody, arguing, scaring the wits out of the locals. Miraculously he closes the gap, admiring the spectacular isolation of the hill exactly as we do and talking to us as directly as a close friend. Having satisfied himself on identity he remembered that he'd seen it described in an old Welsh poem as "Arennig ddiffaeth", barren Arenig. "Arennig is certainly barren enough," he reflected, "for there is neither tree nor shrub upon it, but there is something majestic in its huge bulk. Of all the hills I saw in Wales none made a greater impression on me."

For myself, from 1994, the Arenig became the great place to climb.

In the autumn of 1995, by telephone, by letter, and by not quite adequate photographs, we tried to fit together what we knew. Winter snow fell and melted, fell again and cleared again. In March 1996 I met in turn John Appleby and Terry Taylor on the hill and we began to reconcile our names and explorations. I teamed up with Appleby and we resumed the campaign. In June we climbed Simdde Ddu, the Black Chimney itself, joking that we might at last have closed the Gully Era of Welsh climbing. Perhaps this feature and Twll Du, the Devil's Kitchen at Idwal, are the only Welsh climbs actually named by shepherds. A hundred and one years had passed since the ascent of Twll Du, and fifty since I started climbing. We succeeded on a number of more modernistic lines, once enlisting David Craig. Meantime Terry Taylor, often partnered by Norman Clacher, had had an even more productive year so that by the autumn the list of climbs had doubled. As I write the hills are deep in snow again. I look forward with delight and with impatience to spring on the Arenig.

TO WHOM IT MAY CONCERN

I am well aware that the reader does not require information, but I, on the other hand, feel impelled to give it to him.

Rousseau, Confessions

ACCESS

Not long after the end of the Second World War, just about the time I started rock climbing, in the year and above the town in which *A Private Function* was set, I attended a public function at the Cow and Calf Rocks. It was a walkers' rally organised to demonstrate support for the idea of creating National Parks, of establishing the Pennine Way, of gaining a more comprehensive access to the countryside of Britain. The postwar government had pledged itself to secure these aims but its resolve was seen to be weakening and a grass-roots campaign to re-energise it was being launched.

Tom Stephenson was one of the speakers. Behind us stretched the wide expanse of Ilkley Moor, a War Department Firing Range, unfenced but its perimeter lined with warnings to keep out. It was known to have been cleared of unexploded ammunition but the military had declined to release the area, possibly having plans for future use. Stephenson worried himself with the further thought that if the army chose to relinquish the range without prior public notice it might be converted immediately to a strictly keepered grouse moor, though it was crossed by ancient rights of way. Perhaps emboldened by his audience of many hundreds, seeming to come to decisions as he spoke, he said that he was going to take a walk across it anyway and he grumbled that the signs shouldn't really be there, that somebody ought to do something about them.

199

At this, little knots of somebodies began to detach themselves from the gathering which grew leaner by the minute. I had the impression that he was obliged to wind up more quickly than he'd intended, in order to find out what was going on. I still remember the strong satisfaction of wrestling a sign out and heaving it into a wet ditch. Before night fell, parties had crossed the lovely moor from side to side and from end to end. Of the millions who've enjoyed it since then, I wonder how many knew about that sunny afternoon. Forgive us our trespasses.

It was a time of unbounded optimism. During the war, as during the First World War, the spokesmen of all political parties had promised a fairer society as the reward of victory. These promises sometimes included rights for all citizens to walk more freely about the land of their birth. Through the previous sixty years some twenty attempts to get an Access to Mountains Bill through Parliament had failed or had been blocked until a final successful attempt produced in effect, through amendment at committee stage, something like a Landowners' Protection Act. This time we'd get it right.

What we wanted, and what we still want, can be said very simply. The freedom to walk anywhere on uncultivated land; some means of following, off the road, all self-defining natural routes like rivers and coastlines; the enjoyment of a degree of access by pathway through the nearest fields, woods and parkland to every household in the kingdom. We don't need reminding that rights are accompanied by responsibilities.

There are only a limited number of ways in which title to land is gained. It can be acquired by seizure, that is, by discovery or first settlement, by right of conquest, or by squatters' rights; the fact that successful seizures are usually subsequently ratified in law doesn't alter the means by which possession was gained. Or it may be gained by agreed legal transfer, when two parties consent voluntarily to change of ownership through inheritance, marriage, gift, purchase, and so on; in Britain this is how most private landowners would explain title, though all these titles actually originate from some form of seizure. Or it may be gained by enforced legal transfer, when the attitude of the relinquishing party is irrelevant, as in compulsory purchase.

I've outlined these three methods of gaining title since they offer a means of reviewing past attempts and future strategies to secure access. However, it's convenient to take them in reverse order so as to answer with less delay the question I ask myself: After the War, what went wrong?

The planners of the National Parks and Access to the Countryside Act of 1949 set up a machinery by which Park Planning Boards and Local

Authorities could extend public access by acquisition, by Access Orders and by Footpath Creation Orders. These powers have been used to a limited extent in the Peak District. Over the rest of England and Wales they've hardly been considered. Many County Councils, disregarding noisy local protest, reported that they saw no need for further open access or for new footpath provision. Footpaths, together with roads, have always formed a part of 'the Queen's Highway'; yet whilst the use or the threat of compulsory purchase is normal in road improvement schemes it's regarded as almost unthinkable as a means of extending walker access.

At first glance these results seem surprising and hard to understand. They're comprehensively examined and explained in Marion Shoard's magisterial study of land tenure, *This Land is Our Land*. The Attlee Government, seeing the task of reviewing access needs to demand very detailed local knowledge, chose to delegate the work. The demand for access came mainly from the cities: but that access was required mainly in the country and there it was assessed by a variety of local institutions. Within such bodies as County and Parish Councils landowners and farmers had a traditional and hugely disproportionate representation and influence. That influence continues to the present day in the councils of rural areas and it's also strong in almost all the statutory bodies responsible for land, not excluding the mutilated Forestry Commission, still Britain's largest landowner with well over two million acres. Further, the power of the landowning and farming lobby is felt even in the agencies dealing with amenity and conservation, such as the Park Planning Boards and the successors and assigns of the original National Parks Commission and Nature Conservancy. This lobby resisted calls for further access by simple obstruction at every level and also promoted an alleged incompatibility between conservation and recreation.

In short, the prospect of securing access unilaterally, by law, came to nothing. It had rested on the illusion that power lay only in Parliament. And for the future in any case, it's impossible to imagine that a Conservative government, or, for that matter, any Coalition or Labour government we can conceive of at present, would legislate access by enforcement.

What are the chances, then, of securing further access by the alternative of legal agreement? In fact it was the hope of the architects of the 1949 Act that confrontation could largely be avoided. They assumed that where de facto access existed it would remain unchallenged and they hoped to move ahead mainly by Access Agreements and by similar arrangements to establish voluntarily dedicated footpaths. (Sufferance access, courtesy paths, permissive paths: the stinging expressions tell us where we stand.) They made provision for compensation for damage which developed mainly into annual payments for use.

This approach has proved quite productive in the Peak District and it's been used in a few other areas but it has clear limits and disadvantages. Payments escalate steadily and they're being forced up to prohibitive levels. Some agreements operate only on a year to year basis. The rights gained rest on the landowner's pleasure, whilst what we want are rights in perpetuity on a basis felt as more durable than law. In some cases permissive paths would be best described as rented paths. (We don't rent the land of the motorways.) In many areas landowners have flatly declined to enter into agreements. With any sharp reduction in Authority budgets agreements may have to be rescinded. (But might this not be a good thing? The collapse of agreements would show the public how little has been won.)

Through much of Britain work towards access agreements still goes on and when it succeeds the gain, considered in itself, is visible and encouraging. Yet negotiations on which many years of effort have been expended have often failed or have produced unsatisfactory results. And set against the larger goals of open access by right and a more useful footpath system the process is hopeless. The agreement of the Pennine Way took seventeen years; the Cambrian Way proposal was abandoned after ten years of obstruction; the post-purchase negotiations on the Vaynol Estate lands in Snowdonia, bought outright 'for the benefit of the nation', demanded over twenty years. Certainly the effort will continue. But it seems to me that decades of struggle will be needed to win proper representation on the appropriate bodies. The young and the optimistic may be prepared to soldier on. The old, and those who want it all and want it now, can't wait for the millenium.

This largely unsuccessful enterprise was the State's attempt to secure access for the people by agreement. That aim can equally be pursued by the private purchase of desirable open country on everyone's behalf. At first thought this seems an unrealistic option but here it's relevant to consider the record of Britain's largest private landowner, the National Trust.

The founders of the Trust, a century ago, saw the problems clearly. They were confident that they could rely on a strong vein of Victorian philanthropy and idealism to support a national effort to safeguard fine buildings and beautiful landscapes for posterity. Prospective benefactors, however, would need and deserve the strongest assurance that these acquisitions would be held and cared for in perpetuity. With a surprising prescience the founders felt that it would be unwise to entrust the State with this task.

They therefore proposed an independent charity to hold properties anywhere in England and Wales forever. At the same time, the State's approval would be essential. And in a master stroke they succeeded in getting the Trust incorporated by Act of Parliament. In effect they obtained the strongest powers available in law to protect the Trust's holdings, even to the extent that they'd be permitted to write their own bye-laws and to declare land inalienable. That this last expression is a legal nonsense, since law can always be rewritten, doesn't alter the fact that the right has been largely effective. It set daunting obstacles for private developers and it caused serious headaches for Government departments. Seventy years were to pass before Parliament authorised, for motorway construction, the compulsory purchase of an area of 'inalienable' land. Subsequent reverses, though deeply depressing, have been few. In fact the State is almost proud of the Trust.

There can be few more striking examples of pure altruism than this hundred-year story. The Trust's support has come from the very richest and the very poorest. (In 1902 the first appeal to buy land in the Lake District drew a much-quoted response: "I am a working man and cannot afford more than two shillings but I once saw Derwentwater and I can never forget it.") Astonishingly, large areas of land and substantial donations of money have actually been given anonymously. Membership now exceeds two million and the Trust holds over 600,000 acres, aside from that held by its sister organisation in Scotland. To a half of this land, mainly lowland farms maintained as traditional estates, access is restricted to rights of way; to the remaining half there's open access and this half includes some of our most spectacular mountain and coastal scenery.

The security of Lake District landscapes is now monitored by the Park Authority but effectively the Trust has been and remains the real protector of the heart of Lakeland. Officers of Snowdonia's Park Authority have been known to remind climbers and walkers that only one of the fourteen three-thousanders, Snowdon itself, can be climbed by rights of way. Luckily for us, rights of way are irrelevant for many of these summits since they can be approached over National Trust open access land. If this weren't the case I'm sure that the Authority would be telling us to be grateful for what sufferance access we have and warning us not to upset the applecart by pressing for access where it's denied.

All this said, many walkers and climbers feel an unease about the Trust. Its upper echelons seem mainly to be staffed by mandarins with strong links with the landowning and military establishments and anxious to accommodate their wishes. The composition of the Council is extraordinarily unbalanced. (In 1992 only three of its twenty-six nominated members represented interests in public access.) The Trust's first official historian, a climber as a matter of fact, warning of the dangers of a large membership, remarked that "the tail has been been known to wag the dog." That's a revealing view of the felt status of supporters and officers and one rift actually resulted in the formation of an internal opposition, the Countryside Protection Group. The Trust's image, perhaps inevitably, is that of a paternalistic body generously providing something for the public. Let's not forget that that something was given to all of us by individual benefactors and the Trust itself is no more than our agency, staffed on a temporary basis. Lately its management has become infected with a marketing philosophy, establishing gift shops and touting for trippers.

With benefit of hindsight, it seems to me a pity that the Trust's work wasn't divided between three independent bodies: one dealing with high culture in the form of historic houses, parklands and gardens; one dealing with the traditional rural landscapes of farmed countryside and vernacular building; and one restricting itself to landforms unchanged or not much marked by man. (The time has now come, I believe, to start working towards this breakup.) All three purposes are admirable. But the Trust sprang from the Commons Preservation Society which concerned itself with freedom of access. As time has passed it's become chiefly a collector of stately homes. These, and farm estates, have turned into a terrifying financial responsibility demanding an enormous supporting machinery. If we'd had a body confining its aims to acquiring untilled land I'm certain that it would have united the efforts of outdoor people to an incomparably greater degree and would have been immeasurably more productive.

However, the Trust isn't the only agency protecting land for the benefit of all of us. Others include the Open Spaces Society, concerning itself with the remaining commons, and the Woodland Trust. In Scotland the John Muir Trust seems to be close to a model of what's needed for England and Wales. The British Mountaineering Council Trust has come into possession of two or three cliffs but it hasn't any wish to start buying them and launching a speculation in rock faces.

Here, a brief summary of attempts to extend access within the law becomes possible. With the establishment of the Trust a hundred years ago, with the work of other voluntary bodies both younger and older, and with strong legislative powers from fifty years ago, the first assumption ought to be that a good deal of ground must have been gained. In fact, over much of the unimproved land to which access has been secured de facto access already existed; local studies often show net losses of rights of way; and though more than a dozen long distance footpaths have been opened it's usually overlooked that all of them were formed largely, and some of them almost entirely, by linking pre-existing rights of way.

In any case, it's clear enough that the possibility of making real the dream of access to all untilled land and of establishing a web of routes through all our river systems by any legal avenue is remote. There remains the option of taking it without the law's approval, by seizure, if you like. This will sound extreme and revolutionary to those who feel that in any conflict between what is lawful and what seems right it's critical to change the law before acting rightly. The strategy, however, has a long history.

It would be easy to parade a line of eminent thinkers who assumed freedom of access to uncultivated ground to be a fundamental moral right, so self-evident that no case need be stated. In fact attempts at justifications run into difficult obstacles and involve material foreign to the character of this book. However, I want to put this matter into context and to mention a remaining constitutionalist approach so I'm forced into a hazardous reference to human rights.

The words are hard to handle. Rights can be clarified as legal or moral but the moral rights start arguments between contending moralities. Other expressions cause the same confusions and they're often used carelessly: freedoms and liberties; demands, claims, needs, entitlements.

There's a crude modern division between first, second and third generation rights. The first generation rights are the civil and political rights, sometimes called 'bourgeois rights', fought for in the eighteenth and nineteenth centuries: extensions to right of property, equality before the law, fair trial, freedom of conscience, speech, assembly, and so on. They're typified in national statements, the American Declaration of 1776 and the ensuing Bill of Rights, the French Declaration of 1789. Justification was easy: the Americans got their rights as an endowment from a Creator; the French rights came under the auspices of a Supreme Being.

The second generation rights relate to the economic, social and cultural goals struggled for in the nineteenth and early twentieth centuries. They're sometimes called 'socialist rights' and they're linked with the

Industrial Revolution. They deal with suffrage, with minimal decencies and safeguards in work and housing, with education, health, abolition of child labour and so on. They begin to look beyond national boundaries as in the Communist Manifesto of 1848. The basis is a reading of history, sometimes projected into fortune-telling.

In the fifty years since the United Nations Charter and the subsequent Universal Declaration of Human Rights there's been an attempt to codify whatever 'rights' could gain majority assent into International Law, to develop regional Treaty Law, to establish supranational courts of appeal, and to press nation states into incorporating these principles into their own legislation. This utopian programme has actually made some modest gains. During this period a call for third generation rights, sometimes called 'solidarity rights' or 'peoples' rights' has arisen. It's of a different order to the earlier groups which (with the single exception of the right of peoples to self-determination) dealt with individual rather than collective rights. There's some resistance to this development, it being held that individual rights should guarantee collective rights and that the balancing of the rights of individuals and of collectivities is tricky. The search for a basis for human rights has largely been abandoned and now they're simply asserted. Attempts to organise rights into a hierarchy, establishing working priorities, have failed; any rights recognised are regarded as having a provisional parity of status.

Rights of free movement haven't appeared in this programme. The closest approaches have dealt with what, to those who've suffered, have been more pressing matters: rights of asylum for political or religious reasons; abolition of slavery and more recent forms of restriction to work and place; and the third generation literature has included claims for a satisfactory environment. There are simple historical reasons for this blind spot. Two hundred years ago, hostile Indians or unfriendly peasants may have given cause for thought to American or French travellers but there weren't any legal impediments to their journeys. The development is a comparatively recent one and Britain is an extreme case. In our small densely-populated island, increasing leisure and ease of transport have collided with Right of Property. In fact, many Third World peoples enjoy freedoms we've lost.

In Britain the argument for access reduces to an insistence that there's a spectrum of types of ownership, which is rarely absolute. At one extreme, certainly, there's an uncontested right of total disposal, even of destruction, as of some artefact which I've made with my own hands but which fails to satisfy me. At the other there are resources like the sea, the air we breathe, owned in a sense in common so that, for instance, the law now keeps some watch upon pollution. Cliffs and mountains not made by man stand at that end of the scale. Importantly, and centrally in this spectrum, there's the ancient concept of *usufruct*, the use of a resource for a restricted purpose without interference with its use for other purposes.

However, it might be profitable to shift the argument sideways and up. There's now a international cadre of well-paid lawyers specialising in human rights issues. They can fit our problem into a larger context and I think that constitutionalists ought to drop it onto their desks. In recent years several High Court judges in Britain have made note, in summings up, of European views or decisions, even where these were at variance with present British law. External support is always helpful.

That's one background against which claims for access to wild country might be made. Here I offer two simple observations. First, the primary enabling skills or capacities we all start to struggle for in the first year of life are walking and talking. Second, all civilisations have sprung at some point from freedoms of communication and movement. These principles are themselves without necessary moral bias. Therefore logic suggests, opposing the working rule that rights have parity of status, a general presumption in favour of freedom of speech and movement as the neutral foundation for all human rights. Essentially, to curtail either is to thwart human nature and the drive of civilisation.

Governments, of course, often insist on rights of curtailment in order to protect the stability of the regime but each instance ought in principle to be subject to periodic review. And our case should be that within one's own country a fundamental principle of right of access on something like the Swedish model ought to be recognised. It's astonishing that governments fail to see that despite a widespread collapse of faith in most of our institutions a strong sense of citizenship can still rest securely on attachments to landscape and to what is best in the built environment; further, that indifference to the condition of either is a recipe for social disaster. Having said this, it's possible to support the claim to right of access simply by summarising the virtues of walking and by insisting on its harmlessness.

In praise of walking. It can be used simply as exercise. Enjoyed as a regular habit, without reconnaissance of the pain barrier, it can help keep the body in working order through a lifetime. If there are recurrent and troublesome surpluses of energy, however great, big walks can be used to eliminate them. Most walkers, on the other hand, find some interest in the scene around them, either of an aesthetic character or in the study of nature or in both. The therapeutic properties of walking are considerable and cost nothing. It may be a slow cure but it can be used to deal with grief, unhappiness or ill fortune. It's often helpful as a means of escape, leaving work and the mass media far behind. "Happy is the land, my young friend, where one need not seek peace in the wilderness," said Rousseau: "but where is that country?" he added, a surprising question to issue from the pastoral Europe of two centuries ago. On Thoreau's release from his memorable night in Concord Gaol he led a party of friends up the highest nearby hill, the obvious place to go: "and then the State was nowhere to be seen." (But he hadn't yet finished with the State and his reflections on civil disobedience were quick to follow.)

The claims made for walking are sometimes extreme. Bruce Chatwin declared that he shared with the film director Werner Herzog a belief in its sacramental value. In the winter of 1974 Herzog walked from Munich to Paris, where his guru Lotte Eisner was said to be dying, in order to "walk away" her illness. By the time he'd got there she'd recovered and was to live another ten years, so proving his point. George Steiner has asserted that the main part of Western humanist thought stems from the physical experience, the actual pulse and pace of walking.

In the Lake District, with better public access and heavier use than anywhere else in England, conflict between resident and visitor is exceptional. In less frequented areas, by contrast, a rich choice of objections to the arrival of the walker have been put forward. Farmers and foresters say that walkers will cause damage and endanger their own activities and if this is contested they say that their own activities will endanger walkers. In the meantime both farmer and forester accept the subsidies the public endlessly provides. Landowners with grouse moors and deer estates echo the same two arguments. But the few systematic studies carried out haven't found observable damage to shooting and stalking interests.

For decades many water authorities insisted that free access to their gathering grounds would threaten the purity of their supplies. This argument was maintained even where rights of way were already in use over the land, even where it was crossed by roads or by railways discharging sewage, and even where grouse shooting and angling were permitted. As late as 1939, in opposing the Access to Mountains Bill, the British Waterworks Association referred to "the tendency of such areas to become a resort for undesirable characters among whom immorality and licentiousness is rife." In later years, following public pressure and recognising improved purification techniques, most authorities relaxed their opposition and some began to make wider provision for public access. The effects of privatisation haven't yet begun to show.

The erosion of footpaths has been promoted as a central matter of debate on account of charges of ecological damage and unsightliness. The footpath reconstruction programme has now built up such momentum that it's absorbing large sums of money and has permanent staff with vested interests in its continuation. It shouldn't be overlooked that the problems are localised. At a few unique places — Scafell, Snowdon, Stonehenge — there'll always be a concentration of activity, though solutions other than restriction of access, access by parking fee, and heavy construction work are obvious enough. Similar signs of wear appear wherever access is limited, the basic principle being simple: the less access, the more erosion. Some stretches of the Pennine Way show evidence of wear which would never have occurred if there'd been a half dozen continuous unranked options. The money already spent on the damaged sections would have bought up these options.

It's unfortunate that in some of our mountain regions the work done to combat erosion has been badly carried out: inappropriate materials have been used; the construction has been unsympathetic; a rigid width specification has been imposed; attractive natural obstacles have been destroyed; winter hazards have been built in by summer workers. The cure has been worse than the disease. Compared with the grosser changes in our mountain landscapes — conifer blocks, pumped-storage schemes, windfarms, denudation by overgrazing, ground cover differentials imposed by new fencing on hilltops, modern roadworks, unscreened carparks, campsites and Eurobarns — footpath erosion is invisible and irrelevant. When a steep section degenerates to make a scree, when an entrenching length captures small streams to form a tiny gully, what results, after all, imitates a natural mountain feature. No large-scale experiments have so far been made to find out to what degree erosion has been exacerbated by the overgrazing stemming from the payment of headage grants. In the Pennines the damaged ground has been found to be negligible in area compared with that due to natural causes and, it's believed, with that due to vegetation changes from atmospheric pollution and acid rain.

It's clear that no-one's offended by ancient walls and sheepfolds, the remains of abandoned smallholdings, old mineral workings, mine trackways and drovers' roads. That's because there's no sense of present human purpose about them. The new paths, by contrast, send out a signal that the agencies of the state want nature, and all personnel using the hills, under surveillance and control. A dictatorship of managers has been imposed.

Of all the traces men leave in wild country a naturally developed foot-path is the most acceptable. It's tempting to see it not for what it is (it is a tape encoding generalised information about the minds of men) but as if it were imbued with a discrimination of its own. Hill paths strike varieties of subtle accommodations between economy of effort and im-patience of aim, between wayward curiosity and prudent calculation. They make aesthetic choices and they yield to risk-taking impulses. They have second thoughts. Every step is different but they talk to us non-stop, quietly, soothingly, in an idiom, a body language, as natural as our mother tongue.

Litter gives a final cause of complaint. This is a trivial matter since it can be cleared up anyway. The average walker cares more about the appearance of the countryside than the average farmer, whose plastic nutrient bags (and, sometimes, pesticide containers) can be found in many streams and hang in most hedges.

So if, broadly speaking, walking is the most innocent of occupations and if it's valuable and if it's seen as good by a large part of the popula-tion; if our forefathers were shifted not so long ago from the land, often against their wishes; if we've been deprived of right of movement over land once accessible; if, for half a century, we've subsidised farming and forestry without any concession in return or the slightest sign of gratitude; if it's proved impossible to extend access by lawful compul-sion; if the process of gaining it by agreement is too slow, and uncertain, and costly, and if comprehensive purchase is an impossible expense:— what are the chances, then, of gaining access by seizure? This question suggests high drama but on a moment's reflection it's obvious that it's been going on since the establishment of the Norman deer park and since the Enclosures in the form of simple trespass.

At its extremes trespass aims for one of two styles: the trespasser takes good care not to be seen or he makes quite sure that he is seen. I find two interesting features in the undetected trespass. The first is clear if I abandon any moral standpoint and look at the substance of law. (Law is, after all, only the front line between the existing power and the public temper.) Most criminal or civil law concerning the person deals with actions involving both material loss, damage or change and the corre-sponding sense of grievance in the complaining party; also, less fre-quently, with either the change or the grievance alone. There exists a rare fourth class of action of which the undetected trespass is an exam-ple. It causes no material change and it leaves the landowner with his happiness unimpaired. This surely means that it represents the lowest and defining limit of what the law sees as anti-social behaviour. In fact,

until the time of writing, English law was fairly tolerant of casual trespass. The trespasser might be sued under civil law if he caused damage;
he might be ejected "with sufficient force" if he refused to leave; he
might have an injunction taken out against him if he persisted in a
favoured trespass. But, despite what was said on the notice boards, he
couldn't be prosecuted.

The second odd feature of the discreet trespass is that when it does
happen to be detected it sometimes arouses an astounding fury. The
rage seems wildly disproportionate to the offence and it's clear that for
many landowners self-esteem is crucially dependent on a sense of full
dominion. They are their land. And the need to retain this dominion is
desperate since private land is the outstanding symbol of wealth and
privilege that can't be stolen, trashed or imitated by the envious and the
poor. This is sad but it has to be taken seriously. The xenophobic landowner may be accompanied by dogs or waving a shotgun so that solo
trespass can feel, in some areas, like a dangerous game. Land rage came
before road rage. For this reason it seems wiser to trespass as a small
group. But the larger the party, the more likely it is to be seen.

As long as men enclose wild country the evasive trespass will go on
and every time it passes unobserved a tiny victory has been won. The
trespasser has become a folk hero, taking on the mantle of the poacher
and superseding him in the landowner's anger. He's a part of English
history.

The confrontational trespass must have as long a history as the discreet trespass but until fairly recently it took place in the name of livelihood. The most famous cases of recreational trespass are from this century, the Doctor's Gate raids on Bleaklow from 1909 onwards and the
mass trespasses on Kinder Scout and at Abbey Brook in 1932. It's worth
pointing out that some have been misdescribed since the footpath or
land at issue had been closed illegally. Even at the time of the Kinder
Scout affair the public had held a traditional freedom of access until the
far edge of living memory. As a tactic these demonstrations were condemned at the time by many of the outdoor movement's own leaders
and spokesmen, though with friends like Sir Lawrence Chubb walkers
needed no enemies. However, it's impossible to avoid the suspicion that
in the dismissiveness of even so revered a campaigner as Tom Stephenson
there was a sense of pique that he hadn't helped organise the Kinder
Trespass himself and wouldn't go down in history as one of the martyrs.

It's never possible to weigh the relative contributions of direct action
and political agitation to a particular outcome but the real significance
of the mass trespasses was that they stirred the outdoor community's

imagination and inspired what became almost a myth. They also put on public display the solidarity of the establishment. The composition of the civil jury which caused five of the Kinder trespassers to serve prison terms should be kept permanently in print. It consisted of two Brigadier-Generals, three Colonels, two Majors, three Captains and two Aldermen: more officers than gentlemen.

From 1980 onwards a growing impatience has become obvious in the outdoor community as the actual titles of recent publications make clear: *The Theft of the Countryside* and *The Theft of the Hills*; *Forbidden Land* and *Our Forbidden Land*; *Whose Land Is It Anyway?*, *This Land is Our Land*, and *Them's Our Hills*. Even two books with the same title, *Freedom to Roam*. The Kinder Trespass is now remembered annually in an anniversary ascent. The Ramblers' Association, which has led the access agitation for half a century, took to promoting an annual Forbidden Britain Day. As a body climbers have taken a shamefully small part in these struggles. In earlier times access to the bigger and more remote crags was rarely contested and in the hills — except for the arrival of the conifer block and the windfarm — we haven't seen anything quite comparable with the total destruction by agricultural technology of a large part of England's traditional countryside. But in the past few years conflicts over lowlying crags are becoming more frequent and climbing magazines are reflecting an increasing concern. In 1991 a climbers' trespass on MoD property at Range West in Pembroke secured some concessions.

It seems possible that the demonstrative trespass will continue to be seen in the future, particularly where there's any attempt to restrict de facto access or to charge for air and exercise on newly privatised land. These areas, together with large estates and forests, are obvious targets. Modern forestry, farming, and water gathering need fewer people on the land than ever before. At the moment it's proving impossible to control serious crime on the doorsteps of police stations in the cities. It wouldn't be easy to do much about dispersed simultaneous trespass in remote places unless the trespassers were to announce their plans beforehand or to leave unattended cars parked at the roadside. It may be that the movement is now strong enough to risk publicised confrontational trespasses. However, the organisers would lay themselves open to the range of legal reprisals now developed to control, it's said, music festivals, New Age Travellers and Gypsy settlement.

In discussing the risks of trespass the experience of Earth First! groups in America and elsewhere can't be ignored. It's a wry comment on English society that the most extreme direct action it's recently produced has been that of the Hunt Saboteurs and the Animal Liberation Front. We care more about animal rights than about human rights. The purpose of Earth First! groups is simply the defence of nature and it might be thought that we've nothing to learn from them. That's not so. Everyone involved in the access struggle should read *Ecodefense* (and that deceptively surfaced novel, *The Monkey Wrench Gang*) for comprehensive views of the strategies of protest and for the fact that the recommendations on secure organisation didn't keep one of the co-authors out of harm's way. With the abandonment in British politics of any attempt towards consensus, and with the growing sense of the powerlessness of the individual, it's quite possible that responses will be seen here in the cause of access as well as in that of the remembered countryside.

In opposition to ecotage and to the demonstrative trespass the constitutionalists will labour on. The dream of an Access to Mountains Bill hasn't died. I find it hard to believe that anything useful might come of it and I have to remind myself that both Lloyd George and Winston Churchill voted in support of one of the earlier bills. Also, centrally, the casual trespass will go on, avoiding confrontation in order to maintain, as someone wrote seventy years ago, "that philosophic and tranquil demeanour which should always characterise the super-trespasser." And think of this: Wordsworth declared himself a trespasser; in the thirties a British Prime Minister and a High Court Judge publicly confessed themselves persistent trespassers; a few years ago a former chairman of a Regional Development Board gleefully described to me the ritual of his fortnightly and startlingly audacious trespasses. The best of company.

CONSERVATION

The climber is anxious to retain and to extend his freedom of access to hills and cliffs; he must also want to protect the surroundings he enjoys. I'd like to express some of the pleasure the mountain scene itself, rather than the activity, has given me. I can't do this by generalisation, I have to bear witness to things seen. This leads on to the dilemmas some of us have to face.

In fact, the grandest impressions and most arresting sights, those offered by the sky and the weather, aren't much at risk. Man-made climatic change is imperceptible. The arrival of the jet and satellite, however, is a disturbance in the night sky. It means that there's now no wilderness on earth safe from visual intrusion. We've messed up the stars and no-one seems dismayed.

Start, then, with the sky and its rarer displays. Start with a June evening on Snowdon, three women contouring the cwm to the foot of Clogwyn du'r Arddu, myself dawdling behind. They were looking for *Lloydia serotina*, the mountain spiderwort, the Snowdon lily, in bloom; it's the most famous of all our rarities, confined in Britain to a very few locations in this area. I was using the excuse to admire once again the finest cliff in Wales and to acknowledge its great routes.

Two hundred yards behind the botanists, my eye was caught by an iridescencent patch on the still surface of Llyn du'r Arddu, five hundred

214

feet beneath us. I stared at it, puzzled. It wasn't until I began to move that I realised I'd been looking at a reflection from the sky, where, in concentric rings, a perfect rainbow-coloured disc was visible. I saw that it stood at the altitude of the declining sun though it was a diameter or two larger. A moment later I noticed a companion, flanking the sun on the other side at the same height and distance. A memory came back of something I'd read: 'false suns'. Estimating a right angle, halving and halving again, I took rough bearings. And after long search I rediscovered the account; mock suns appear at 22 degrees of arc and they're caused by refraction from ice particles in the upper atmosphere. I felt absurdly privileged, never having met anyone else who's been favoured with this manifestation on British hills. The Snowdon lily was just a bonus.

The more unfamiliar these atmospheric displays the more startling they seem. There's a considerable literature on glories and Dolores La Chapelle has brought enough of it together to show that the haloes of religious figures probably derive from them. In sparsely settled desert mountains the extreme infrequency of sighting must give them extraordinary impact. Here, against the deep ice-carved, sun-shielded corries of our cloudy hills, they're not uncommon. The regular hill walker is bound to encounter his haloed shadow on a number of occasions though I've never starred in one with the mist-screen diffuse enough to promote me from saint to Brocken spectre.

The night sky can offer spectacular portents. I've only seen auroras a few times in Scotland and once or twice further south. They were weakly conceived and didn't impress me so powerfully as lunar rainbows seen in the west of Ireland. Why the moonbow should be observed so seldom is a mystery. Presumably a certain level of illumination has to be reached, restricting its incidence to a period about the full moon, and there are fewer people about through wet nights than through wet days. Possibly they're mainly seen on misty and hilly western coasts. I've hardly come across a mention in climbing literature though I'm tempted to guess that a moonbow inspired the opening of a seventeenth-century poem probably written in Wales, 'The World' by Henry Vaughan: "I saw Eternity the other night / Like a great Ring of pure and endless light / All calm as it was bright..." I can't remember any sight so transfixing as a double moonbow I saw in Donegal, the immaculate white arches high and complete.

The effects of light on mountains have often been celebrated in the form of the alpenglow. With luck, once or twice in a lifetime, these effects will seem to enter the realm of the paranormal. Other than on snow and outside the repeatable effects of very stable climates, as described on Hymettos, I've seen two astonishing sunset transfigurations. One was of the north wall of the Tre Cime in the Dolomites. The other was of the Cuillin of Skye. These two were grossly different in character yet in each case the light seemed an active property of the rock. I'd degrade these epiphanies if I were to apply to them the commonplace names of colours.

On British hills the weather often changes or frustrates the plans of climbers and sometimes those of hill walkers too. Rain rules out any climb near one's best limit and wind can be a problem. For a reader who doesn't know the inconstancy of our hills I can best convey it as I see it from where I live. The summit of Snowdon, the highest hill in Wales, stands fifteen miles to the west; the coastal resort of Llandudno, a Victorian spa nestled between the limestone headlands of the Great and the Little Orme, fifteen miles to the north. Llandudno has an annual rainfall of less than thirty inches and it's one of the sunniest spots in the west. Snowdon, not reaching much over 3500 feet, also has many sunny days a year and is climbed by countless family parties. A mountain railway lifts trippers to the summit. But its highest slopes take more than two hundred inches of rain and in the winters I've been living here this only half-tamed hill has killed more than a hundred climbers and walkers.

That's a tremendous rainfall gradient. Roughly, it might be said that for every mile and hundred feet of height gained from Llandudno to the south-west there'll be an extra six or seven inches of rain a year. So the higher crags are often wet and in recent years indoor walls and the previously unexplored seacliffs have become extremely popular. Yet the effects of rain can be admirable and awe-inspiring. We count rain in a simple arithmetic of inches though its results show in phases. It goes on for days and the hillside streams run steady but unchanged. Then at some critical increment they visibly swell, multiply, curdle. And beyond this, on rare occasions, the mountain's character alters, its whole relief is suddenly defined as new cascades show everywhere and every slope is laced with plunging threads of water.

Waterfalls. The most impressive I've ever seen was that of Gavarnie in the Pyrenees which seemed in a category beyond Niagara or Yosemite Falls, all three as visited in late summer or autumn. Niagara drops into a basin and Yosemite into carved channels or pools. No doubt Gavarnie shows a trough in normal conditions but we approached it after several days of downpour and it appeared to be striking well out onto a simple talus. From the whole huge area of impact it was exploding out and up again, a Hiroshima of water struggling to cross the cirque. Now it might be assumed that compared with scenes like these the waterfalls of Wales are derisory. That's not the case. The smaller the fall the more closely we approach in safety and in fact a point is reached at which the sensory effect is equalised. If snow melts rapidly the Aber Falls, its main drop only a hundred feet or so, can be probed and its margins entered to offer an equally memorable sense of the power of water.

No need to go to Patagonia to learn about the strength of wind. I've never been forced to crawl on British summits as, on odd occasions, strong and experienced friends have but I've often had to push and sometimes to support myself. A few years ago we made up a party of three to climb an ancient classic, the Cyfrwy arête of Cader Idris. None of us knew the climb, the other two didn't know that side of the hill. Confession: I'd never been up this celebrated mountain.

It was a wild autumn day but the date couldn't be changed since the ascent was a sixtieth birthday request by one of the party, the escorts being a year or two either side that age. The rain fell and the wind blew. At five minutes from the road my boots were swilling. An hour up, halting in the shelter of boulders by Llyn y Gadair, water was trickling in culverts beneath my waterproofs. The birthday boy was heard to say a second time that in view of the conditions he'd do whatever we thought best. We weren't having that, he'd got us out here. The cloud was disturbed for just long enough to allow us to identify the steep base of the ridge. We didn't really climb it, we out-manoeuvred it, having to bypass or vary the first direct pitches, even though briefly somewhat sheltered from the wind.

The plateau, in the howling gale, was another world. We were each thrown down two or three times, alarming on this boulder-covered ground, and frequently we were stampeded. Outcrops unknown to me bowed out of the cloud and disappeared. And then we were in the old roofed shelter at the summit, doorless but its back to the wind, a haven of comparative calm, quiet and indulgence, enjoying coffee, food, even a bottle of champagne. Later, leaving cloud and wind again, the always marvellous rite of passage displayed beneath us the satisfying shape of an unfamiliar cwm. It had been a brilliant day and Wales offers equal opportunities to everybody every year.

The winter climber can usually find a suitable project in Scotland but in Lakeland or Wales he'll often be frustrated. Snow falls irregularly on the highest hills over six months or so but except in mid-winter it's normally quickly removed. From my own house, however, I'm able to watch the small twin snow-patches persist on Carnedd Llewelyn:

1994, last seen on June 11th; 1995, June 5th; last year, displaced some distance, June 5th again.

The variability of our weather means that in a bad spell we often get a glorious winter day. That's good but it isn't everything. Bad weather is bad in so many different ways. From countless winter ascents of Snowdon I've no generalised image. The snow line, the depth and texture of snow, the direction, force and character of the wind, the sky, the reach of vision, never combine in the same manner twice. The only consistency comes from the counting out of the stations of the way, the brief halt at the Pyg Track col, the break for food and drink by the desolate frozen pool beneath the Zigzags, the recognition of familiar rocks. If, for really hard conditions, there's a single common denominator it's the frost flowers at the summit, miracles of organisation, feathery blades and arrowheads aimed straight at the wind, sometimes more than a foot in length, once maybe eighteen inches.

The onset of snow on the hills is always enlivening. This is especially so for the climber if it arrives without warning. There was a day on the Ordinary Route on the Idwal Slabs when, magnificently, huge soft flakes fell vertically in an absolute stillness and I was swept with happiness. (In the pub that night as locals groaned about the weather I tried to convey that delight to a near neighbour, Owen Wynne Owen. An engineer, his chief interest is the reconstruction of veteran cars. He was staring at me intently through his thick-lensed glasses. "Harold," he said, in a low and urgent voice, "you must see a psychiatrist. Without delay.")

A day on Lliwedd when a furious hailstorm hit us. Hail ran down the cliff like water, banking every ledge deeply and freezing to vertical rock. In twenty minutes it was as if the mountain had been shifted two thousand miles northward. A day on the Blaitière on my first trip to the Alps. I was in the charge of Alf Beanland for whom this was perhaps his third season. On the upper glacier it began to snow quite hard. We continued, climbing the rocks to the Rocher de la Corde in crampons. The snow was angled by a strong consistent wind. Alf was in a fix. He could see that I was enjoying myself and he was wrenched by temptation. The summit was only a few metres higher but the route along the ridge might be difficult in these conditions. Already our track up the glacier might be obliterated. He had to set an example of alpine judgement. Telling myself that the Rocher could really count as a summit in itself I acceded to his decision. We went down very quickly, seeing no trace of our route of ascent but coming on each feature easily. I'd felt great pleasure at pushing the rules already.

What is it with a storm that gives us such delight? Maybe I ask this improperly, never having experienced conditions in which I've felt my life on the line, never having worked in an occupation in which earnings or livelihood might be threatened. Noticeably, at scenes of natural disaster people not only collaborate and take risks to help each other but are often cheerful as well as excited. Storms energise and unite us and I'm sure that many feel an affirmative response. It's not just the sense of awe at the power of nature as rivers burst banks, winds throw trees, snow proclaims the independence of each village. There's also a thrill at the interruption of the numbing routines of cities when factories, offices and schools shut down, all the purposes of men are vetoed. Our over-organised civilisation needs an occasional good shake. Roads close, drivers abandon their cars. Good: let's see them walk. I rarely feel so much at home, so much myself, as in tolerably vile conditions.

On British hills one of my most memorable bad weather days was in the Cairngorms in midwinter. In the fifties while Gordon Mansell and I were working as instructors in Derbyshire our leader, Geoff Sutton, decided to mount an expedition into the land of Picts and Scots. None of us had been into this area before but we'd made winter incursions into other parts of Scotland, we'd climbed in the Alps, we weren't scared. At our base Geoff sat at a table frowning over his maps like Caesar. Finally he drew a line and told the pair of us to take six volunteers on a scouting excursion, reporting back to him on what the country looked like. He might follow with another party on hearing our account.

Through soft snow we'd trudged up to Derry Lodge and, now thigh-deep, now waist-deep, we'd continued to the bothy in Coire Etchachan. Here we found that the door had been left open, snow had blown in and had melted and refrozen so that the floor was now a deep and perfectly level slab of ice. We applied our axes and cut out enough to get the swollen door almost shut but we couldn't make much impression on the floor. The place afforded shelter and nothing else. We had a competent and sensible party and some daylight remained. Leaving them to cook their food we set off for the Shelter Stone at Loch Avon. If it offered better accommodation we'd accept. Although we'd have to take them over in darkness we'd have done the route twice in daylight if we moved fast. We were lucky to find the Stone, which was almost buried, but traces of a recent track revealed an access to the chamber down a deep narrow shaft through the snow. Rejecting the idea, we returned to settle down for a poor night. Gordon wrestled endlessly with an improvised hammock knitted from a climbing rope. The rest of us, despite all the padding we could arrange, sank slowly into made-to-measure pools in the ice.

The morning was cloudy, the wind gusty, visibility poor. We made a way up to Loch Etchachan where, in a moment of alarm, we realised that we'd strayed onto the verge of the smaller lake, the ice concealed by drifts. Ascending Ben MacDui we were in the lee of the hill, comfortable almost to the top. There we ran into a hard cold consistent wind, blasting us with tiny ice particles, visibility down to a few strides. From here onward we'd have to navigate with the utmost care. At the summit, fingers freezing, I set a compass course and strode out. I went resolutely forward for thirty seconds and all the time the wind was screaming something that made no sense. Just as I slowed in confusion I heard Gordon, at the back and checking me, shouting urgently. I'd reversed the compass and was probably heading for a precipice. Deeply embarrassing. I turned round, tried again, and within a minute found myself in the only perfect whiteout I've ever experienced.

In a landscape of matt white it was as if we were walking in pitch darkness. The ground was almost level but quite invisible and I found myself testing its solidity unsteadily with my axe and my feet. It was as if we were on a slightly rolling ship. From time to time I turned, hoping that the shapes of the others, all just visible, would give a clearer confirmation of the vertical and of any slight rise or descent than my own bodily sensation. I had to laugh. They were staggering like drunks, arms outstretched, some axes waving dangerously. Dimly, Gordon's bearded, snow-encrusted figure might have been the Great Grey Man of Ben MacDui. We went very slowly forward for several minutes until, without any perceptible change in wind speed or direction or in the spindrift content of the air, near surfaces suddenly became visible again and confidence was regained.

We were making for the March Burn and the Pools of Dee. As we lost height, on a new bearing now, a window opened to reveal some hundreds of feet of the right flank of our spur. From the map our line had seemed the safest way off the hill, reducing steep descent to the minimum possible. Now we saw that the slope itself presented a novel problem.

I'm not certain that at that time we'd ever read the term 'slab avalanche'. I'd certainly never seen the mechanics described. However, a perfect illustration lay directly beneath us where an acre or two of snow had sloughed cleanly off. At the top, as well as I could judge, the fracture lip seemed to be about two feet high. At the bottom, where the perfectly smooth slope ran out, thousands of tons of snow had shunted to a standstill in a heaped chaos of slabs and blocks. It formed a ridge perhaps twenty feet high and some hundreds in length. We understood the effect and the cause instantaneously and we stopped and conferred.

We hadn't enough daylight to start exploring other descents all of which seemed more problematic. The bared surface must be safer but it might be hard enough to require time-consuming step-cutting for our cramponless party and the descent to the shear line would risk a further avalanche. To continue along our present course seemed equally dangerous.

We decided to continue along our present course. The reasoning was that with every step our height above the runout would decrease and that if the whole slope went, with luck, we'd all ride the top edge down. We roped up at short intervals and continued along our slowly descending traverse. As we moved delicately across and down, not speaking, hardly breathing, the snow began to make strange creaking noises and a thin continuous crack, two or three inches wide, opened up to link the feet of the whole party. Snakelike, this crack began to creep forward a little faster than myself until its head lay at twelve feet before me. For several long minutes it held this advantage and, moving with great caution, I didn't dare attempt to overhaul it. Slowly the height of the slope and the possible slide began to look more reasonable. Finally, a foot at a time, I began to gain on the living fissure until at last it halted and we were off. We continued rapidly, now on safe ground, and took a short break at Lochan Buidhe. Only a generalised memory of the wild and satisfying scene and of the making of hot drinks on our primus stoves remains.

The Lairig Ghru is perhaps the finest major pass in Britain. Down at its summit by the Pools of Dee we imagined that our trials were over. Hardly four miles of gentle descent or level walk remained and we were now below the cloudline and more sheltered from the wind. In fact the snow was still very deep. Our party was tired and Gordon and I took turns at breaking a route through endless drifts, corniced like Hokusai's wave. We seemed to make painfully slow progress and it was almost dark when we came within sight of Corrour Bothy. We still had to cross the river, running strongly despite the sub-zero temperature. A frustrating distance downstream two steel cables were strung from bank to bank, each clad in a three-inch sheath of ice. Clipping a sling round the upper I took a rope across, breaking the ice off in chunks with axe and boots and finding the final slippery ascent quite trying. And at last we were in the security of the bothy, enjoying the sound of the wind outside, preparing hot drinks and food, reliving the massive gratifications of the day, sinking down into a deep dry bed of soft heather for what I'll always remember as one of the most comfortable nights of my life.

For the lover of theatre, after rain, wind and snow, nature has a final resource: the electric storm. It reaches the same intensities in plains as in mountains but mountains give better viewpoints and more appropriate backcloths for the spectacle. For detached enjoyment it's best seen from shelter. It's urged that this shouldn't be the mouth of a cave or the roof of an overhang since the human body can play spark core electrode with the rock lip. In this one uses one's discretion. In Crafnant three years ago, having finished our climb with just minutes to spare, we lunched in comfort and at leisure. We were sitting against the back of the undercut base of Clogwyn yr Eryr. Above the initial overhang the wall itself is vertical or overhanging and our balcony remained bone dry. We felt secure and exhilarated as, through a sheet of water fifteen feet out, we watched strike after strike hit the slopes and the lake beneath us. For myself, although I've several times felt the urge to hurry downward from exposed situations, I've not once registered the physical warnings of mounting electrical charge. A remarkable photograph of my wife, taken on the north ridge of Tryfan, disturbs me. She smiles happily, her hair raised in a corona. A few minutes later the party was taking shocks from the rock.

For special effects the electric storm is best enjoyed in darkness as well as from shelter. A memorable night in the Dolomites. Soaked to the skin in walking up to the Rifugio Lavaredo we treated ourselves to an expensive meal, eating by candlelight and watching sheet lightning through the big picture windows. For a good two hours the entire mountainscape was revealed and held for seconds at a time under an almost unflickering ceiling of white.

Lightning can be useful. To summarise my acquaintance with the Nantillons glacier: I've jogged down it in perfect conditions, not worth description; I've fallen down it; I've descended it without crampons and with a stone-age dagger in lieu of a steel-age ice axe; I was groping down in a snowstorm a page or two back. And once my way was lit by lightning.

As we'd regained the lower glacier, after a day of intense excitements and just as night fell, Keith King had burrowed into his rucksack for our only torch. It had mated with his peg hammer and we had no spare bulb. Almost immediately rain began to fall in torrents and to run down the ice, embedded at this level with rock debris. Drenched to the skin in minutes we felt our way more and more slowly as the last light faded. But just at that moment lightning began to advance up the Arve valley and quickly the storm concentrated itself around us. Soon the strikes, discharging for several seconds, were at half-minute intervals. Shortly we had a system. One looks right and down, the other left and down. Someone declares, we move rapidly while the electric light is on, then cautiously from memory. Drawing to a halt we ready ourselves for the next strike. It didn't seem to take any longer than a daylight descent.

Perhaps the rarest and most curious of nature's electrical phenomena is the fireball. It remains a mystery to meteorologists and little is known about it except that it's said occasionally to descend the chimneys of houses and to chase very old ladies out into the street. To this old wives' tale I lend my support, having once had a perfect sighting.

At the time I had an upper-floor flat on the edge of the Gwydir Forest. On a warm sunny afternoon an off-colour cloud rolled over the summit of Moel Siabod and within a quarter-hour a violent thunderstorm had begun. I stood at a window, watching the rain drive down. Lightning was stabbing into the woods and the strike to thunder interval was tending to zero. The temperature had fallen dramatically. Between the trunks of some massive beeches I could see the start of a track two hundred feet away. At its entry a parked car sheltered a young couple who, shaken by inner tempests, apparently hadn't noticed the storm. The steep slope beyond the track was covered in young birches.

Simultaneously there came a blinding flash and a deafening crack. In the tops of the birches, say at thirty feet, a globe of fire had appeared and it hung there motionless for several seconds. It appeared to be rather larger than a beach ball and to cast some light. Quite slowly it began to descend as if almost weightless, following a curious wavering course until at four feet above ground level, eight to ten seconds elapsed, it halted for three or four seconds. Then it drifted sideways for six or seven feet. And then, without any prior change, without sound, instantaneously, it dematerialised.

"I have seen the flake of fire fall, miraculous and pentecostal," says one of Golding's heroes. That's not good enough, I want to know how things work, what the trick is. In shirt-sleeves I charged downstairs and out into the hammering rain. With the bank behind and the distribution of the trees I'd positioned the descent path almost exactly in two dimensions and within a few feet in the third. All I needed was a cross-sighting. The lovers would have been recalled to the outer world, the ball having hung finally only twenty feet in front of their car. But before I was under the beeches I heard the car revving up. I changed course for a gap in the wall, waving my arms, but they were descending the lane at suicidal speed. The girl, who appeared to be getting dressed, flashed me a brief terrified glance as they passed by. Too late. I trotted up to the trees, clambered around, examined leaves, looked down from higher up the slope, searched the dirt of the track. Nothing. The fresh green leaves of the birches were unscorched. I noticed the near interlacing of the branches and could only conclude that some principle of aversion, some negative polarity in this tiny orange-red sun, had steered its erratic track, resisting any contact with substance and earth.

Attention turns naturally from the activity of the heavens to the creatures of the sky. In roped climbing the belayer often follows the flight of birds and admires their mastery over the downward drag that's forever clawing at his back. When low-level cliffs stand in woodland and he can look down on the canopy he gets a privileged view of treetop life. Some seacliffs hold enormous colonies, fascinating and entertaining to watch. Who doesn't stop for a moment to gaze at a line of cormorants drying their wings, at ridiculous puffins, at the crowded tenements of auks? In recent years, on sea cliffs in particular, ornithologists have sometimes made heated criticism of climbers. In fact very few climbers would choose to make an ascent through a dense colony but occasionally it's been done and has been seen to cause consternation in the barrio. It's hard to judge how seriously to take this criticism. When an exploratory route was made at Bempton, on the Yorkshire coast, an RSPB representative alleged that recovery would take years. Yet from this same cliff, a century ago, several thousand eggs a year were collected for human consumption without destabilisation of the colony.

Many birds sit tight anyway or will only leave a nest very briefly. I pulled up onto a ledge on a classic Cornish climb on Chair Ladder to find a sitting seabird before my face. It was a common gull, or an outcast kittiwake maybe. In my haste I noticed behaviour rather than detail. It rose stiffly to its feet, pointedly turned its back on me, took a couple of steps away and, trembling with indignation, stared at the back of the niche. As I bridged quickly past it resumed its position, only to have to go through the same outraged performance for my companion five minutes later.

In the interests of science and conservation I'll now supply a complete list of every species I've actually disturbed from a nest by rock climbing. First, then, on a single occasion, let's say a kittiwake. Second, on several occasions, jackdaws. The jackdaw doesn't know it's had the misfortune to be classified as a pest and may be shot without a license. Pest or not, any alarm felt by the jackdaw can be no different to that felt by peregrine, eagle or osprey. The distinctions we make relate more to our thirst for the unusual than to our concern for the creature.

In fact my check list of birds started from their nests, always in innocence, by fifty years of rock-climbing numbers just four species. For the other two I have to move a little higher up the hill. These two are kestrel and (dare I say it?) peregrine. We disturbed one of each in the Lakes in the early fifties and one of each again in Wales in the late eighties. The peregrine, incidentally, said to abandon its nest at a distant threat, rose in each case from three feet above the leader's head.

The peregrine is now re-established after near extermination by insecticides; yet though we see it everywhere in the hills it remains something special. It's the fastest creature in the whole of nature. It's said that it can chase a swift down in level flight and it's been observed to hit small birds with such force that the head detaches. The stoop is a breathtaking sight, the folding of the wings into a heraldic fleur de lys, the easy overbalancing, the astounding plunge. No watcher can withhold admiration. However, it's to be hoped that, as in Manhattan, these predators will start to colonise city buildings rather than restrict us on every crag to a six-month season.

Mountain tops aren't rich in birdlife but a few birds seem so much at home in these bare places that even if they're common at lower altitudes they come to characterise the scene. Sometimes they suggest associations with other hills far away, a community of mountains. The choughs occasionally seen around Welsh hilltops bring to mind their relatives on the highest alpine summits. The alarm call of the ptarmigan, rising from Cairngorm snows, takes me back to the cries of red grouse, started on the Pennine moors. The alpine swifts cruising the Dolomite faces look very like those seen hawking along the Yosemite walls.

It has to be admitted that the birds most commonly seen on British hilltops nowadays are the scavengers. Hill walkers and climbers from the Continent are bemused to find themselves escorted to Welsh and Lakeland summits by seagulls hoping for scraps. The raven is a scavenger too but it can do without man and it seems more at home on the tops than any other creature. In the strongest winds and the deepest snows it sails around, an ancient enigma. The Welsh name for Snowdonia is Eryri, the eyrie perhaps, the place of eagles. If, with any luck, the golden eagle re-establishes itself here after an absence of at least three hundred years it will be welcomed with delight by all but a few hill farmers. But it will be here in condominium with the raven. "The eagle knows the place but not the time: the raven knows the time but not the place."

A climber's bestiary. The senses always quicken on sighting even the smaller animals, as if a hunter's instincts as well as the reflexes of self-preservation are buried deep within us. In a snow-covered Lakeland, at the very summit cairn of Fairfield, I met a stoat in ermine face to face. We stopped in our tracks and took a long and careful look at each other.

I was too big to eat and too slow to be a nuisance. Mysteries: on the first climbers' inspection of Glen Veagh in Donegal we found a freshly killed badger half-embedded in the grass at the foot of the five-hundred foot cliff. How had it chanced to fall? What was a woodland creature doing on the bare top of this rock wall? Later I learned that badgers occasionally live in high cairns on the hills. In the Pennines I've sometimes seen blue hares in winter white, caught out by the absence of snow. They were introduced from Scotland and can't get used to the short winters.

Like these arctic hares, a number of our animals aren't aware that they've been associated with man. In Wales a few strays amongst the feral goats occasionally come down to the road but the largest flock, in the Rhinogion, seems to keep to itself. Once we saw it, a hundred strong, on the rough terrain to the north of the Roman Steps. A marvellous subtlety of whites, creams, browns and greys, even while grazing it flowed over this nightmare of boulders and heather-filled pits much faster than we could walk. The wild ponies of the Carneddau, still claimed as stock by the local farmers, are perfectly adapted to the tops. Once, in brilliant moonlight at two in the morning, walking the broad whaleback towards Foel-fras, a group of half a dozen came from nowhere. For an hour they accompanied us northward, whinnying wildly, circling us at a gallop, retreating into darkness and plunging towards us again, a fantastic sight. To the English climber the red deer of Scotland and of some Donegal hills are equally gladdening, especially when met unexpectedly in an impressive herd, profiled on a mountain skyline or caught by headlights blocking a snowy winter road.

Higher mountains overseas are never rich in animal life if they reach above the treeline but the longer approaches offer exotic pleasures. In the Alps the first sightings of marmot, chamois and ibex are especially memorable and their very presence makes us feel more at home our-selves. Their assurance can surprise us. High on the Hörnli ridge of the Matterhorn we looked down and across the east face to see a dozen chamois or ibex, the range too great to be certain, on ledges at the foot of the further ridge and high above the snowline. They were straying out onto the slabby lower rocks of the face which, catching the first sun, was releasing heavy stonefall. Perhaps a quarter hour later I looked down again and couldn't find them. Then I saw that in that brief interval they'd traversed the whole face, a suicidal mission to a climber's eye.

Naming the animals. Before the inspiration of making a woman came, God saw that he'd made an appalling mistake. To stop Adam breaking things, in a desperate, panic-stricken attempt to keep him occupied, God paraded all the creatures. Here's a nice game for you. What would you like to call this? And this? And this? His severely limited attention span overridden, Adam was amused and produced his whimsical names: chipmunk, ground squirrel, dormouse, chameleon. Even the smaller beasts can be curiously engaging. The animals took one look at Adam and dispersed as fast and as far as their legs could carry them. We had to go to North America to find the ground squirrels and chipmunks. In France we camped at St. Martin Vesubie, nice little town, lively, an attractive walk up to the starts of alpine routes in the morning, a wild drive down to Monte Carlo at night. On our return, night after night, we shone lights into the trees, trying to find the sources of loud, unearthly, piercing whistles. Finally we fixed on some unexpectedly tiny creatures, big-eyed, clinging like koalas to the smaller branches. We couldn't believe them the authors of these penetrating shrieks until we noticed that the throats pulsed visibly with each cry. Tick off some kind of dormouse.

Somewhere in Turkey, or in the Islands perhaps, we found the chameleon. We walked down a hillside to some ancient ruins to see a group of people admiring it at thirty feet. Brilliantly coloured in shocking taste, more than a foot long, it was lying on a rock. From amongst the watchers, with infinite patience a photographer tiptoed very slowly forward, camera pressed to his eye. Nobody spoke or moved. The lizard watched him. Some minutes later at five feet he clicked the shutter, the creature flicked away, and the man leaped into the air with a shout of triumph. What he'd failed to notice in his concentration was that with every step the colours were bleeding away. Before he got his shot the chameleon was almost invisible against its rock.

The climber may disturb birds on occasion but animals are just as likely to disturb the climber. Snakes. I've almost stepped on adders a few times in Wales and Cornwall, once some way up a rock climb at Tremadog. In Greece I sat on my heels by a stream, staring into the water. From the reeds brushing my shoulder a thin green and yellow snake launched itself high into the air and splashed down inches before my toes. It lay undulating in the current for several seconds, then cracked like a whip and was gone. At that I was released, leapt to my feet and ran a few paces back, heart pounding. It had been too sudden. In Gibraltar an amazing tangle of jet black snakes basked in the sun near the top of the Rock. From Big Sur we made a short excursion into the Pfeiffer Park after reading the various posted warnings. As if bears and snakes weren't enough, at the turn of the century some wealthy lunatic rancher had introduced a herd of wild boar. They'd settled in easily and now they had Residents' Visas. "If seen, stand perfectly still for some time, then back away slowly and silently." And as I strained my eyes through the trees and into clearings ahead, a small snake tumbled down the steep bank beside me to land at my toes.

Beneath Glacier Point Apron in Yosemite, boulder hopping at some speed, I changed feet in midair to avoid landing on a fat, muddy-coloured snake. By the time I turned round it was sliding under a rock. That same afternoon I was following Maureen down through the woods when she stopped abruptly and began to make small noises of distress. I saw that she was standing on the tail of a five-foot snake, brilliantly coloured, astonishingly thin for its length. It lay perfectly still, pretending it wasn't uncomfortable. On my advice she stepped back and, released, it slid swiftly away.

In Yosemite, too, we had our confrontation. At Sunnyside Camp in the woods one night, we were in for a big surprise. I'd no old line long enough to hoist our food sack up to the bear wire but I'd found a piece of cord about thirty feet long. Every night, sack on back, I climbed the awkward tree and clipped the sack to the wire. Then I shot it out thirty feet attached to the line. Every morning I had to climb the tree again to retrieve it. On the tenth night rain fell in sheets, water ran everywhere. I couldn't face the whole performance in the dark so I simply climbed up twenty feet and hung the sack on the stump of a branch. In the small hours we were awakened by a terrific thump and heard a loud ripping noise. I unzipped the tent cautiously and shone a light. Five feet away, the bear had torn the sack top to bottom at a stroke. Now it chomped its way through our delicious stock of fruit, casting a red and scornful eye on me from time to time. I urged Maureen to take a look but, face down, she was trying to shrink through to the Antipodes.

Everybody loves the megafauna, especially the elephants and whales. As the scale reduces the interest tends to slacken until only the specialist and young children are captivated by insects. It's said that a mere fraction of these have yet been classified and the evolutionary biologist J.B.S. Haldane grumbled that the Creator seems to have had an inordinate fondness for beetles. The same things might be said of the world of vegetation. We all admire redwoods and ancient oaks but there's just too much at the other end. God didn't push his luck by inviting Adam to hand out names for the kingdom of plants. He left that task to Linnaeus who found it more than a lifetime's work.

Within a few miles of my house the north flank of Creigiau Gleision forms a mile-long wall of untidy broken crags, hardly ever visited by rock climber or scrambler. A year or two ago, looking for solid rock amongst this chaos, I came on a steep vegetated gully inaccessible to sheep. I could see that it was filled with large disc-like yellow flowers, oddly out of context amongst these mainly acid rocks and above long slopes of impoverished heathery screes. Without a rope, and with difficulty on this insecure ground, I managed to get close enough to persuade myself that I was looking at Welsh poppies, commonplace in gardens but a plant I'd never heard of high on a hill. It was another reminder of the privileges of the climber whose zoom-lens eye is forever ranging between the horizon and close focus.

I don't know how long ago or by whom the removal of vegetation from rock climbs was first called gardening, nor whether the expression was used mischievously; if only he'd called it weeding. In recent years this practice has begun to upset conservationists and an ethical distaste for destroying living things has been instilled in most of us so that the explorer of new routes may feel pressure without and guilt within as he bares a vital handhold or rakes out a crack to try to find protection. However, the urge to clean up climbs doesn't just spring from the wish to make them safer or to fix the permanent standard. And if I can't justify this practice I'd like at least to put it into perspective and to look at motive forces.

It appears that the spectrum of taste in human responses to place is a straight match for the whole range of the earth's landscapes. At one extreme some people are enchanted by the fertility and profusion of tropical jungles and they don't feel the slightest sense of claustrophobia. At the other, there are those whose spirits lift in the barren spaces of deserts and high mountains and who aren't in the least repelled by the sterility of rock, snow and ice.

These extremes of taste are also on view in the domestic garden. Sometimes it's a riot of contending plants, hard to sidle between. Sometimes it's formal and controlled with clarified geometries and space for human beings to move freely. Rock gardens, pavements and screes are in themselves an interesting study. The first rock garden ever seen in Britain is said to be that created by the explorer and naturalist Sir Joseph Banks about 1770, a vast heap of black basaltic lava. In Victorian times rock plants were sometimes set on huge models of the Matterhorn with the top painted white. Generally, nowadays, the material is used as a neutral background to give display space for alpines rather than for its intrinsic interest. In Japan, on the other hand, the virtues of rock are recognised and the rock garden may be just what it says. A winding line of stepping stones, perhaps emphasised by the equally elemental substances of sand or water, may lead the visitor into an unexpected encounter with a massive boulder which is intended to be considered for its inherent appeal and impressiveness.

The domestic gardener in Britain isn't troubled by the scruples climbers suffer. He tears out whatever interferes with his vision, classing wild flowers as intrusive weeds and hardly ever attempting to raise our native rarities. Nearly all our garden plants are exotics or cultivars. Kew Gardens may not be natural to Britain but it's what many gardeners want to see. The climber is in a similar position. Clean cliffs aren't natural for much of Britain but they're what many climbers crave. That's because we're attracted by structure. I look at a nicely built corner, the walls bare but the angle choked with pennywort and stonecrop. These plants grow by the thousands in the woods all around and one clump is just like another. But in that corner I know there's a crack, every move, every hold, interesting in itself, describable, the line a unique aesthetic statement in a language I understand. I want to undress it. The first pitch of Great Slab on Clogwyn Du'r Arddu started life as the "Green Caterpillar"; nobody in his right mind would want to see that magnificent pitch under grass again.

Jesus used rock to stand for eternity: "and on this rock I will build my church." Dr Johnson used it to stand for reality, kicking a rock to disprove the theory of Bishop Berkeley: "I refute it thus!" William James used it to stand for the unknowable, a haunting significance in nature forever just beyond our grasp: "there it remains, a mere boulder of impression." It's odd to reflect that there may be disadvantaged peoples on this earth who've lived out their lives without acquaintance with this primal material — in the Congo and Amazon basins maybe, the Marsh Arabs perhaps. Once the Tate Gallery paid an enormous sum to an avant-garde sculptor for his display of a random heap of common bricks. As might have been expected this caused a furore. Perhaps the Directors had never handled a house brick or seen its six sides. They should have examined a single square yard of unquarried Yorkshire gritstone or of any of the rock types mentioned in passing in this book. Those surfaces are more detailed, more fascinating, more mysterious, more organised, than any abstract painting.

Our particular problem is that some of our cliffs, those high mountain crags that happen also to be rich in lime, are the only refuge in Britain of an arctic-alpine flora, relict of the last ice age. In fact it's at the absolute limits of its range here. Of course, if there is a greenhouse effect, and if it works as some scientists predict, this flora may be doomed anyway. And presumably, if it goes, it won't be replaced by other rarities; more familiar lowland plants may simply move up the hill and any new arrivals in Britain will come in at the other end of our climatic range. However, owing to our island situation, this might not happen within the same time-span unless there were human intervention which in one sense is as unethical as gardening. Therefore the climber must feel some responsibility in the present towards this flora.

On the whole, the flora is hanging on remarkably well. *Lloydia* retains its grasp on its three well-known cliffs, each climbed on for sixty to a hundred years. In fact the rise in climbing standards has shifted activity from the gullies which best support plant life. Where particular gullies are used as descents the fastest, easiest and safest line quickly becomes well-marked and divergence is seen as a mistake to be avoided. Nearly all new routes nowadays take rock so steep that it offers no purchase for plants. It's true that trees on popular climbs succumb. Holly Tree Wall has lost its holly and Birch Tree Wall has lost its birch. But these demises have been felt more keenly as sentimental blows to the climber than as regrettable losses to the conservationist. (A subsequent direct on Birch Tree Wall was named, with wit and feeling, Bring Back the Birch.) In any case, trees on sloping ledges which haven't been able to secure themselves by finding anchorage in deep cracks will sooner or later be thrown by their own weight as is evident on walking the foot of many unclimbed crags. The greatest impact made by the climber is probably the baring of earth at the start of well-used climbs, though this effect is also produced wherever sheep take shelter under overhanging rock.

Generally, as every domestic gardener knows, nature can only be defeated temporarily with the bare hands. For more decisive victories, teams of draught animals or plagues of grazing animals have been the traditional solutions. Now we have the final solutions of machinery and chemicals. Read the description of a Victorian meadow at the end of A.S. Byatt's *Obsession*. Read the description of a chalk down in Marion Shoard's *The Theft of the Countryside*. Each of these is a loving portrait of an earthly paradise and something analagous was once to be found within walking distance of almost everyone's house. Agri-business has already destroyed most of that lowland England. In the mountains these effects aren't quite so obvious since the landforms can't be changed and dominate the scene. But there's still something missing.

Where have all the flowers gone? Well, where I live we've eaten them in the shape of Welsh Lamb. We've subsidised the devastation of our flora and the confinement of survivors to our cliffs. Most of our hills now show as a plain quilt of anonymous grasses, ornamented so discreetly that we hardly notice it with tormentil, clubmosses and heath bedstraw. The remedy is clear. We need some sheep-free mountains.

To walk up to Cwm Idwal through woods of birch, hazel and rowan, to continue up slopes luxuriant with flowers, would give some taste of another model of paradise, what it's like to climb in the Alps. And management wouldn't be needed. Nature knows best how to manage herself and her resilience is amazing.

I was on Hydra five months after the island burned. My wife and I reached the heights of Eros and then we cooled off. Mt Eros is the culminating point of the island and from this summit we could see something of the extent of the conflagration. We also noticed a col offering a way over to the uninhabited south shore and the following day walked over for a swim. Our route took us through some miles of the wasted forest, a graveyard of endless blackened stumps. There was no trace of greenery to be seen and everywhere the fine grey carpet of ash still lay three to six inches deep. Yet in every square yard, a miracle of rebirth, a little posy of delicate pure white cyclamen had risen through the ash.

On a small cliff in Wales I once climbed a fifty-foot new route and to satisfy my curiosity I made this childish experiment. Just above the start I cleaned off, washed and scrubbed a flat ledge about three feet by one, marking the wall above it with a little quincunx of dots in case anyone might like to identify it in the future. For some years I climbed the route from time to time but now it's never used. In fact the process of recolonisation began within weeks of the original ascent and the first step in the rehabilitation programme was a surprise to me. It was carried out by spiders. They ran webs across the inner corner of the ledge and these webs were intermittently damaged by wind or rain. However, collapsed almost flat, they served to collect and seal down tiny fragments of blown vegetation, small leaves, seeds, washings of grit. Within a quite short time this compost or humus was glued solidly into the back of the ledge and finally began to produce a growth of its own. When I last looked the ledge was buried again.

Recently I seem to keep running into a two-thousand-year-old observation by a poet I've never read, Horace, in a language I don't know, Latin. *Naturam expellas furca, tamen usque recurret!* You can drive out nature with a pitchfork, but she'll always come back. For hand tools, I believe that this is largely true. And I think it's possible to worry too much about a modest amount of gardening on our crags.

Clogwyn Du'r Arddu

THE ORDINARY ROUTE

In the nineties I consider this proposition: that as far back as the fifties I started to opt for the Ordinary Route.

No, that won't do. It makes a neat device for this book and I've supplied a wealth of evidence but it's not the whole truth. Like most climbers I've usually gone for the hardest and most attractive route I thought I just might manage in the day's context. Still, I feel an affirmative sentiment, a real affection for the concept of the Ordinary, which, together with its climbers, is often patronised. I want to set a proper value on it, raising its status. So I ask myself once again, what makes a good climb anyway?

Climbing selects from three obsessions: the Stage, the Line, the Move. Many climbers tend to the near-sighted or the far-sighted and downgrade the parity of the stage or the move. Working the extremes, the young rock-climber hardly seems to notice his familiar surroundings, maybe the most derelict of quarries. A surprise is in store. If he returns to this arena after an absence of thirty years he'll find himself stabbed to the heart. (Small quarries have a cosy intimacy: from the moment industry ceases they start to imitate nature and the echo of human abandonment adds a distantly solemn note. Big quarries have a real grandeur. Not long ago, on a grey autumn day in Garrett Quarry at Llanberis, the strong wind started small scree slides at the top of the huge debris-littered spoil slope known to climbers as the Oil Drum Glacier and properly divided by its Rognon. These slides gathered material and momentum as they ran the six or seven hundred-foot slope to an easement and the wind winnowed out rolling grey-white clouds of powdered slate. The replication of snow avalanches was startling and the ambience seemed of the Alps rather than of Wales, distracting me from the task in hand.) The alpinist or the expedition climber may feel that the stage and the line are everything. But even as he reviews his chosen route, through the synapses something stirs his body, making simultaneous translation into known codes of physical effort, of the moves we make.

What makes a good climb anyway? The essential requirement is continuous inescapability at the standard of the route itself: the first steps taken, it has to be easier to continue or to descend than to reach the top or get back to the ground by any other line. (Variations are often given names of their own but they remain variations, not climbs, themselves subject to the same rule. Some variations, of course, may be longer than nearby climbs and it's hard to compare climbs of different lengths directly.)

This condition satisfied, other requirements follow. The climb needs unity in the form of a reasonable consistency of standard. The apprehensive will want any crucial difficulty at the start so that, success probably assured, the rest of the climb can be enjoyed. The bold will prefer it at the end so that the outcome is held in suspense. But both need some continuity in the demands of the climbing.

The climb must also have apparent permanence. We want to feel that, conditions allowed for, we're making the ascent our predecessors made; on a new route, the ascent that those who follow us will make. So in general and in detail the material must feel reliable and durable. Perhaps my own generation was the first to learn that no cliff, however securely built, can be guaranteed free from change within a lifetime: the Great Flake of Scafell's Central Buttress loses its chockstone, killing an ill-starred young climber; the West Buttress of Clogwyn Du'r Arddu suffers a major rockfall, destroying whole climbs. In geological time, of course, even El Cap is a sand castle.

All rock climbs age with use. When the nailed boot was thrown away we could never have guessed that, by sheer weight of numbers, the rubber-shod foot would imperceptibly buff up the holds of Welsh and Lakeland mountain crags. On sandstone and the softer grits very small holds wear out and on limestone they may be brittle or take on a glassy polish, so that the hardest and shortest modern routes may be subject to rapid change and their celebrity might not last. Snow and ice climbs exempt themselves from this requirement since conditions are expected to vary and they're renewable resources anyway. However, a single ascent may spoil a snow climb for those who follow and can even destroy a fragile British ice climb until nature resurfaces the line.

It might seem odd that I haven't included the appeal of the line itself in these requirements when I've centred it between the stage and the move. The line, after all, is what first arrests the climber's eye when he looks at a cliff or mountain, even when he examines a photograph. He can't help trying to connect weaknesses and possibilities. (I met an old friend who'd packed up years ago. He was into golf now. Golf! I was amused to see that he was still loping around in the beaten-up kletterschuhe he'd been wearing when we'd last climbed together. "But I still think of myself as a climber," he said, baffled, amused, exasperated. "I walk along the main street here and I keep eyeing up the buildings. I can't stop joining up the bits I know I could do. It's maddening." This was Geoff Roberts.) In fact the striking lines we see at a glance aren't always the best the cliff can offer. Some possibilities are hidden, design secrets revealed only by the attempt. In retrospect these ingenious discoveries are just as good and they're much more intriguing to trace from the ground.

In general, it seems to me that if the climb satisfies these requirements the quality of the line, its presence and character, will be guaranteed. There's a bit of trading off. We can settle for a felt inescapability if a known escape isn't too obvious and if the continuity is unbroken. We might accept some discontinuity if the route presents the perfect corner crack or the textbook hand traverse and so on. However, I don't believe a variation or escapable line can ever deserve the three star accolade.

These requirements are objective qualities but something else intrudes. It's necessary to introduce a particular climber, you or me. Then the good route will have to fall within a specific and appropriate range of difficulty. That ought not to need saying but it's often overlooked since only the hardest climbs engage the expert's close attention. Guidebook writers often ignore the fact that by its nature the guidebook is addressed to climbers of all standards. Guidebook judgements of what is good ought therefore to be made independently of standard.

A good climb, or a very good climb, is often described as a classic. That means that it's known by reputation to show the required characteristics and it's already achieved popularity and prestige, even a written history. Resistance to the tendency to describe a new route as an instant or even a future classic seems unjust in a sense since the objective characteristics are seen immediately. In another sense it's correct since the act presumes future response, even though nearby climbs which show the same characteristics more perfectly might yet be found.

Now I want to measure the Ordinary Route against these standards and to write a tighter specification. By definition there must be at least one harder route up the same cliff or mountain and in fact the more there are the better, since the more its uniqueness is underlined. It's true that there exist poor Ordinaries on cliffs, though seldom on mountains. The climb might sneak up the edge of the cliff and permit escapes. But when the Ordinary is well placed its inescapability is absolute and I think there's a rule of thumb about its necessary psychological or aesthetic space: it should be flanked by margins of more difficult terrain at least as broad as the climb is high. In fact this setting is often available to it and displayed on this backcloth it reveals itself as the central feature with a purity of intention its neighbours can't hope to rival.

Although I'm talking about the easiest route I didn't say it has to be easy. It can be of any standard except harder standards local to it. The Ordinary on Everest ("the cow track", to French and German mountaineers), the Abruzzi Spur on K2, call for more than luck with the weather and route condition. The 1938 Route on the Eigerwand, the Triple Direct on El Cap perhaps, may have been put down by the odd expert party after ascents in good conditions: not before starting. With a selected list of Ordinaries a man might well be the world's most experienced climber. "Oh, we just did the Ordinary." Why is this said so diffidently when the Ordinary is often the best?

Harder and longer routes abroad can look after their own reputations. It's our domestic Ordinaries in Britain that I want to promote and to make more visible. Here they're often disguised. A quick glance through the index pages of a dozen Welsh and Lakeland guidebooks listing many thousands of climbs collects less than ten with this title, though some are hidden by indexing under the crag or buttress name; whilst, in fact, good Ordinaries are numerous. Some are masquerading as the Original Route or Route 1 but the discovery of later climbs doesn't necessitate that change of status. On so acccessible a cliff as Raven Crag Buttress in Langdale it needed nineteen years from the ascent of the Original before the Ordinary was found. It goes under the name of Holly Tree Traverse though it's lost its principal holly and it isn't essentially a traverse. It's as good as any route on the buttress.

I think we ought to copy a practice used abroad. For most important summits the first routes are named by aspect or by orientation. But in a French guidebook, for the Western Alps perhaps, the expression "voie normale" will appear in brackets for one of the routes, following its title of East Ridge or whatever. It's too late to change old names in Britain now, and I think I'd resist the attempt myself, but whenever the easiest route is finely set we ought to direct attention to it. So, for instance: Holly Tree Traverse (Raven Crag Ordinary).

Before the Second World War rock climbing was nothing if not a minority sport and few beginners were recruited during the war. The great rise in numbers began abruptly in the next decade. That postwar generation is now queueing up for its pensions and it has the leisure to climb whenever it wishes so that for the first time in our history the old-timers, "the coffin dodgers", are becoming a significant presence on our crags. Many of these climbers are discovering that thanks to modern footgear and protection the inevitable decline in standard hasn't been quite so dramatic as they'd have expected. They're not likely to be satisfied with the Milestone or Middlefell since they've been around a bit and they've developed a taste for more stirring surroundings. However, they may well have climbed all routes locally accessible to their slowly reducing abilities and they face a frustrating problem. And, after exclusion by landowner or by bird-watcher, I want to address that final problem: exclusion by the elite, in the name of climbing ethics.

Nearly all new development in climbing is of routes close to or at the upper limit of the moment and hundreds of new extremes are now produced in Britain every year. Few amenable crags have remained unnoticed or untested for a century, except perhaps in Scotland, and good routes in the lower and middle grades are hardly ever reported. Worse, some have been lost. A sizable number of excellent postwar climbs in the very severe range used a modest amount of piton aid. Subsequently virtually all of these were freed and the tendency of the competition ethic, together with an aroused awareness of the disfigurement the removal and replacement of pegs can cause, made it seem improper for later parties to revert to the use of aid. In some areas good climbs have even been hijacked, suppressed in the guidebook when a more difficult variation has been found in order to appropriate start or finish or both for a new route under a new name. Routes with vegetation also tend to be omitted, though some of the finest lines in Britain were first climbed mainly on grass. As the average standard has risen, so guide-writers have begun to reject the easier crags by formula: "here the climber is left to discover his own routes."

Apart from drawing attention to those fine Ordinaries in disguise we ought to be producing more. An obvious place to look for them would be on the harder cliffs, of which many may never have been checked for the easiest line; it wasn't what the modern explorer was looking for. In the sixties there was a small movement towards the rationalisation of existing climbs by drawing attention to recombinations of routes. The proposal was made in the name of consistency of standard but effectively it was used to promote the harder option. On the prestigious cliffs the opposite project ought to have equal appeal, the fitting together of the easiest possible line. I'd like to know where to find the West Buttress Ordinary on Clogwyn Du'r Arddu. Is it one of the listed routes or is it some recombination I haven't yet worked out? A V Diff up the West Buttress would be, absolutely, Britain's finest climb. Is the Ordinary in Huntsman's Leap simply that with the lowest technical grade? Or might I find something else with a bit of lateral thinking? There's a joke Ordinary at E5 at Gogarth but might not a serious Ordinary be threaded up the Main Cliff?

There's another way in which good easier routes might be produced on the harder cliffs and that's by changing the rules. Remember: the purpose of the competition ethic is two-fold, the arrangement of a contest of which the outcome is in doubt and the sorting of competitors into order of size.

In Britain we acknowledge a traditional and ideal ethic: the route should be led on sight and no aid should be used. Call this the hero ethic. In fact, many ethics are recognised. There's a whole spectrum of new route ethics, observed in particular areas and styles of climbing. At one extreme there's an attempt to tie the new route ethic to the hero ethic. I think it's probably true to say that most climbers who've been able to adopt that approach have been those lucky enough to be operating without intense competition. At the other extreme local new route ethics sometimes permit whatever tactics are needed to allow the production of new climbs. Here we get abseil inspection and cleaning, rehearsal, preplacement of protection. And we get argument.

To most climbers it doesn't matter how any particular route was originally climbed. It exists and we enjoy it for what it is. To the contenders it's a cause for great concern and protest follows whenever the tactics used have been heavy enough to mask differences in performance levels. All argument would end if new routes weren't credited in guidebooks and magazines, an unenforceable policy. It would be reduced if precedence in guidebook credits were given to the first sight solo, followed by the first sight ascent, and so on.

In effect, on existing routes most climbers are simply competing against the guidebook grading. Usually the leader accepts the hero ethic yet there are situations in which he ignores it. On outcrops climbers often follow or top-rope routes before they lead them and nowadays it's common enough to see short hard routes rehearsed with self-protected top rope systems. It's understood that the competition is largely with oneself or that the activity is regarded simply as training.

I'd like to extend this flexibility of approach to bring routes on the more difficult cliffs within the range of the middle-grade climber and I'll outline two possible styles. I'll call the first of these the pioneer ethic. In the earliest years of rock-climbing the game consisted of getting up by any means offered by the body, the rope, the sling and, later, the snaplink. It would seem quixotic to reject the use of modern ropes, snaplinks and footgear. This approach would permit the use of combined tactics, rope moves, lassoing, aid moves on slings, protection from inserted pebbles and jammed knots. The restriction of equipment to this basic arsenal is fanatically stringent but the techniques allowed would make some more difficult routes accessible.

In fact I'd recommend a further step. I'd add to these resources the nut, the great equaliser, as the key weapon in what might be called the clean aid ethic. From the full range of equipment I'd only be rejecting bolts, pegs and chalk (as showing weakness and as offending environment ethics) and, probably, camming devices (as showing weakness and as machines with moving parts). It's true that even the nut will eventually polish slots and cracks but this is visually minimal. I'll admit that a nut that's taken a fall might be unextractable though as a matter of fact I've never failed to retrieve an abandoned nut, usually without much effort and without a nut key. With this approach large numbers of more difficult climbs become accessible and now I can list one or two severes on the West Buttress, amongst which I think the easiest ought to be pointed out with two grades shown. So, let's guess: Longland's (West Buttress Ordinary); Very Severe (Hard Severe with clean aid on Overhang). If I'm alive, well, and still leading there in my seventies it looks as though it's bound to be in this style.

To suggest that this approach removes the element of doubt is absurd. Many climbs are invulnerable to nut aid or to rope tricks. The justifications of the approach are several. It would reduce the difficulty of some magnificent climbs, making available, perhaps at the price of only one or two moves, hundreds of feet of fine free climbing. The dampening of the main difficulty of the climb moves it nearer that desirable consistency of standard. It's a practice many of our most famous explorers took as their right anyway, seeing difficulty adjustment as well as risk adjustment as privileges restricted to the elite. And nuts can involve real skill in placement so that an aid move on a micronut can feel quite as exciting and precarious as the most limiting and delicate free move.

In the past, except as a special dispensation for the expert, these tech-niques have been regarded as cheating. But this isn't a case of the cheat or the spoilsport, as Huizinga defined them. It's another form of the game, a democratisation. And these practices bring back into climbing an element — farce, horseplay, pantomime — which to a degree it's relinquished, and to its own cost. Climbing can offer fun as well as the spice of fear. The spirit in which the Ordinary should be approached is that of the large party, even the good-natured queue, of talking, meeting interesting people, advising others or assisting them, of cries for help; of watching, in amusement, disbelief and awe, the maniacs on the nearby extremes fighting it out or tumbling off. The Ordinary is the route on which most climbers start and to which they'll one day return. It's the route I wish I could climb again with Keith Carr or Andrew Maxfield and might yet climb again with Gordon Mansell.

I've described some good Ordinaries of a variety of grades at some length in this book and I've touched a few more in passing: the via Original o Normal on the Cavall Bernat, Royal Arches, the Grépon from the north, Hangover on Dove Crag, the Ordinary on the Idwal Slabs. A handful to represent a thousand days I remember with equal pleasure. I could list others I haven't climbed but which I've nursed as images of the spirit — on the Devil's Tower in Wyoming, on the Naranjo de Bulnes in the Picos de Europa, on the Sella and Vajolet Towers in the Dolomites, on Mont Blanc, a summit I happen to have missed. I see now that I might not climb any of them. That doesn't matter. With only four or five people exploring the Arenig, almost within sight of my house, why pine for the Devil's Tower? New possibilities keep coming up to offer dreams to live for. Climbing is, after all, substantially an activity of the imagination.

LAST WORD

In 1994, aged ninety, my father died, resisting this obstruction of his plans. He'd lost his sight a year earlier and for two or three years he and my mother hadn't left Bradford. Prior to that, from time to time I'd been collecting them and bringing them to North Wales for a few days of fresh air. On one of the last trips, casting around for something new, I drove them through the hills and out to the tip of the Llcyn peninsula, the most westerly point of Gwynedd. The weather was perfect. In those conditions the coastal scenery matches the Mediterranean. I was able to take the car to a parking area on the top of the final headland, Mynydd Mawr — Big Mountain: what does it stand for at this point in this story? — and we strolled around the coastguard lookout taking in the views.

He was always a strong walker, driven by physical restlessness rather than by any interest in landscapes. He was a tireless explorer of towns and public houses and he needed people. Suddenly he'd become bent and slow, having to push as, puzzled, he'd come up against the head wind of his middle eighties. On the headland now, he resettles his flat cap several times in a characteristic gesture. His eyes drift over the surroundings briefly and incuriously. What's he thinking of? Remembering far-off racecourses and football fields, looking forward to the big fight in a few days' time? Wondering how long we'll be hanging around here?

A group of walkers on the coastal path, including a couple of attractive girls in very brief shorts, approaches us. With a studied indifference the old man turns round to inspect them the second they've passed. (Allowing a decent interval, the son turns round too.) If only one of the lads could've been a famous cricketer or a snooker player or a darts champion. They'd spent their lives climbing up rocks; or, one with his head bent over a book, the other a microscope. He gazes back the way we've come. Nearest bookie must be thirty or forty miles away. There was a nice-looking pub in that last village. Probably the lad will be ready for a drink when he's finished here. There he stands, staring down at some bits of cliffs as if there were gold there. Then the son turns and thumps the old man on the back, a bit harder than is necessary for a grudging display of what has become something almost like affection.

He's anticipated me and braced himself. He's still amazingly strong. He smiles, not put out.

> "You all right, Bill?"
> "All right, lad."
> "Enjoying yourself?"
> "Wouldn't mind a pint on the way back."
> "A pint will be arranged."

Vaguely frustrated, I pace around. There's some difficult climbing on a sea-cliff somewhere near here, Cilan Head. No chance to locate it today. Outside the little wall defending the lookout there's a level grassy trackway and from its unprotected further side the slope, interrupted by short hidden buttresses, falls precipitously for five hundred feet to the sea. I approach the brink and look down with the born cautiousness of one half of my inheritance. Two ridges, Braich y Pwll, Braich y Noddfa, enclose a small bay directly beneath, not too easy of access. The warm sun brings up the smell of heather, gorse, the sea.

The mother's face is alive with pleasure as she savours the views. (She doesn't know yet that she, under strong protest, and her husband, in scornful acquiescence, will be made to walk unaccompanied up the little companion summit, while the son and the son's wife run down to look into the little zawn to the south; afterwards she'll feel pleased with herself, as the son knew she would. The son doesn't know yet that after a few drinks at Aberdaron, father and son will start shouting at each other so loudly that the manager will approach and give them a look; for obstinacy they're an equal match. Peacemaker, the son's wife will calm them.)

All her life she's loved the countryside while sharply aware of its perils; the dangers of getting wet feet, of catching a chill, of being caught out in the dark. Her limited travels have sharpened her perceptions. She feasts her eyes on Ynys Enlli, two or three miles out across the blue and placid Sound, the first faint stirrings of the fierce tide race just beginning to trace a line of disturbance through the strait. She's been there in her reading and certainly knows more about the monks of Bardsey than the son. Her thoughts bring back the romance of the Dark Ages. The unruffled sea stretches across to Ireland, to Wicklow Head, only fifty miles away. Behind, the tiny but shapely hills of Lleyn lead up to the Rivals and above and beyond them to the mysterious heights of Eryri. She feels a strong contentment, qualified by a single worry clouding this fine moment. She keeps glancing round at her admired but difficult child. She tries hard to control the anxiety but it can't be suppressed. He may shout at her. He may laugh. He may put his face in his hands and groan in mock despair but it has to be said. With a huge effort she keeps her voice steady and gives the remark a perfectly casual tone.

"Don't stand so close to the edge, Harold," she says.

GRAMMAR

"But the point of the ladder is surely," and [the Failed Sage] said this as if it were something he had not considered before and was not entirely convinced about, "to oblige us to notice enterings and leavings. The point is not the difficulty. The point is the point made by the difficulty."

Paul Griffiths, *Myself and Marco Polo*

The writing of a comprehensive grammar would be an intimidating task. It would have to consider motivation and reward, history and technology, ethics, risk, skills and social factors. Most of these matters have been touched on in this book but here's a simplified grammar for the beginner. It starts with a note on the scene and an explanation of the use of the rope. The quotation above is a reminder that metaphysical descriptions of climbing are also possible and have often been attempted.

Every climb is unique and has title, presence and reputation. Usually it's named by the first party to ascend it. In remote areas or on bigger mountains the first names may be purely topographical; on popular cliffs they become fanciful as development progresses. The climb is claimed in a club journal, a local log-book or a climbing magazine, is written up in sufficient detail to allow others to follow the route, and is given a grading for difficulty. Eventually it finds its way into a guidebook for the area where it's credited to the originators, and redescribed and regraded if felt necessary.

Various national and local grading systems exist and from time to time unofficial rates of exchange are offered. In Britain rock climbs are given an overall classification ranging from Easy to Extreme, the top category now having a number appended to allow for new worlds. At the time of writing E9 has been reached. This overall grading masks problems quite different in character. Probably it's best to think of it as representing the degree of likelihood that other climbers will succeed on the route, on the assumption that other climbers will judge the route worth repeating. It's usually supplemented with technical gradings which purport to rank the physical difficulty only. Great prestige accrues to those who succeed on the most desperate enterprises and good communications networks keep contenders informed of the latest developments. "Climbing pre-supposes a certain language-game," Gordon Stainforth said. "Its names, its grades, are important to us."

Usually, in addressing any serious difficulty a pair of climbers will be wearing harnesses and will be tied to either end of a rope of perhaps fifty metres in length. One climber will secure himself (belay himself, anchor himself) on a suitable ledge (stance). He may tie on to a rock spike, a chockstone, even a tree or bush in some areas, with a bight from his end of the rope. More conveniently he might use a short loop of tape or rope (a sling), clipping into it with a snaplink (karabiner). If the cliff doesn't offer any such anchorage he'll inspect any cracks or pockets for constrictions and he'll insert one or more of a sized range of small wedgelike alloy blocks (nuts, chocks) pre-threaded onto slings or wires. Or a camming device expanding to lock in parallel-sided cracks might be used.

In some areas, and subject to considerations raised later, he might drive in a metal blade or wedge (a peg, a piton) provided with an eye into which he can clip. As a last resort he might carry the equipment to drill a hole and insert a bolt.

As the leader advances his rope is paid out by the belayer (the second), usually through a purpose-designed rope-braking device (a plate, a tube). When he reaches the next suitable stance he in turn belays himself. On the most difficult climbs the lack of a good ledge may compel him to anchor more or less suspended in his harness (take a hanging stance). When secured he draws in any slack and he takes in the rope continuously as the second climbs the intervening distance (the pitch).

In this routine, in a direct ascent, the second could fall only a very short distance, that of the slight stretch of the rope together with that of any slack the leader has failed to take in. The leader, on the other hand, might fall twice the length of rope he's run out, together with the considerable stretch of the heavily loaded rope. The thought alarms him so as he climbs he seeks interim points of security (protection). He places slings, wires, cams (or again, in some areas, pegs or bolts) and he clips his rope in with a snaplink so that it slides through freely as he moves (he fixes running belays, runners). Any fall is now reduced to twice his distance above the runner, plus stretch. A climber leading at his limit laces the pitch with all the protection the rock allows, restricting any fall. On pitches demanding any more or less horizontal movement (traverses) the leader will also place protection for the second's benefit to reduce any swinging fall.

That's a description of roped rock-climbing but the same general method is used on snow and ice. Further equipment is brought in (ice-axe, crampons, ice screws) whilst some rock gear will be unnecessary. A difference has arisen. On rock the climber uses natural holds and he'll be criticised if he attempts to improve them; on snow and ice he may carve holds or stances as freely as he needs since he's working a renewable medium and ascent is otherwise impossible.

Now we can make distinctions. First, any attachment which offers protection might itself be used to pull up on or to provide foothold (for aid). A move, then, is usually made using the hands, the feet, the body itself (free climbing). But in extremity a climber may use his equipment to assist himself (aid climbing) permitting the overcoming of difficulties otherwise beyond his and possibly beyond anyone's powers. Second, climbers don't always operate in teams (parties). Occasionally they choose to climb alone (to solo). At any moment, then, we're free climbing or we're using aid and we're climbing as a party or climbing solo.

These two sets of options allow four possibilities. But the use of the rope or its relinquishment must also be considered and this gives eight theoretical styles of climbing or at least of accomplishing a move. The crossword-puzzler may like to write these out before reading on, and to envisage situations. Further explanation may be needed. The Indian Rope Trick isn't yet understood, though it's possible to ascend an already fixed rope with the aid of friction hitches or clamping devices (ascenders, prusikers). However. the rope itself may be used for aid in lassoing, in lateral movement by laying away against it (tension traverse) or by pendulum (pendule), and in the descent and subsequent retrieval of the doubled rope (abseil, rappel, roping down). The body of a companion might itself occasionally be used for aid to provide foothold (a shoulder, combined tactics). And, by time-consuming systems, roped solo is possible.

The experienced climber who's been unable to resist the vetting of this chapter may have been halted here and might finally declare that in practice these eight possibilities don't all exist. That's too hasty, though some are most uncommon. In Britain, anyway, the normal form of the sport is free climbing by roped parties; unroped free solo is often seen on short climbs and on the easier longer climbs but is not so common otherwise; and roped parties on free climbs may in extremity make an aid move, but usually try to avoid this if witnesses are present.

Now it's possible to make a note of the sets of skills involved in climbing. I say that these are basically four and that they form a hierarchy: movement skills; judgement skills; protection skills; aid skills. Further, that they're ordinarily built up in the order given, irrespective of whether the introduction to the sport is on man-made climbing walls, on the harder scrambles on mountain walks, or by seconding longer climbs. The spheres of protection and aid have been outlined but some notes on movement and judgement may be called for.

Climbing may be broken down into repeated sequences of assessment, movement and recuperation. The first and third often combine, and with practice or on easy rock the pause is unnecessary so that the action becomes fluid. It's a kind of dance with cues from the rock rather than from music. (It would be technically possible to represent crucial passages in adapted forms of Labanotation or Benesh Dance Notation but this misses the point; even difficult obstacles sometimes permit a surprising variety of attack and most climbers want to work out a personal solution. The very hardest boulder problems, however, may succumb to only one sequence and are now being coded in some specialist guides.)

Learning to climb involves acquiring a repertoire of transfers between one resting position and another, together with an appreciation of the characteristics of different rock types. The problems set may be hybrid in nature but can often be generalised as strenuous, delicate, technical, awkward, and so on. The climber learns to overcome them by a wide range of techniques: he balances up slabs, he pulls over bulges, he bridges up corners, he chimneys up clefts, he jams up cracks, he mantelshelfs onto ledges; and so on. On softer snow he may kick steps, on harder snow he may cut steps with his axe, on ice he may front-point with his crampons. (He sounds hyperactive; but in a roped party he'll have plenty of time to enjoy his surroundings while he's belaying his partner.) Beyond this there's an argot of finer distinctions, expressive and often amusing, but it's not worth introducing it here; as one of the means by which each new generation seeks to distinguish itself from its elders, it changes every five years.

No two moves are ever quite the same but by patient experiment the body learns an infinite variety of adjustments. The climber, in using any technique, tries to conserve the resource most easily exhausted: strength. He learns, too, how to use poor resting positions at the least physical expense.

Judgement has two faces and looks out and in. Externally, the climber learns to judge gross technical difficulty, including problems of escape and retreat, to weigh the probable consequences of a fall, and to estimate the hazards posed by insecure material, possible stonefall or avalanche, bad or deteriorating weather and so on.

The inward aspect of judgement is equally important. Initially the climber tends to objectify difficulty as a quality inherent in the climb itself. It's often difficult not to feel that a particular route is easy and another hard, though one climber makes the latter look simple while another makes the easy route look desperate. Quickly, then, the climber learns to grade himself and later to understand that guidebook ratings (whether the opinion of a single writer or of a wide consensus amongst earlier climbers) can never be a perfect fit for any individual. He makes, then, dispassionate estimates of his ability and of his form of the day and he judges to what extent his physical and nervous resources have been depleted by his exertions. Beyond this, and more difficult, he should be conscious of his own psychological make-up and characteristics. He must try to consider, for instance, whether he allows his self-image or the view others hold of him to shape his actions; whether the fact that he's being watched influences him; whether, when tired, he permits the scale of high probability low pay-off risks, and low probability high pay-off risks, to tip too far; and so on.

Having listed these four basic fields of expertise I can now say how we recognise a skilful climber. We can do it from a brief observation or by considering known achievements. In the first case the observer notices two obvious characteristics. First, ease of movement, confidence, and also perhaps, the amount of protection the leader of a roped party finds it necessary to allow himself. Second, the length of time spent in solving the problem: since, although on short climbs we rarely consider speed as an end in itself, it gives a crude index of competence. In similar conditions two climbers may make their first leads of an unfamiliar pitch and both may appear in perfect control throughout. Yet it detains one for fifteen minutes and the other for ninety. The initial assumption has to be that the former is the more skilful.

It might be thought that there's little difficulty in judging skill by the record. We notice a series of difficult first ascents; the first ascent of any 'last great problem' and its early repetitions; solos of high standard climbs, especially when the soloist hasn't seen the route earlier as a member of a roped party (an on-sight solo, a sight solo); the reduction of aid used by previous parties (the 'freeing' of a move or of a route); and, of course, any kind of grand slam of an already defined list of hard climbs or any comprehensive familiarity with a particular area.

A large problem in making overall judgements is that of how much importance should be accorded to survival or to the avoidance of accidents as a criterion of skill. The wastage of experts goes up steadily in proportion to the seriousness of the routes embarked upon. It's impossible not to speculate on whether those who've died in the mountains have been less good at reading the risks than those who've survived. At the same time, almost every expert climber has had unforeseen falls, has had near misses through stonefall or avalanche, or has had a close call in bad conditions at some time or other. Finally, the question of whether the expert is entitled to a share of good luck remains unanswerable.

Many of the matters already touched on provide the material for furious argument. These disagreements stem from diverging views on what are called 'climbing ethics' but I think it's essential to look at the debate in a wider perspective. Matters of right and wrong in climbing actually involve actions with effects of two quite different classes. First, those which may be said to be detrimental to the scene in its widest sense: environment ethics. Second, those relating only to transactions between climbers: competition ethics. (These last are unrelated to the rules of organised climbing competitions.) Some actions offend both ethics and some offend only one or the other. Some actions are temporary in effect, some are more permanent but reversible, some are irreversible. But it's important to separate the two categories.

Briefly, offences against the environment ethic comprise ecological damage, aesthetic damage, pollution, vandalism, and any sort of erosion of the natural integrity of the scene. Outside these there's a contamination of local cultures in some parts of the world. The general type of offence is disturbance.

In this sphere the activities of climbers are a proper concern of the non-climbing public who have a perfect right to complain or to take action. In Britain, in recent years, botanists and ornithologists haven't been alone in lodging protests. Climbers can have only one initial response to these attacks: they're entitled to check or to monitor claims of disturbance, since these claims have sometimes been alarmist. It might be added that the climbing world itself includes all manner of specialists and that first reports of ecological disturbance have often come from climbers.

Competition ethics, by contrast, are the concern mainly of the competitors and their supporters. Climbing, in its essential nature, isn't a spectator sport though it has to be admitted that public bitching between aggrieved prima donnas offers endless delight to unengaged readers of climbing literature. The general type of offence is resort to unfair advantage.

It's true that there are climbers who don't climb competitively in any real sense. They may choose to restrict themselves to ascents they know to be well within their powers or to climb only as second. They still reap many of the rewards touched upon in this book. However, it has to be accepted that competition has always been a motor of advances in climbing.

It's seen to take a variety of forms. A climber may see himself as competing simply against the route and his present limits, using whatever advantage he feels essential. It's hard to find any just objection to this if the environment ethic isn't offended, except in the special case of first ascents. In that instance, simply by claiming the route the climber enters a public competition and any resort to advantage ought at least to be declared. Here, though, it's pertinent to notice Huizinga's remarks, in *Homo Ludens*, on the cheat and the spoilsport. The undetected cheat doesn't matter, he says, since he doesn't threaten the nature of the game. The spoilsport, on the other hand, should expect to arouse annoyance or anger: by openly flouting the rules he reveals the artificiality and fragility of the game.

Essentially the sport rests on two other forms of competition. The first is that practised by the great majority of climbers. They may well enjoy a more or less friendly comparison of their own performances with those of their close circle of companions and acquaintances; but their competition is essentially with the received form of the sport as expressed by the area guidebook or in local tradition.

Finally, there remains the obsessive race for successes and public prestige waged amongst local, national and international elites. This is the dynamic of climbing and involves first ascents or the mastery of a particular form of the sport. The prestige gained, incidentally, isn't so dissimilar in each sphere. In all intensively climbed areas local heroes produce local problems which might stop a visiting world expert. The same single-mindedness has been called for and the same length of time demanded in the ascent of the world's greatest peaks, in the freeing of American big walls and in the subjugation of British boulder problems. One can't imagine that the world's most famous postwar Himalayan climber, Reinhold Messner, and the world's most famous postwar boulder problemist, John Gill, might conceivably have envied each other's successes.

The first description of competition ethics was made a quarter-century ago in a lucid and elegant essay, "Games Climbers Play", by the Bolivian-Californian mountaineer, Lito Tejada-Flores. He described several characteristic terrains of climbing and the practices common in each, ranked in order of size and seriousness from boulder problems to Himalayan ascents. He called these a spectrum of "climbing-games" and pointed out that a handicap-system had evolved "to equalise the inherent challenge and to maintain the climber's feeling of accomplishment at a high level in each of these differing situations." The rules, he said, are expressed negatively. In other words, the less serious the ascent (as measured, perhaps, by ease of escape) the less advantage climbers allow themselves until the boulder problemist is permitted only his specialist footgear and his hand chalk.

The purpose of the ethic is "to conserve the climber's feeling of personal (moral) accomplishment against the meaninglessness of a success which represents merely technological victory"; it serves "to maintain a degree of uncertainty as to the eventual outcome...." Tejada-Flores further concluded that "good style" is defined by the average amongst competent climbers in each sphere of climbing. The function of the elite in setting higher standards is to show how performance might evolve. This is done by applying the more stringent prohibitions of a lower game in the spectrum to a more serious game.

Here, it's easier to express the mechanism of competition ethics in terms of the skills and styles described. We have the example of the ways in which earlier ascents have been made; we have rising standards through technological innovation, population pressure, and the greater ease and frequency of access allowed by increased wealth or leisure or both. We have a need to exert ourselves; we have a need to scare ourselves; and we have a craving to demonstrate expertise. However, those who went before us tried very hard and, aside from finding more difficult new routes, the most obvious way in which we can display superiority is by relinquishing advantage. Therefore the territory of the aid climber is always under attack from the free climber and the province of the roped party is always threatened by the unroped soloist. In practice and in detail, however, the shapes of these attacks are complex and a practical illustration is useful.

The Nose of El Capitan in the Yosemite Valley is perhaps the world's most famous rock climb. This 3000-foot ascent was first made by Harding, Merry and Whitmore in 1958. After several probes, the fixing of ropes to allow rapid re-ascent to the high point and the establishing of caches of equipment (siege tactics), the party succeeded in a single eleven-day push using a great deal of aid. Within two years it was shown that siege tactics weren't essential to success. Robbins, Fitschen, Frost and Pratt climbed the route almost without reconnaissance in seven days. They had the advantage of a proven line to follow, of in situ aid and of superior equipment.

With the subsequent introduction of nut protection and aid, and of better and lighter equipment, it became obvious that there were a number of ways in which greater expertise might be demonstrated. It might be possible to make an entirely self-reliant ascent and in 1969 Tom Bauman made a roped solo in six days. It might be possible to make a freer ascent; bit by bit the amount of aid thought essential was reduced until in 1993 Lynn Hill led a continuous free ascent. It might be possible to make a faster ascent; by 1975 Bridwell, Long and Westbay had completed the climb in a day and in 1993 Peter Croft and Hans Florine took it down to less than five hours.

These ambitions were mutually exclusive, each involving relinquishments. In an undertaking at this level of difficulty a solo ascent is unlikely to be the fastest since rope manoeuvres seem necessary and roped solo is slow. Neither is the freest ascent likely to be the fastest, since the crucial sections may involve falls or repeated attempts. The fastest ascent must use aid if that saves time and will inevitably rely on prior familiarity. And with each success new goals arise: the fastest on-sight ascent, first feminine ascents, first national ascents, and so on.

Most difficult rock climbs show a similar history but on the highest mountains this life-cycle isn't so apparent. There, stable weather and good snow and ice conditions are of crucial importance. If the first ascent was made in perfect circumstances much stronger parties may fail year after year. Even the ordinary route on Everest, climbed in 1953, wasn't made without oxygen until 1978, by Messner and Habeler. And the mountain wasn't soloed until 1980, again by Messner though by a different route.

It was obvious a hundred years ago that British rock climbing was a purely recreational activity. Larger claims were made for alpinism and for greater mountaineering but with the appearance of the aeroplane exploratory and scientific pretensions began to be undermined. With the arrival of the helicopter it became clear that all mountaineering was to be reduced to the status of sport.

Technological intrusion is a potential threat to all recreation. In formal games it's blocked by rule-book and in most informal sports it's resisted by gentleman's agreement. Climbing, the most diverse and the least disciplined of all sports, is hard put to control it and at all levels there's been a degree of acceptance. Even the boulder problemist avails himself of hand chalk and has been happy to change into footgear of more adhesive rubber.

The deep logic behind the vetting of technological innovation rests on environment and competition ethics but in detail it remains obscure and unpredictable. It favours modesty and tends to resist the mechanical. It accepts improved design in clothing and footgear and it admits the safety helmet (permitted, in disguise, even in so traditional a field sport as English fox-hunting, which has a parallel debate on "hunt ethics"). It allows harnesses, welcomes any lightening of loads, and is happy to see advances in the classic tools of climbing such as rope, snap-link and iceaxe. All these items seem to be classified as parts of the body since they make no essential difference to the physical action of the climber. But the logic looks carefully at any apparent extension of the body.

Of recent years, in rock climbing, the boundary seems to be drawn at about nine inches, the distance at which a wired nut placement might be made. This distance is within the range of reach in climbers, though shorter climbers aren't given any special dispensation and must just do the best they can. (Curiously, lack of reach rarely seems to be critical.) Beyond that boundary the climber must resort to traditional rope tricks. The logic has ratified camming devices, though with moving parts they'd appear to be machines. But it's deeply worried about the battery-powered drill which allows the placing of bolt protection without much physical effort. It has nightmares about glues. On high mountains it's ignored the avoidance of dangerous descents by the option of the paraglider, itself involving risk and skill. It's made no special pronouncement on short-wave radios or mobile phones.

The competition ethic may be seen as to some degree a self-organising system and to date it's resisted simple technological intrusion fairly well. However, when that intrusion is linked with strong population pressure the ethic shows signs of strain. Wherever cliffs are so accessible and the infilling of variations is so advanced that further progress in the existing styles is beyond the limit of the day, new practices, apparently retrograde, start to evolve. Wherever a mountain has a huge historical significance the ordinary route will be subjected to abuse. In either case the environment ethic will also be disregarded. Some notes on instances of these pressures at each end of the spectrum will round off this description.

Twenty years ago, in a lively essay on future directions in art, Clive James included a discussion of what he called 'the art-sports', principally ice-skating and gymnastics. He was led to this reflection:

> It's possible that an art that depends so largely on the conquest
> of difficulties will rapidly become decadent when the limitations
> of the human body allow no further difficulties to be conjectured
> except by freaks.

Similar fears about the specialisation of climbing have been expressed almost from its beginnings.

Of all sports, games and pastimes, rock-climbing and mountaineering may have the strongest claim to the title of art-sport. This claim wouldn't rest entirely on movement aesthetics, far more pronounced on steep rock than on a Himalayan ascent, nor on the drama and beauty of their staging, unsurpassed in the high mountains but less evident in an abandoned junk-filled quarry. It would also consider the residue of recreational activities. Some produce artefacts (dart board, pool table), others construct arenas (football stadium, ice rink), and others again create concepts made real only in performance (the hunt, the dance). We can describe a form of dance abstractly, as easily as a climb without the climber. Yet climbing, uniquely, also produces something analogous to material works of art, the climbs themselves. And it's a fact that in discussing particular climbs we use a language like that of aesthetics, valuing them on scales of seriousness, complexity, integrity and individuality; setting them in relationships; rejecting them for artificiality or impermanence.

Amongst recent developments arousing charges of decadence the appearance of the organised climbing competition is interesting in this context. In Britain major events take place indoors on uniquely prepared artificial walls which are afterwards dismantled. The throwaway culture has produced the disposable climb. However, whilst the permanent availability of the climb has been sacrificed (together with all values of setting, once considered the chief inspiration of climbing) it's worth noting that one of the original rewards of climbing has been reclaimed and guaranteed, the pure on-sight lead.

The sight lead of a difficult first ascent still holds a central esteem in climbing. If a single model had to stand for all climbing and mountaineering it might well be the 1938 ascent of the Walker Spur of the Grandes Jorasses by Cassin, Esposito and Tizzoni. Two of the Italians crossed the frontier to learn the approach to this notorious north face and retraced their steps immediately to await the third man. On his arrival the three returned and without any reconnaissance of the line made the hardest ascent of the area and of the era in three days. In Britain, sight first ascents at the extreme limits of difficulty for their areas were still achieved regularly as late as the seventies. This hardly ever occurs now and the change seems to some to mark an age of decline.

In fact the more accessible of British crags are a special case since some reconnaissance is involuntary. The hardest routes are likely to be climbed by local experts who can't escape the advantage of familiarity. In ascending existing routes the climber notices new possibilities, often looking down on them to see small ledges, even useful holds. Some of our cliffs support loose rock and tiny fingerholds may be lichenous or dirty. Beyond the vertical, with the climber unable to stand in balance or even to hang on for long, these problems become impossible to handle in ascent and an argument for prior inspection by abseil, with the cleaning up and the brushing of key holds, is immediately available. These tactics have occasionally been practised even on mountain crags almost from the beginnings of British climbing and by the fifties a divergence of approach was very clear. Some climbers wanted the challenge of the relatively unknown and climbed their routes from the bottom up, prepared to use some aid to permit a sight lead. Others, declining aid at any price, prepared climbs by abseil or even rehearsed the route, belayed from above, before leading it free. The first approach regards the new route as the living of an experience, the second as the production of a commodity.

Rehearsal has reached an extreme position on some of our limestone crags and slate quarries where it's now the norm and bolt protection for new routes is usually pre-placed. This practice has been forced by population pressure. (It's interesting to consider the dynamics of climbing in the light of the theories of Malthus and his critics.) All naturally protectable lines at the available level of expertise having been climbed, new ground can only be opened up safely by recourse to the 'dirty' protection of the bolt. This development is referred to as 'sport climbing' as opposed to 'adventure climbing', characteristically found on the volcanic rocks of the mountain crags and most sea-cliffs. There's a temptation to link these two styles with rehearsal and the sight lead but this is incorrect since the adventure climb is sometimes rehearsed nowadays. The difference lies in whether movement skills or judgement skills are most admired and in the attitude to pre-placed protection and the environment ethic. The adventure climber emphasises inescapable seriousness, saying that the activity is diminished by defensive risk adjustment and that the sport climber tests only a narrow and specialised range of strengths. The sport climber emphasises pure difficulty, saying that he's exploring absolute physical limits.

Neither side has attended seriously to the crucial questions. For the adventure climber the question is: what's the moral justification for recommending a style of activity which will inevitably kill people? For the sport climber the question is: on what authority do you claim the right to leave visible litter on cliffs which aren't just the heritage of climbers?

Unhappily, the act of placing bolts is deeply satisfying in itself to a generation for which society hasn't been able to arrange useful physical work and they've appeared in areas where the environment ethic is respected. Response has varied from the guerilla action of chopping the bolts, still leaving a scar, to the sanction of excluding bolted routes from guidebook histories and credits. And whilst it appears that the arrival of the bolt has reversed the general drift of the competition ethic it's noticeable that within sport climbing itself an ethic reasserts itself. Attempts to protect the status of existing routes are made. It's urged that there should be no retrospective bolting, reducing the seriousness of the original lead; similarly, that bolts on new routes on tightly infilled crags shouldn't be placed where they can be reached and clipped from existing routes. And since a lengthily rehearsed first ascent puts later parties under a colossal handicap a range of sub-classifications in the abandoning of advantage has appeared: 'dogging', 'redpointing', 'flashing'. And, just as guidebook credits for the freeing of old aid routes have been established, this hierarchy of styles of ascent is now noticed by climbing magazines.

In contrast to the effects of pressure on small crags by experts there's the effect of pressure by moderate climbers on high mountains. Whenever a mountain is celebrated in climbing history and has a significance even to the general public, a value attaches to the summit independent of the route of ascent. Here the competition ethic loses strength and the easiest route comes under pressure.

The Matterhorn gives an obvious example. In good conditions the Hörnli Ridge is technically easy and it's climbed every year by countless guided parties which may include clients almost without mountain experience. As everywhere in the Alps for routes used by guides high accommodation is available (hut, hütte, cabane, refuge, rifugio; usually a substantial building) so that the ascent may be made without a bivouac. But well-defined ridges may offer few variants to the easiest line and a slow party may cause congestion. This creates a problem for the professional guide, whose aim must be to get his clients up and down as fast and as safely as possible. He also wishes to keep the route open for as many days of the year as possible. In the main the Hörnli is simple enough to allow most parties to advance at a brisk trot and to permit the overtaking of any slow group. But at one point the ridge becomes narrow and more serious in less than perfect conditions. This bottleneck is therefore equipped with fixed ropes and an emergency hut with rescue telephone is sited not far beneath. Clearly, the guiding system itself, resting on the needs of those who've come a long way to climb the mountain, exerts a strong influence on how the Matterhorn is climbed. This influence has shaped alpine climbing to an extent we no longer notice. And it may yet prove to have a more baleful influence on Himalayan mountaineering.

Concerning the greatest peaks, there's been some controversy in recent years between advocates of large and small expeditions. The small expedition follows the direction and prescriptions of the competition ethic and may have less environmental impact. (It burns little or none of the diminishing firewood supply of the approach valleys, though when it gets home it may write a book about its adventures made, like this book, from other peoples' trees.) The large expedition uses all the equipment it can afford and carry and any means it can think of to try to ensure success. (It says that the odds are with the mountain anyway. That some of its members do useful work for a living and may only get one or two chances in a lifetime. It wonders whether five four-man teams have much less impact than a single twenty-man team.)

Astonishingly, the ordinary route up Everest has now come under pressure with the appearance of guided expeditions, congestion, parties breaking the trail and fixing ropes, other parties taking advantage of this softening up. In this decade there have been days on which more than thirty climbers reached the summit and queues formed at the Hillary Step. Inevitably, equipment is jettisoned as it always has been on exhausting or dangerous retreats. As early as 1978 Messner noted two hundred abandoned oxygen cylinders at the South Col. Recently a few expeditions, one at least with this sole purpose, have devoted themselves to the task of attempting to clear up the debris left by earlier parties but haven't felt able to claim much success. However, a sense of what's proper still resists the ambitions of commerce. A proposal to build a huge hotel beneath Everest was defeated or withdrawn, as were proposals to construct a cable-way up the Matterhorn and to floodlight the mountain.

This description of climbing (a problem-solving dance with nature as choreographer; a set of methods to deplete physical and nervous energy) says nothing about spirit or about the natural world's magnificence. It may seem outside the experience of other mountaingoers. In fact, walker and climber often share the same large scene and there aren't any clear boundaries between mountain walking, scrambling and climbing. Further, it's apparent that the smaller details of environment and competition ethics are only special cases derived from general principles, recognised by the fell-walker too, in our attitudes to nature and to difficulty. Whenever, in British hills, the walker resists the extension of a road, whenever he complains about the removal of natural obstacles to ease a footpath, he's saying that he prefers to keep the scene undamaged and to climb his hill without help.

ACKNOWLEDGMENTS

It would be hard to make a good guess at the number of companions I've shared a rope with and few of them are named in this book. It rests, however, on the sum of those relationships.

The manuscript was read by David Craig, Terry Gifford and Peter Hodgkiss. It seemed unreasonable to expect the first two, with heavy writing and teaching commitments of their own, to supply detailed annotation as well as generalised comment. Their careful readings, politely couched reservations and consistent encouragement were what I needed. With my editor, Peter Hodgkiss, I had stimulating exchanges on English usage and on what constitutes a proper respect for the language. John and Sue Gittins located material on access issues I'd been unable to obtain.

Some parts of the book appeared in earlier drafts in the *Fell and Rock Journal, Mountain*, and *High*, under the editorships of Terry Sullivan, Ken Wilson and Geoff Birtles. I'm grateful to them for giving me space in the first place. A first version of the chapter "On Falling Off" was read at the International Festival of Mountaineering Literature at Bretton Hall in 1991 and was included in *Orogenic Zones,* ed. Gifford and Smith (Bretton Hall 1994).

Acknowledgment is made to Iris Murdoch and to Chatto and Windus for permission to use the lines quoted from *The Sea, The Sea* (1978).

Finally, it may have been noted that the chapter-head vignettes which lend grace to the book aren't even initialled. The artist, who wished to remain anonymous, is Gordon Mansell. Spoiling my joke in the Foreword, he shows that he can handle the oval of vision and the fractals of chaos as easily as the rectangle of control.